RESURRECTION FERN
Tales of a Dominican Friar

ALSO BY THE AUTHOR

1973
Environmental Awareness through the Arts

Taste and See: Louisiana Renaissance, Religion and the Arts

1980
Releasing the Artistic Talents of Our Handicapped

1984
Editor and Contributor
Treasures of the Vatican: The New Orleans Vatican Pavilion

1987
Editor
Renewing the Judeo-Christian Well Springs
Volume 1: Tulane Chair of Judeo-Christian Studies

1989
To Rise with the Light: The Spiritual Odyssey of Jack Chambers

1992
Editor
New Visions: Historical and Theological Perspectives on the Jewish-Christian Dialog
Volume 3: Tulane Chair of Judeo-Christian Studies

2005
Editor
Re-Imaging God for Today
Volume 6: Tulane Chair of Judeo-Christian Studies

2010
Editor
Renewing Hope in the Judeo-Christian Dialog
Volume 7: Tulane Chair of Judeo-Christian Studies

RESURRECTION FERN
Tales of a Dominican Friar

Val A. McInnes, O.P.

SOUTHERN DOMINICAN BOOKS
NEW ORLEANS

Copyright © 2010 by Fr. Val Ambrose McInnes, O.P.
All rights reserved.
No part of this book may be reproduced, stored, or transmitted in any manner whatsoever without prior written permission from the publisher, except in the case of brief quotations embodied in critical articles and reviews.

Library of Congress number applied for.

DOMINICAN SHIELD

The shield symbolizes Dominican life in a graphic way. The black of the shield indicates the vow of poverty; the white, the vow of chastity; and the cross, the vow of obedience. The fleur de lis emanating from the tips of the cross symbolizes holiness. This ancient shield or coat of arms of the Order of Preachers has been adapted in its present design by the contemporary Dominican artist, Angelo Zarlingo, O.P.

For further information, please address
Fr. Val A. McInnes, O.P.
775 Harrison Avenue
New Orleans, LA 70124

Grateful acknowledgement is made to the Henry Moore Foundation, Henry Casselli, and photographers Chris Pizzello and Matt Anderson.

TO

my Mother and Father,
Genevieve Rodgers McInnes and Angus J. McInnes, Sr.,
who have given me life, love, and faith

&

my McInnes / Rodgers Families
who have given me my Scottish/Irish roots

&

my Dominican family
*who have given me my preaching and teaching
mission in the Church*

&

all others I have come to know and love
in my Dominican ministries and
who have shared their love and friendship with me

ACKNOWLEDGMENTS

Without the help and encouragement of the following, this memoir would never have seen the light of day:

My dear friend, Julia Woodward Burka, who kindly volunteered to spend a couple of hours each weekday in the summer of 2009 for me to dictate my stories.

My special assistant, Nancy Tatarski, who has helped me organize my materials so we could make some sort of sense out of them.

Emilie and William Griffin, old friends who have much experience in editing and bringing things to final completion.

My Dominican community at St. Dominic's in New Orleans for helping to support me by their fraternal concern and love in good times and in bad—Fr. Mark Edney, Fr. Daniel Shanahan, my prior, Fr. Michael O'Rourke, Fr. Chrys Finn, Fr. Roger Shondel, Fr. Sergio Serrano, Fr. Victor Celio, and Fr. Richard Bontempo.

My provincial, Fr. Martin J. Gleeson.

Finally, I acknowledge the generosity of my family and friends who have helped make this memoir possible.

All funds raised from the sale of this volume go to the Southern Dominican Retirement Fund.

CONTENTS

	ACKNOWLEDGMENTS	vi
	ILLUSTRATIONS	x
	PROLOG	xv
	INTRODUCTION	xvii
1	*Life and Death*	1
2	*Lost and Found*	3
3	*Moving to South London*	5
4	*Discovering the Arts*	7
5	*Breaking the Race Barrier*	10
6	*Ursulines and Intellectuals*	13
7	*College in Windsor*	15
8	*Summer School in Switzerland*	17
9	*Pilgrimage to Rome*	20
10	*Nice in Nice*	22
11	*The Grotto and the Grotesque*	24
12	*Summer School in Holland*	26
13	*Back to Assumption*	28
14	*Monastery Crawling*	31
15	*Novice in Winona*	34
16	*Philosophy in River Forest*	39
17	*Theology in Dubuque*	44
18	*Assignment in the Twin Cities*	47
19	*Canada Council Grant*	51

20 *Tulane Catholic Center*   56
21 *Chair of Judeo-Christian Studies*   61
22 *Dominican Teaching and Pastoral Life*   64
23 *The Vatican Pavilion*   75
24 *Backstage at the Vatican Pavilion*   83
25 *Promoter of Development*   90
26 *Vatican Museums and Medjugorge Visions*   103
27 *The Pope Visits New Orleans*   114
28 *California Retreats*   117
29 *From Socialite to Carmelite*   121
30 *Order of St. Lazarus*   127
31 *Displeasure and Dysplasia*   131
32 *Katrina*   138
33 *St. Thomas Aquinas Environmental Award*   144
34 *Surprise Birthday Party*   148
35 *Avocations*   152

EPILOG   155

APPENDICES

A *International Dominican Foundation Board, 2003*   159
   International Dominican Foundation Advisory Board,   160
   2007
   International Dominican Foundation Board, 2009   162

B *"My Medjugorge Experience, 1988"*   164
   by Cherie Banos Schneider

C *Tulane University Chair of Judeo-Christian Studies:*
   The Public Lectures, 1980-2009   171

D Books Published by the Chair of   188
   Judeo-Christian Studies
E Recipients of The St. Martin de Porres Award, 189
   Southern Dominican Province, U.S.A.
F Recipients of The St. Thomas Aquinas   190
   Environmental Award, Southern Dominican
   Province, U.S.A.
G "Passion for the Arts Plays Big Role in Pope's 191
   Teachings": Interview with Fr. Val A. McInnes, O.P.
H Curriculum Vitae of Very Rev. Father Val   193
   Ambrose McInnes, O.P., Ph.D.
I Patrons of the Vatican Museums in the South   203
   and Southern Dominicans Present Canadian
   Serigraphs to the Vatican Museums

INDEX   205

ILLUSTRATIONS

The illustrations appear in a 32-page insert between text pages 102 and 103. The following is a list of captions as they appear in the insert.

1. Ambrose fishing in the Thames River outside of London, Ontario in 1933 – "The Foreshadowing of a Future Vocation—Fishers of Men."
2. Father Val's parents, Angus J. McInnes, Sr., and Genevieve Rodgers McInnes.
3. 1954 graduation with M.A. in philosophy from Assumption College, University of Western Ontario.
4. Photo of the author and his brothers during their time in London. Left to right, Angus J. McInnes Jr., James A. McInnes, the author, Patrick R. McInnes, and John Charles McInnes.
5. The author's Dominican class of 1955 for the Province of St. Albert the Great, St. Peter Martyr Priory, Winona, MN. The photo is the simple profession of vows on August 31, 1955. Father Val is left front (in white since he was not professed until November.)
6. Seated after his simple profession of vows and reception of the Dominican black and white habit, November 18, 1955, at St. Peter Martyr Priory, Winona, MN. He was given the religious name of Valentine after the Dominican Basque martyr, Bishop Valentine de Barrio Occoha.
7. The Genevieve Rodgers McInnes Memorial Chalice designed by Fr. Val and executed by Hamers Chalice Company of Belgium celebrating Fr. Val's ordination day, 3rd of June 1961. It was a gift of his father to the Dominicans.

8a. Angus J. McInnes, Sr., at the time of his son's ordination, 1961.
8b. Ordination class of 1961.
8c. Govenor General Georges P. Vanier of Canada laying a wreath in honor of Ensign Henry Edward Dormer at the War Memorial, Victoria Park, London, Ontario during the Centenary Celebration of Dormer's death, October 1966.

9. Professor W.D. Davies, opening lecture for the Chair of Judeo-Christian Studies at Tulane University, April 14, 1980.
10. President Herbert Longenecker of Tulane University greeting Professor W.D. Davies with Fr. McInnes at the conclusion of the inaugural lecture.

11 Mr. John Bricker, one of the major benefactors for the Chair of Judeo-Christian Studies, speaking to Evelyn Gaudin, a Southern Dominican patron.
12 Sir John Haught, the first recipient of the St. Thomas Aquinas Environmental Award.
13 H.R.H. The Prince of Wales receiving the second St. Thomas Aquinas Environmental Award from Fr. McInnes at his official residence of Clarence House in London, September 9, 2008.
14 Award designed by the Dominican sculptor, Fr. Thomas McGlynn.
15 Photograph of His Holiness Pope John Paul II, by Karsh of Ottowa granted with his special permission for the Vatican Pavilion at the Louisiana World Exposition.
16 The Vatican Pavilion at night.
17 The tapestry of the Risen Christ, Vatican Pavilion.
18 A series of six photographs of Henry Moore's preliminary sketches for the Crucifixion study ending with the finished sketch. The photographs reveal the evolution of his inspiration and, as he said, "I must respect the sacred moment of sacrifice without taking too many liberties from the conventional portrayal of Christ's death." Unfortunately, he did not find time to execute a maquette for the Vatican Pavilion. (With permission of the Henry Moore Foundation.)
19 His Excellency Archbishop Philip M. Hannan, His Holiness Pope John Paul II, Fr. Val A. McInnes following the meeting for the arrangements for the Vatican Pavilion at the Louisiana World Exposition, December 2, 1981.
20 The Woman at the Well, the centerpiece of the Vatican Pavilion, created by the internationally famous Croatian sculptor, Ivan Mestrovic.
21 Very Rev. Valentine Ambrose McInnes, O.P., EGCLJ, GCMLJ, SMLJ, PhD. Senior Chaplain for the Military and Hospitaller Order of St. Lazarus of Jerusalem at the St. Lazarus National Shrine in the Old Ursuline Convent in New Orleans.
22 Fr. Val McInnes presenting Chevalier Dr. Hans von Leden, Grand Prior of the Military and Hospitaller Order of St. Lazarus of Jerusalem, to His Holiness, Pope John Paul II, 1992.
23 The solemn profession of Lee Martin Martiny, August 15, 1993. Left to right: Fr. Val A. McInnes, O.P., Fr. Lee Martin Martiny, Fr. Timothy

Radcliffe, Master of the Order of Preachers, Ambassador Vernon A. "Dick" Walters.

24 First recipient of the St. Martin de Porres Award Loretta Young and Fr. Val A. McInnes, 1986.

25 Houston 2000 St. Martin de Porres honoree Mrs. Rose Cullen with Fr. Val A. McInnes.

26 Some of Fr. Val's family celebrating at the 2000 Houston Dominican Gala. Left to right: his brother, Angus J. McInnes, Jr., his niece, Maureen McInnes, Angus' wife, Ann McInnes, their daughter, Carol Ann, and Fr. Val McInnes.

27 Father Roberto Rodriguez, Southern Dominican Provincial, presenting Fr. Val with the 2000 Fra Angelico Award on behalf of his Southern Dominican Friars for his work with the arts and spirituality. The citation reads, "A visionary, transforming the world through art and spirituality."

28 New Orleans Southern Dominican Gala 2008. Father Val with his niece, Marilyn Coles Calderone.

29 Harry Connick, Jr. accepting the 2008 St. Martin de Porres Award in recognition of his help in the recovery of New Orleans after Hurricane Katrina.

30 2001 General Chapter, Providence College. Southern Dominicans gathered with the Master, Carlos Azpiroz Costa, in the center. Fr. Val is on his immediate right and Fr. Rodriguez on his immediate left.

31 The 2009 members of the IDF Board. Left to right: Dr. Gene Stark, Very Rev. Fr. Michael J. Mascari, O.P., Dr. Patrick Jordan, Mrs. Lou Jordan, Very Rev Fr. Marty Gleeson, O.P., Fr. Val A. McInnes, O.P., President Emeritus, Rev. Msgr. James F. Checchio, Bishop Kevin W. Vann, Archbishop Robert J. Carlson, Archbishop Thomas J. Rodi. Seated: Father Mark Edney, O.P., President, Archbishop Donald W. Wuerl, Chairman, and Francis Cardinal George, O.M.I., Honorary Member.

32 The original members of the IDF Board of Directors. Front row: Most Rev. Robert J. Carlson, Very Rev. Fr. Roberto Corral, O.P., Francis Cardinal George (honorary member), Very Rev. Fr. Martin J. Gleeson, O.P. Back row: Very Rev. Fr. Edmond C. Nantes, O.P., Rev. Mon. James F. Checchio, Very Rev. Fr. Val A. McInnes, O.P. , President, Most Rev.

Donald W. Wuerl, O.P., Most Rev. Timothy M. Dolan, Chairman, Most Rev. Thomas C. Kelly, O.P., Most Rev. Edward F. O'Brien, O.P., and Very Rev. Fr D. Dominic Izzo, O.P. Missing from the photo: Theodore Cardinal McCarrick, Ms. Donna Miller, KC, Very Rev Fr. Neal W. McDermott, O.P., Sr. Rose Marie Masserano, O.P., and Most Rev. Michael J. Sheridan.

33 The International Dominican Foundation Advisory Board and Associates greeting Christoph Cardinal Schonborn at his residence in Vienna.

34 Wolfgang and Judith Feuchtmuller, former Tulane students of Fr. Val's from Vienna, in Christoph Cardinal Schonborn's study, Vienna 2008, showing the bullet holes shot into the painting by the Nazis when they stormed into the building in 1938.

35 Father Val McInnes presenting his monograph, To Rise with the Light, to Pope John Paul II.

36 Fr. Val presents Jack Chambers' Dormer Tribute to the Vatican Museums. Receiving the serigraph is Dr. Walter Persegati on behalf of the museums with Helen Boehm looking on.

37 The "sporty" Father Val in Capri.

38 Father Val in front of Dolores and Bob Hope's new home in Palm Springs.

39 Portofino photograph: On the famous yacht trip, Mrs. Louise Russell (mother of Sr. Mary Joseph) and Fr. Val at Portofino, Italy with Valentino's yacht in the background—similar to the one they were on.

40 A general view of the futuristic Hope home.

41 Dolores Hope and Father Val.

42 Father Val, Bob Hope, and Ann Miller's son, Donald.

43 Ann Miller with Father Val and her mother, Mrs. Louise Russell with an interloper.

44 Ann Miller, Father Val, and Walter Annenberg.

45 Ann Miller, now Sister Mary Joseph of the Most Holy Trinity, on the day of her simple profession of vows. As one of our mutual friends on hearing of her new religious name said, "Only Ann Miller could manage to include all the principles of salvation in her religious name."

46 Jo and Bob Ponds' Ponderosa estate in Palm Springs where the annual retreats are held.

47 Dolores Hope, the widow of legendary comedian Bob Hope, looking on as guests sing "Happy Birthday" at her 100th birthday party in Los

Angeles, with Fr. Val helping hold up the cake, May 27, 2009 (AP Chris Pizzello).
48 Fr. Benedict Groeschel, CFR, Fr. Val and one of Fr. Groeschel's good friends, Fr. John Lynch at Dolores Hope's birthday party.
49 Cover for the program of the Hurricane Katrina Benefit Concert in Santa Fe, New Mexico, designed by Brett Landry of San Francisco.
50 Sketch by the author: "The Tree of Life" (1999).
51 Sketch by the author: "Mount Vesuvius from Capri" (1999).
52 The official photograph of the members of the International Dominican Foundation Advisory Board and Associates with the Latin Patriarch, His Beatitude Archbishop Michael Sabbat, in Jerusalem, April 18, 2008.
53 Fr. Val with Dick Colton, at his 80th birthday party.
54 Portrait of Fr. Val A. McInnes, O.P., by the American artist Verna Arbour.
55 "Madonna and Child" watercolor created by Henry Casselli for Our Lady of Hope Chapel in St. Dominic's Church, New Orleans. Photo courtesy of the artist.

PROLOG

Resurrection fern (*Pleopeltis polypodioides*) grows on the upper side of the branches of live oak trees in the southern part of the United States, especially in Louisiana and Alabama. It flourishes in the wet season and dies in the dry season. However, as soon as the rains come again, the fern sprouts up with new life and vitality.

I have chosen this title for my memoir because it illustrates the ongoing saga of the death and resurrection that occurs in everyone's life. Therefore, it is a visible sign of the invisible spiritual realities that lie hidden in our daily lives.

The resurrection fern embeds itself in the great live oak. It finds its home and life there. In some ways, it is related to the Tree of Life. Through baptism and faith, we too are embedded into that tree. And our faith springs up as living water inside of us—to life everlasting.

> Val A. McInnes, O.P.
> *Feast of St. Dominic*
> August 8, 2009

INTRODUCTION

I have been urged by family and friends to write down some incidents of my life that reflect and reveal the way God works in the lives of his people. Many of these would never have occurred if I hadn't been raised in an atmosphere of faith. Faith was as natural to my way of life as breathing.

I hope that, by sharing these tales with you, I might let you experience vicariously many joys and sorrows of the daily life of a Dominican religious. Perhaps it isn't exactly the typical life of a Dominican, but each of us Dominicans has a unique story to tell.

As the Portuguese say, "God writes straight with crooked lines." Nothing ever happens the way you think it's going to happen. Later on, you usually look back and say, "Oh yes, if that hadn't happened, I would not be here today."

The Church into which I was born (1929) was a very stable one. Things hadn't changed for years. That distinct sense of stability was like standing on a firm, very supportive rock. No doubt Christ's words to Peter come to mind, "Peter, you are rock and upon this rock I shall build my church."

For the first twenty-four years of my life, I grew up in this kind of atmosphere. Everything was well-ordered, very much in place, and consistent, providing a comfort level that I and many others enjoyed. It wasn't until I had finished graduate studies and made the decision to become a Dominican that things in the Church began to change. There were two mentalities at work, the one that encouraged the stability I just described; the other that saw the need for change. Emerging from this period of my life, I can now see four movements that would eventually be incorporated into the Second Vatican Council.

The first was the Liturgical Reform Movement. This had to do with the desire for native language in the liturgy with greater participation of the people in the liturgical celebration. In some places, experiments were allowed; for example, the altar facing the people; part of the Liturgy of the Word was in English while the Liturgy of the Eucharist remained in Latin. In other words, the liturgical reform was at heart an attempt to make worship more relevant and meaningful to the people. Changes were introduced to remove certain obstacles to understanding. Other changes enhanced communication and participation in the liturgical action itself. This movement culminated in the Second Vatican Council with the Constitution on the Sacred Liturgy.

The second was the Ecumenical Movement. This was first instituted by Protestants, Episcopalians, Anglicans, and Lutherans who sensed that the great divisions in Christianity were sapping the energy of the faith and dividing it rather than uniting it. There had to be a new quest for Christian unity. As a result, the World Conference of Churches on Ecumenism was organized, chiefly focused in Europe and later overflowing into North America. This found its way into the Second Vatican Council in the Decree on Ecumenism; it stated, "There can be no ecumenism worthy of the name without a change of heart." The Council called that "spiritual ecumenism." It required dialog, joint study, as well as cooperation and social action.

Many religious leaders believed that, unless dramatic actions were taken, the various churches would drift more apart and the cause of unity would suffer even more. For this reason many different ecumenical groups began to develop. National and international conferences took place in an effort to address these shortcomings.

By this time, the Roman Catholic Church sent invited observers to many of these meetings. They in turn became more aware that Christian unity had to become a primary goal of all the churches of Jesus Christ throughout the world. In fact, I was a delegate at the World Conference of Religion and Peace in 1969, as a Catholic representative, invited by Cardinal Wright and Bishop Dozier. Archbishop Dom Elder Camara rose at one point and said, "Until Christians unite, we are a sign of contradiction. We are witnessing to the non-Christian world that we cannot put our own house in order. Until we do so, we will have no impact upon the vast numbers of people waiting to be exposed to the Good News of Jesus Christ."

By the time of the Second Vatican Council, the Ecumenical Movement had taken front stage and provided one of the great documents of the Ecumenical Council on ecumenism. The separate document on Jewish-Christian relations, *Nostra Aetate*, was unprecedented in its implications for the renewal of Jewish-Christian dialog. This document in fact was the germ for our Chair of Judeo-Christian Studies at Tulane University.

The third great movement was the concern for Social Justice in a world increasingly divided between the haves and the have-nots. The question of social and economic justice became a major issue in second and third world countries as well as in the first world. Too often the wealthier countries ignored the common good of their own poor. Also they failed in their wider responsibilities for the common good of the poorer nations.

The concern for the poor was manifest in our own country, the United States, through a wide variety of programs. One example was the life and work of Dorothy Day and others like her. Even the government programs coming out of Roosevelt's New Deal showed a concern for the poor. Public Works Projects helped people to get back to work and make a reasonable living during and following the Great Depression of the 1930s. Angela Gregory, New Orleans' own nationally and internationally known sculptress, was a beneficiary of the Public Works Projects. Subsequently she became a great friend of mine.

In the Roman Catholic Church, Pope Leo XIII's innovative encyclical *Rerum Novarum* set the stage for a re-evaluation of the gospels' message for justice, taking care of the poor, the elderly, and the infirm. These programs have been manifested in works of mercy such as hospitals, homes for the poor, soup kitchens, etc. So strong was this movement that it reshaped the Church's image of itself. Social justice issues have become primary concerns of the Church the world over. Our own Dominican saint, Martin de Porres, was canonized on May 6, 1962, by Pope John XXIII as the Universal Saint of Social Justice.

The fourth great movement was the revival of interest in Biblical Studies. At the turn of the twentieth century, a Dominican by the name of Pere Joseph Marie Lagrange received permission from Pope Leo XIII and from his French Dominican superiors to study higher literary criticism in Vienna. Just at that time, the development of Protestant biblical scholarship spurred on Roman Catholics to dedicate themselves to a more detailed study of the historical origins and sources of the Sacred Scriptures. Fortunately, Lagrange was able to establish a school for biblical and archeological studies in Jerusalem, simply called *Ecole Biblique*. The full name for that school is *L'Ecole Biblique et Archeologique Francaise*.

This stimulated in the Roman Catholic world a whole new interest in biblical studies. Scholars were drawn to examine the historical, philosophical, and literary backgrounds out of which the Old and New Testaments had emerged. The culmination of the success of this endeavor became evident in the late 1950s when the Jerusalem Bible was published by the Ecole Biblique.

Overnight, it became the best edition of the two testaments, providing a wealth of footnotes concerning the internal aspects of the texts as well as the historical and literary background.

At the same time, many institutions, Catholic and Protestant alike, began a revival of biblical studies focusing on the origins of Christianity in the Jewish scriptures—thus enhancing the long-neglected dependency of Christianity upon its Jewish antecedents. Like the other movements, this revival fed into the Second Vatican Council deliberations; the document on Jewish-Christian relations, *Nostra Aetate*, as I mentioned above, became one of the great documents of that Council.

When I entered religious life and began my studies as a Dominican, these ecclesiastical movements were major influences. When the Second Vatican Council was opened at St. Peter's Basilica on October 11, 1962, Pope John XXIII proclaimed to the world that it would be the beginning of the new age of the Holy Spirit. The Pope said there would be a renewal and reform of the Church to update it and to bring it into contemporary times.

This new awakening, however, was a challenge to the established order of the Church and the stability of the Church. Many people found the idea disquieting and wanted to know why anything had to be changed. As a result, there was immediate tension in two camps of the Church: one in which people wanted their comfort level undisturbed, and the other consisting of those who saw the need for updating as the Pope himself had proclaimed. It is a curious fact that Pope John XXIII, one of the oldest popes in modern times, was the one who saw the need for the change and actually introduced the changes.

Reflecting over the years, I have come to the conclusion that the challenge was too much for many people. They had what I have come to call "a buttress mentality," much like a Gothic cathedral with its flying buttresses holding everything in place. However, the challenge that Pope John XXIII gave was that we had to learn how to internalize the faith and make it alive; we had to learn not be content with thinking that simply going to Mass on Sunday and other fixed celebrations was a sufficient exercise of the faith. Yet many priests, religious, and lay people fell away from the Church precisely because of this challenge. They simply found it too difficult to change.

The wonderful cathedrals of the Middle Ages provide an example here.

They were built with flying buttresses and Gothic arches to house the drama of the sacred liturgy that took place within its precincts. Yet it was all too common for medieval people to identify the church with the building rather than the worship that went on inside. Today this is well illustrated in closing down churches out of necessity. People allow the sentimental attachment to the building, the fixed romantic image in their minds of where they worship, to become more important than the act of worship itself. Yet it must be recognized that a church building can reflect the dignity and inspiration of the worship going on inside it.

One of my Dominican professor friends, Fr. Jude Nogar, O.P, has written an influential work, *The Wisdom of Evolution*; in it he has coined two phrases that epitomized this conflict of mentalities and reflected the two distinct positions. He called the first group who did not want any change "the picture people"; he defined them as the people who, once the building or the painting was completed, were not willing to change under any circumstance. On the other hand, the people who saw the need to internalize the faith and lead people from a superficial practice of the faith to a deeper internalized one he came to call "the drama people." They were able to envisage the mystery of salvation as an unfolding drama in which we all participate through the various conflicts of our daily lives. The daily encounter with Christ celebrated in the sacred liturgy and sacramental life of the Church constitutes the very inner vitality feeding the people of God.

For me personally, this distinction helped a great deal. I came to understand that the internalization of the faith was a sine qua non for the renewal of the faith. If the Holy Spirit were to renew the Church, we had to be open in a new way to the movement of the Spirit, not trying to control the faith solely through external forms but through a deeper motivation. We had to allow the Holy Spirit to possess us more in the inner depths of our hearts.

I discovered later that Fr. Nogar's two terms aren't mutually exclusive, but rather analogous to the matter and form theory of Aristotle in which they are intimately inter-related and in which they need one another. However, if taken separately and without their complements, confusion, antagonism, and violence may follow.

Looking back on these tumultuous years, I think the liturgy was too quickly transformed into English or other native languages. The change came about without the gradual process of adaptation and orientation; it was done without proper intellectual preparation. As a result, many who were reactionary became even more so. The avant-garde types, seeing the reactionaries and their behavior, were moved to be even more avant-garde. This created more and more tension and less mutual understanding. When the sweeping changes came quickly, many were at a loss to explain them. Others were impatient and wanted to know why change didn't come sooner.

Many liturgical theologians tried hard to bridge these gaps of misunderstanding; yet polarization began to take place. Conservative and liberal groups began to replicate, producing more confusion than light.

Perhaps the worst scenario involved those who didn't agree with the explanations they heard but decided to stay and undermine the very foundations of the Church with their half-baked ideas. They expressed strong egotistical interpretations of what they thought was right as opposed to the teaching authority of the Church. Many masqueraded under the guise of change to introduce their own individual interpretations of renewal, especially in the liturgical celebrations and matters of moral doctrine.

The consequence of all this disorder was that there was no clear vision acceptable to all of the direction of the moral life of the Church. Many bishops themselves either became confused or allowed themselves to be co-opted into one or another conservative or liberal camp. Unfortunately they didn't transcend these parochial issues and keep the Church on an even keel, balancing off unreasonable demands and pruning extremes from the membership of the Church.

I experienced all of this from inside of the Order of Preachers, first in the province of St. Albert the Great when I entered, then later in the province of St. Martin de Porres in the southern part of the United States, which I was instrumental in helping to found.

Fortunately, in the early stages of my formation in the Order, I was surrounded by gifted and intelligent professors. They were able to transcend many of these parochial issues and keep us balanced in our dogmatic and moral studies; they showed us how to integrate these studies into our spiritual lives. The faith-need to internalize our spiritual lives was taken up and emphasized. Outside the order, some religious felt that they were living in a God-shaped vacuum without any real deep awareness of their spiritual life, the sacramental life of the Church, and how it was lived out within the community.

We were free of that experience. The schedule for our daily lives was wrapped around the sacramental reality of community prayer, community Mass, communion, and contemplation. These daily exercises freed us up from being pre-occupied with the mundane and gave us a sharp focus on the substantial realities of God dwelling within his people, in our brothers and sisters of St. Dominic. We had a vibrant community life with all of its peculiarities but certainly with the great asset that we shared our life in common. We lived in common, shared our education, and prayed in common.

In this setting our academic life took place. We were given the intellectual tools to understand the changes taking place in the Church, why they had to take place, what their benefits were, and how we all had to let go of the forms of the past in order to grow into the new revitalized ones. This enabled us to hang onto the living traditions by updating them and reshaping them for the present and the future.

In some ways, all of this was rather frightening and tragic. At the very time we were busy internalizing the faith, so many of our brothers and sisters in the Order and the Church began to leave. For some, this time was especially hard. Those who once considered themselves wise in the Order now suddenly found themselves adrift without any anchor of faith or vision to their future. They seemed lost and, in fact, wandered off.

All this confusion created within us a desire to find a deeper renewal and purpose, not to allow the superficial changes, departures, infidelities, and ignorance to discourage or overwhelm us. The sad thing is that for many this didn't take place. The joyful thing is that for many it did take place. It was the price that had to be paid for the renewal of the Church. Without it, the Church would have remained stagnant and incapable of giving its message to the contemporary world. Because the Church did change and grow, it released a new capacity from the wellsprings of faith for the Holy Spirit to take possession of the people of God in a new and deeper way. Pope John XXIII's prophetic message of a new life of the Holy Spirit began to take hold but not without its casualties. Looking back on these years, no one would say it hasn't been worth it.

We can now turn to some of the tales and stories which illustrate these changes in a concrete way. I hope to show how events personally affected me. As a young person growing up in the Catholic Church in Canada and later joining the Dominican Order in the United States, I have prospered in my religious commitment to serve the people of God and to bring the life of Christ to all of those who are willing to listen.

RESURRECTION FERN
Tales of a Dominican Friar

1

Life and Death

Of all the events in my early life, the episode of my mother's death made the greatest and most lasting impression. It was on a Sunday morning when we were at church for Mass. Suddenly my father was notified that my mother was critically ill and dying in St. Joseph's. He gathered us all together, and we made a dash to the hospital.

When we arrived, we were ushered into my mother's room. Since I was only four-and-a-half, I was told to sit in a chair at the foot of the bed and be still. For the next two hours, I sat and looked at my mother's feet, which were uncovered. Doctors and nurses were frantically doing something to help her; gradually her feet turned blue. She had died. Finally, we were told to leave the room but not before we kissed her. I was lifted up by one of my two aunts.

Fortunately, we knew both of these aunts very well. Sister St. Sebastian of the Sisters of St. Joseph was commonly referred to as Aunt Helen; Sister St. Mary, a member of the Sisters of Charity, we simply called Aunt Mary. Both of them had been allowed to come visit us while my mother expected her latest child, who died in childbirth. As my father tried to comprehend what had happened, my aunts took very good care of us and shepherded us about. My main shock was the realization that I didn't have a mother any more. Aunt Helen, who was a very sensitive lady, realized this; while we were crying she brought us all together.

"You now have two new mothers, and you can call us that instead of Aunt Helen and Aunt Mary. You don't have to cry any more."

Those simple words took away the sting and the gloom. They restored the happiness. The sorrow seemed to lift; and I was relieved to have a mother after all; in fact, two. What a stunning and thoughtful thing to say to a little boy and his brothers and sister who had just lost their mother!

Looking back, I learned at a very early age that life somehow includes death and that death includes new life, even though I wouldn't have been able to articulate it. Thank God I did experience my mother's death firsthand! It taught me that we all must face death sooner or later. However, the deaths closest to us such as our mother and father bring home how definitive this separation is. In my mother's case, it was particularly sad because she was only thirty-eight years old when she died. In my case the experience sowed the seeds of wonder about what it all meant, why people had to die, and why people were so very nice to me, consoling me and giving me new hope even when I was sad.

2

Lost and Found

As I was growing up in London, Ontario, after my mother's death, I enjoyed going downtown with my father. Being an inquisitive soul, I didn't hesitate to look at things and enjoy others. I was very curious, like most children. Except on one occasion I did something I shouldn't have done. Without realizing it, I let go of my father's hand and I was suddenly all alone. Fortunately, and almost immediately, some friendly people came along and asked who I was. I was able to give them my name, but that was it.

Soon, a policeman arrived and decided to take charge of the situation. He was very kind and engaged me in a conversation. Since I was beginning to get fearful and panicky he asked my name again and where I lived.

"I can't tell you where I live, but I can show you the way to my home if you will take me."

So we started off with me giving directions. We went straight down Dundas Street, turned right at Maitland, and went all the way over the railroad tracks down to where my home was.

In the meantime, my father had grown frantic and was looking all around the downtown area. When he came home, he was delighted to find me there. Combined with the delight was a severe reminder that in the future I was always to hold onto his hand and not wander off.

This episode has stayed in my memory partly because I think it reflects an innate talent I have been given; I always seem to know where I am and have a great sense of direction. Being lost was fun because I got to meet the policeman and he drove me home in his car. No doubt it was a foretaste of things to come and the seed of my wanderlust.

4   *Resurrection Fern*

From my earliest years we went fishing on the Thames River outside London, Ontario. On one early expedition there was my aunt Sister Helen, my father, Patrick my brother, and my sister Rosemary. They placed me on a rock in the river, and I was fishing away when I caught a fish. It was at least two inches long. I was in fisherman's heaven, at least for a moment. Then they decided it was too small; they unhooked it and threw it back. That marked the beginning of my fishing career and the world of things to come as a *fisher of souls*.

3

Moving to South London

As I was finishing grade school at St. Mary's School in Central London, our family moved to a lovely new home on Elmwood Avenue in South London. It was a Norman style house with a big turret on one side and a large Roman arch entering onto a porch, then leading into the house. It was a grand place. The move brought us into a completely new neighborhood where we made new friends and joined a new parish, St. Martin of Tours.

However, it was hard leaving St. Mary's where we made our early friends, went to Mass, and established a sense of belonging in that community. Such pastors as Monsignor Mahoney and Father Sargawic became good family friends, and we enjoyed the Sisters of St. Joseph's teaching us and, when the occasion arose, disciplining us.

But it was not long after our move to South London that we felt the same sense of being at home in St. Martin Parish. Again the priests and sisters were welcoming. We weren't by any means overly devout Catholics, but we did go to Mass on weekday mornings. Oftentimes we went home with neighbors and had breakfast with them. Starting the day with Mass gave us a sense of joy and comfort.

We found ourselves caught up in a new community with all sorts of interesting things to do. One neighbor, directly across from us on Elmwood Avenue, was Miss Hazel Pound. She was a nurse and worked in East London at the asylum for mentally disturbed people. She and her sister Stella became very good friends; we often spent afternoons and evenings together with them.

One early consequence of this seemingly ordinary experience of going to Mass regularly was to plant the seed of the priesthood within me. I didn't do anything about it until I finished my graduate studies. Nonetheless, at that early age I discovered a mixed motivation urging me to consider the priesthood. Since I was an imaginative child, I would go into our linen closet, pick out one of the best sheets, make a circular vestment by folding the sheet four ways and cutting out a centerpiece, decorating it with Christian symbols, then inviting my young friends into our homemade attic chapel where we all had a grand time celebrating Mass, eating Ritz crackers, and drinking ginger ale. This was a favorite pastime, and it left its mark.

4

Discovering the Arts

One of the wonderful things about our Sisters of St. Joseph teachers was that they were always interested in promoting the talents of the students. When they realized I had some talent for painting and drawing, they immediately took me under their wing; after school they had me doing all sorts of things—posters, decorative pictures for the walls. Suddenly I woke up and found out I really could draw. But without their interest and solicitude for ferreting out the talents of the students, I probably would have remained indifferent to painting and the arts.

When we were in grade eight they also recognized the need for us to develop our speaking abilities. Fridays we had to prepare a two-minute talk on any subject of interest to us. In fact, it was during one of these Friday afternoon oratorical lessons that I gave a little talk on "The Vatican—The Treasure House of the Ages." (I had no idea then that one day I would end up being on the Advisory Board of the Vatican Museums, helping to restore some of the great works of art in the Vatican collections.) If it weren't for such speaking experiences, we would never have learned to stand on our own two feet, talk spontaneously, and overcome our fears.

Often I would buttonhole one of my brothers or sister to listen to my prepared talk. When they weren't available or interested, I'd go across the street and ask the Pound sisters to listen. Always very gracious, they would say yes, but first things first.

"We have to have our afternoon tea."

So we sat down and had our tea with cookies before I could bore them to death with my two-minute talks. They in turn would criticize me gently but firmly. Before long we became best friends. In high school I'd take part in oratorical contests. One year, I was fortunate enough to win the Rotary championship and was invited to the Toronto Fall Exposition Oratorical Competition for the province of Ontario.

Besides teaching us the skills of painting and speaking, the Sisters were intent on teaching us English grammar and spelling. When I went on to the Christian Brothers for high school, I was ready for them. My older brothers had all attended De La Salle, and I was expected to do the same. The McInnes clan descended upon them en masse.

I took history, French, Latin, mathematics, biology, and chemistry. By disposition, I'm not a natural linguist. In fact, I failed my first semester of French. The Christian Brother who taught me, Brother Raymond, took me aside.

"McInnes, this is the last time you're going to fail French."

For two semesters he kept me after classes for an hour every afternoon. At the end of this time, French was my best subject. Again, without this discipline and attention, I probably would have given up all linguistic interests. Later we studied Spanish, Greek, and Hebrew, which were also part of our course requirements.

Fortunately, my older brothers helped pave the way for me. Jack was a great football player as well as my brother Angus. Patrick and I followed up but not with the same talents. We had decided that sports like hockey were a little too much, especially the body checking; tennis was more to our taste and not quite as bruising. Perhaps it's just as well because we kept all our bones intact and came out relatively unharmed.

One of the distinctive characteristics of a Christian Brothers education was that they, like the Sisters, were aware of the wider aspects of education such as drama and woodworking. I enjoyed and began to excel in both of these arts as I pursued my regular courses, but not with the same interest.

We were fortunate enough to have the Grand Theatre, with some of the best drama people in Canada, just down Richmond Street from us. Some of their members would come over to De La Salle to coach and direct our plays. The first drama I was in was not Shakespeare but a melodrama by the name of *Curse You, Jack Dalton!* This was a particularly hilarious production. It required both male and female parts; since we were an all-male school, some of us had to play female roles. The dowager was one of my best friends; when he was made up he looked just like his aunt; we broke out in hilarious laughter.

I was chosen to be maid to the dowager. In one dramatic moment I had to rebuff a suitor by throwing a glass of water in his face. One night, however, the water actually flew all over the proscenium. I was completely nonplussed but, without a moment's hesitation, my dowager friend ad-libbed.

"We must do something about that leaky plumbing. The wall looks awful!"

It brought down the house.

We also starred in the musical *Show Boat* at a time when mimicking the wonderful tunes was the rage. However, the real meat of our drama experiences came from our roles in *Romeo and Juliet* and *Merchant of Venice*.

Soon we were doing plays in collaboration with the Roman Catholic girls' high school called St. Angelus. In *Romeo and Juliet* I was assigned the role of Friar Lawrence and one of my friends, Claude Penza, was chosen as Romeo. Another friend, Mary Helen Sweeney, was cast as Juliet.

Again we had excellent direction from Flo Scott and Martin O'Meara, both from London Little Theatre. They taught us how to learn our lines and how to act well, inspiring our lines with real meaning and emotional tone. This was verified when we opened with *Romeo and Juliet*. One of the local newspaper critics commented in his review, "Rarely if ever in amateur theatre do you find such acting and talent."

One of my good friends, Brian Laragh, who was at the time our stage manager and producer, would later go on in drama in New York City.

We had a great time doing these productions. They implanted in us a love of Shakespeare and a precision of speech that we would never otherwise have had.

As a result, we ended up having a well–rounded education. We were at home in academic subjects as well as the arts. I was certainly blessed in all these endeavors because they prepared me well for so many other experiences such as preaching and teaching.

I will always be grateful to the Sisters of St. Joseph and the Brothers of St. Jean Baptiste de la Salle.

5

Breaking the Race Barrier

In the latter part of high school, the Farrell family moved in next door to us on Elmwood Avenue. Their son John Kevin Farrell was a graduate student in history at the University of Western Ontario. As we got to know them, we found out that Jack was a former seminarian in the Congregation of St. Basil, known as the Basilian Fathers; they ran St. Michael's College in Toronto and Assumption College in Windsor, an affiliate of the University of Western Ontario. Later on these institutions would have a great impact on my life.

Jack Farrell was an only child; he naturally gravitated toward the McInnes household, visiting us often, becoming part of our own family. He intrigued us with his learning and flip sense of humor. We had a lot in common with the Farrells. Like us, they were devout Catholics, part of the history of the Irish in Canada and the United States.

When I came to know Jack, he was working on his M.A. thesis on the history of the Roman Catholic Church in the diocese of London, Ontario. I often accompanied him when he was interviewing notables in the city who knew something about that history. These included Colonel Coles, the main importer of coffee into our area of Canada, Monsignor Mahoney, rector of St. Peter Seminary, and Monsignor Flannery, a seminary professor who became a very good friend. These and other local clergy were involved in Jack's thesis as well; in turn I'd help him marshal some interviews for the final draft of the thesis.

Monsignor Flannery had a radio program entitled, "The School of Christ"; I was invited to take part in it, along with some of my friends from other Catholic schools. It was a half- hour program each Sunday afternoon. He would choose one of the readings of the day. We read it and reflected on it in terms of questions he would ask.

About this time we also came to know Sister Mary Theophane of the Precious Blood Sisters. They were a community of contemplative nuns dedicated to the worship of Christ under his passion and death; they focused on how he had shed his blood for our redemption. She'd been a good friend of my father's; we oftentimes went to their convent on Talbot Street for Sunday Mass and a visit with them followed by breakfast.

Sister Theophane typed the final draft of Jack's thesis. Some years later she would do the same for my own M.A. thesis. When she finished mine, she gave me a little card which I treasure to this day. On the back she wrote the following note.

"Your next thesis under the patronage of Our Lady and entitled, *The Science of the Saints*, will be written by daily living often through perfection in seeming trivialities. Upon its ultimate completion, may the Master deem you worthy of a high Degree of Glory for all eternity. –Sr. Mary Theophane Wallace, 1954."

She was always attentive to our spiritual needs and friendships. She and her community were there for all of us.

Out of the friendship with Jack Farrell and others a very interesting group involved in interfaith, inter-race relations emerged. London, Ontario, was predominantly a WASP community at that time. But there were Roman Catholics, Jews, blacks, Native American, and Indians from India. We were certainly in the minority; prejudice was very much alive. We decided to form a group that would help eliminate some of the ignorance that we felt was the cause of the prejudice. After putting our heads together and discussing what we might do, we formed a small group called "The Interfaith Inter-Race Society." We also decided to go to churches and synagogues on Sunday evenings to address the subject of prejudice. The format was to have at least one minority representative on each panel. These speakers would talk about the main source of prejudice against them. Our discussions were successful and for the most part had a beneficial effect.

One concrete benefit came out of our efforts. We were able to break the race barrier at the Springbank Park Amusement Centre. Friday nights there was a dance band. Two hundred people would come to enjoy a cool evening of relaxation by the Thames River. However, the centre had a definite policy of not allowing blacks. We decided to devise a strategy to confront this injustice and prejudice.

The next Friday night we approached the box office. One of us ordered sixty tickets. The observant ticket seller noticed what we were doing; there were at least five blacks in our group.

"We are not permitted to admit blacks."

Whereupon our spokesperson replied.

"Either you allow the blacks to enter with us, or none of us will enter."

Obviously, he was in a conundrum and had to call the manager. Fortunately, economics won out over prejudice, and we all went in. That was our first great triumph over prejudice. A footnote to our Interfaith Inter-Race Society: One Sunday evening we were supposed to go to a particular church. When we arrived, the church was closed and no one was there; someone had forgotten to call and make the arrangements. Spontaneously, I suggested everyone come back to my house, which was in the neighborhood; we could have a little party and spend the evening together.

My father who was a gregarious character was somewhat surprised to see us all pouring in, but he was gracious and welcomed us. I introduced him to everyone. Then he disappeared. I went upstairs to his bedroom; there he was sitting in a chair.

"What are you doing?"

"I'm reading the paper, can't you see?"

Then it dawned on me that he was not very comfortable with having blacks in his house.

"No, that's not true, I'm just tired."

Later my father admitted somewhat sheepishly that maybe he was prejudiced against the blacks.

6
Ursulines and Intellectuals

As I grew up in London, which was not a very Catholic city, I found superb religious groups; among them, the Ursulines at Brescia, offering college education for young women. The sisters left indelible marks on their students both intellectually and morally.

One story concerning the Ursulines has to do with Mother St. Michael, sometimes referred to as "the Brains" of the Ursulines in Canada. She was instrumental in obtaining accreditation for Brescia College, which became a first-class academic institution affiliated with the University of Western Ontario.

Another of her specialties was raising money. She was always trolling the London community for donations to the college scholarship fund and for gifted young women who needed just that sort of help to get through. She left no stone unturned.

Once she and one of her companions were waiting at the bus stop at North Richmond. A gentleman pulled up and asked if they'd like a ride. They gladly accepted. He was a public relations expert and knew a great deal about the Ursulines, especially how deft they were in raising money from unsuspecting sources. His name wasn't on their rolls, and he wasn't about to give it to them.

Try though she did during the drive downtown, Mother St. Michael couldn't worm the name out of him. As he was letting her and her companion out at the corner of Dundas and Richmond, he felt a sense of triumph over the well known fund-raiser.

"By the way," she said, poking her head back into the car, "to whom do we owe this hospitable ride?"

How could he refuse?

That story illustrates Mother St. Michael's ability to get to the heart of a matter. She was quick and perceptive, yet kind and understanding.

When she retired from the university, she didn't lose a beat. She wrote a major paper on the elderly and contemplation; it secured for her a job in the federal government department on the aging. Later, during the height of the Cold War, she was chosen to go to Moscow to deliver a major paper on the same subject: "Harvesting Excellence: The Spirituality of the Aging."

Over the years she became a dear friend of mine. She was a model of the religious intellectual life and influenced me in my own decision to enter religious life and the Dominican Order.

7

College in Windsor

When I graduated from De La Salle High School in London, I applied to Assumption College in Windsor, Ontario. Run by the Basilian Fathers, it had a very good reputation for the intellectual life, especially in the area of philosophy.

When I was accepted, I was delighted because one of my dear friends and school chums from De La Salle, Brian Laragh, had preceded me by a year. I can remember still the first day I arrived on campus. He showed me around, eventually directing me where to register and pay tuition.

In the process we met Claude Arnold; he looked as though he came straight out of the *Pickwick Papers*. He was rotund, wore a tweed suit with vest, hung a gold chain from his vest, and draped a trench coat over his shoulder. His glasses were octangular, which made him look like an owl. "Who in the world is this guy?" I asked myself.

It turned out he became one of our best and dearest friends. On many occasions his mother and aunt welcomed us, poor starving university students, into their home for Sunday afternoon dinner.

Assumption at this time was the Roman Catholic affiliate of Western Ontario. It provided an excellent education in the liberal arts, which included history, mathematics, English, science, and philosophy. With regard to the last, I didn't realize how fortunate I was. I found myself at the very center of a Thomistic revival introduced and taught by three outstanding teachers, Fathers Garvey and Dwyer and Professor Patrick Flood, who taught me the art of clear thinking and good writing and tutored me for the M.A. thesis; the last became a dear friend. To these I would add the president, Father LeBel, and Father Peter Swan, C.S.B., not to mention various lay faculty members.

During these years philosophers Jacques Maritain and his wife Raissa were following in the footsteps of the famous French medieval historian,

Etienne Gilson. The Maritains were teaching at the Pontifical Institute of Medieval Studies at St. Michael's College, Toronto. They'd helped develop the institute in collaboration with the Basilian Fathers and the distinguished philosopher Anton Pegis, who became head of the institute.

At this point in my life I was looking for deeper meaning. In Maritain's book, *An Introduction to Philosophy*, I began to find that meaning as we studied the quest of the Greek philosophers culminating in Plato and Aristotle. Through my professors I explored the world of being and how the truth would make one free.

These early efforts were peepholes into a world I didn't know, but they aroused my enthusiasm to the point that I decided to major and do a M.A. thesis in philosophy. At the same time I was struggling with questions of faith. I wanted to know the relationship between the "being" of the philosopher and the "being" of the revelation to Moses, that God's name was "I am who am." Gradually I saw the light.

I should mention here that I read, in translation from the French, Jacques Maritain's *Creative Intuition in Art and Poetry* and, in French, Raissa Maritain's *Sense et Nonsense*.

Another book that was a great influence in my thinking was Gilson's *The Perennial Philosophy*.

These works helped round out my appreciation of the differences between discursive intellectual analysis on the one hand and intuitive creative perceptions on the other. They brought together my life as a young student searching for meaning and purpose.

Yes, they were small seeds planted in my mind and soul, but they would bear great fruit.

8

Summer School in Switzerland

During my second year in college, I had the opportunity of going to summer school at the University of Fribourg, Switzerland. I had to convince my father that it would be a good academic experience. He was slow to agree. But when I mentioned that I could make a pilgrimage to Rome for the 1950 Holy Year and that I'd be traveling with a Catholic group under the supervision of priests and religious, he relented and indeed put up the money.

From St. Thomas, Ontario, I took the New York Central railway to New York, where I stayed overnight at the Biltmore Hotel. Next day I went on to Idlewild, present day JFK. There we took off on a TWA flight to Paris. I can still remember TWA's emblem, a slick birdlike design with triple tail. As we flew out of Idlewild, we settled into our seats and were awed by the experience that such a gigantic plane could take off with such ease and soar aloft. As we flew out over New England, I was riveted by the passing landscape below and cloud formations above. We landed safely at our first stop, Gander, Newfoundland, where we refueled.

Just as we were taking off, I noticed gas was flowing out of the wing and the engines were red hot. All I could think of was, one spark and we'd be blown to kingdom come. I called the stewardess.

"Don't worry about that," she said, looking out the window. "That happens all the time."

We arrived safely in Paris and went to our hotel. Within three days we'd visited Notre Dame, Sainte Chappelle, Les Invalides, the University of Paris, the Louvre, and the site of the apparitions to Visitation Sister Margaret Mary Alacoque on the Rue du Bac. In one apparition Christ revealed his sacred heart burning with love for the conversion of all men and women. The image was intertwined with Mary's immaculate heart. These images became the design for the Immaculate Heart medal. I found it strange and surprising to see this very active shrine in the midst of commercial Paris.

By this time our group were well acquainted with each other. There were two older Benedictine Sisters, students from Canada and the United States with special concentration of girls from Dominican Rosary College in River Forest, Illinois. One of these girls was from a very prominent Chicago family.

After four days in Paris, we boarded the train for Fribourg and enjoyed the French countryside, especially as we passed through Grenoble and the French Alps down into Switzerland and Fribourg itself. Some of the Rosary College group went to Freiburg in Saxony and had to return to Switzerland to our Fribourg *im Breisgau.*

The surprise for all of us was that Fribourg was an old Roman town in origin divided between the *basse ville*, the lower town where Julius Caesar had encamped as he passed through on his way to *Gaulle*, and the *haute ville*, the newer part of Fribourg where the modern Catholic university was located.

I was billeted in the apartment of a Swiss family. The husband had been a member of the Vatican Swiss Guard. He'd received many honors from Pius XII and was very proud of his experiences as a Swiss Guard officer. For six weeks I enjoyed their hospitality. His wife prepared my breakfast of hot chocolate, wonderfully fresh homemade bread, and jams. From their home, it was only a short walk to the university.

When our group convened at the university for classes, I was delighted to meet some Dominicans who were in charge of the philosophy and theology departments. Three especially caught my attention and we became good friends. The first was Pere I. M. Bochenski, philosopher and logic professor; in his spare time he flew planes. His specialty was communism. He taught us Introduction to Philosophy and Philosophy of Communism. He read *Pravda* in Russian every day and extracted material for reports he sent to the C.I.A.

When we came to know him better, he told us this interesting story. His parents, noble Poles, accompanied him to the novitiate in Krakow in a beautiful carriage. He was welcomed by the novice master, who later made this wisecrack to the community.

"He'll never last!"

But Pere Bochenski had the last word.

"That was the first and last time we heard of him. I'm still here to tell the tale, and God knows where the novice master is."

We were also taught by Pere Loiten and Father Philip O'Reiley from Ireland. The latter was chaplain; the former taught us French. All the classes were in English and French.

A couple of students would become lifelong friends, such as Kitty Rottier from Fremont, Michigan, and Lorin Filmore from Oak Park, Illinois; and a few others, one from Texas and one from New York.

The summer passed all too quickly. In addition to the courses we had great discussions with the Dominicans and visiting professors, and other notables, such as Frank Sheed and his wife Maisie Ward, authors and publishers of Sheed & Ward. I remember one lecture vividly.

Sheed was giving a talk on the history of the Church between the first and the second world wars. When he couldn't remember a date, he asked his wife. She was knitting away.

"Now, Frank, that happened just before our first son was born, and I know for sure that that date was before the birth of our second son, so it must have been before 1920...."

When she finally stopped, he turned and looked at us.

"As I was saying before I was rudely interrupted by my dear wife, the date was 1921."

On weekends we took off to the country. Once we rented a Volkswagen convertible and drove to the higher mountains where we stayed in a beautiful chalet inn overlooking spectacular views of the Alps. Another time we went bike riding, figuring it was the best way to climb the back roads to places like Gruyere where the famous cheese was made. We stopped for lunch, had cheese fondue, then coasted all the way down to Fribourg.

When summer school finally ended, we made our goodbyes. I was greatly impressed by the Dominicans I'd met. They made a lasting impression upon me. Two things struck me; they were a joyful lot and very welcoming. These qualities have stayed with me to this day and are indeed living realities in the Dominican life.

9

Pilgrimage to Rome

On leaving Fribourg we boarded the train for Milan, where we'd begin our Holy Year pilgrimage to Rome. Along the way we enjoyed the relaxed atmosphere of a holiday with occasional interludes of morning Mass, meditations, and the Rosary.

When we arrived in Milan, the station was packed with people. When I looked for my passport and wallet, they were gone. We reported the loss immediately to the police, but I kissed my articles goodbye. Much to my amazement, by the time we reached our hotel, the police had actually recovered them both, including my money. In time I'd learn that during the Holy Year pickpockets from all over Italy went to Rome; their aim wasn't the pilgrimage, but the pilgrims' pockets.

Once settled in to our hotel, we all took off to visit the "Wedding Cake," the richly decorated Gothic cathedral. It contained the tomb of St. Charles Borromeo in the crypt; at the entrance of the church, in the vestibule, was one of the first elevators ever constructed, designed if I recall correctly by Raphael. It was a big wicker basket controlled by pulleys; it was well anchored and still usable. However, I declined a ride. We traveled by bus to Assisi, Siena, and Orvieto. When we arrived in Rome, the city was swamped with pilgrims and students. Fortunately, in our group there was a young lady from New Jersey whose uncle was an Italian cardinal. He arranged for us to attend an audience with Pope Pius XII and to accompany him on his pilgrimage to the basilica of St. Mary Major. Pius XII was a very austere looking man; he rode in an open car as we followed on foot from St. Peter's, where the audience was held, to the basilica where we had benediction.

It's hard to express the impact that Rome made on all of us. Rome wasn't called "The Eternal City" for nothing. Not only did it represent the ancient Roman and early Christian cultures, but it had such impact upon the whole of the western world.

I experienced one lasting impression. I hoped that one day I could return to Rome and spend more time visiting the many beautiful churches and seeing the treasures they contained. My wish has been fulfilled many times over.

We left Rome convinced that the Holy Year and the celebration of Mass at the tomb of St. Peter were the true high points of our pilgrimage.

10
Nice in Nice

As we made our way home through the French Riviera, we stayed for a few days at the Hotel Busby in Nice. On our arrival, we immediately got into our bathing suits and went for a splash in the Mediterranean. To our absolute horror we discovered there was no beach; we had to tiptoe painfully on the stones before we got into the water. After a refreshing swim we somehow made it back to the hotel, had a rest, and went to dinner.

Later that evening the same affluent girl from Rosary College I mentioned earlier was celebrating her twenty-first birthday. She decided to throw a party in her suite and invited our small group to attend. Of course we accepted; the two Benedictine Sisters thought it might be nice to join the festivities.

A word about the sisters. One was German, and the other was Irish. During our stay in Fribourg, the Irish sister accompanied the German to her family's home in Bavaria with the understanding that the German nun would accompany the Irish on a visit to Ireland. The first trip went well, but when it came time for the trip to Ireland, the German sister said flat out she wasn't interested. This caused a rupture in their relationship. As a result, our little group found the Irish sister with us all the time while the German sister went off somewhere else. It reminded me of the *Canterbury Tales* and the foibles of the pilgrims on that famous journey.

Back to the party.

We gathered in our friend's lovely suite. Champagne was poured into a large glass punch bowl in the center of the table. It was generously ladled out into all cups. The sisters arrived late, but thought it was very good punch indeed. As the party progressed, we had some food. The French doors to the balconies were opened, and we poured out. We were enjoying the evening so much that we forgot to notice we'd become raucous. A sentinel warned us to disperse before the gendarmes arrived. Our rooms were on the first floor, but we couldn't make it down to the lobby in time. Much to our delight, we succeeded in evading the police by hiding behind gigantic flower pots in the patio.

The two sisters, however, not fully comprehending what a police raid was, weren't so lucky. Standing in the lobby, completely tiddled, they greeted the police who demanded to know why they couldn't stand up straight and look them straight in the eye. They proceeded to explain in greatest detail how there couldn't possibly have been anything alcoholic in the empty punch bowl; it was just an old-fashioned punch. Confounded, wondering what the Church was coming to, the police escorted them to their rooms.

Next day we gathered for breakfast, then made our way to the train station. The Benedictine Sisters were nowhere to be seen. They finally showed up on the platform just before the train pulled out. They were none too steady on their feet, and their eyes were anything but steady. For which the rest of us were exceedingly grateful. Previously, at the slightest provocation, they prissily reminded us to behave ourselves; we were on a pilgrimage. But from that point on, the tables were turned. At the slightest whim, we reminded them of their drunken adventure cum confrontation with police, news that their religious superiors would dearly love to know. We had no further trouble from them.

11

The Grotto and the Grotesque

We arrived in Lourdes late afternoon in a steady rain. We made a quick run to the hotel. Later on half a dozen of us ventured down to the shrine. We made our way into the grotto, said a few prayers, and then returned. I decided to go up into the basilica by myself. It was rather gloomy; vigil lights were the only illumination. As I progressed up the nave of the church, I heard someone sobbing behind a pillar; I made my way over to see who it was. There, kneeling before a statue of the Virgin, was a huge Pyrenean farmer pouring his heart out with every expectation of getting a response. I have no doubt his prayer was answered.

Visiting the grotto again, while praying, the thought entered my mind, and a strong resolve entered my spirit, to become a priest, or at least try it. It struck me that if Jesus really was the Son of God, that was the greatest single event in human history, and I should do something about it. So I put myself under Our Lady's patronage; she would help me discern whether that was what I should do and where I should go.

The following day, our group joined in the celebration of Mass at the Grotto. Afterward we made our way to Bernadette's impoverished little house where her parents raised her before she was chosen to be a special witness to the Virgin of the Immaculate Conception. Years later when I saw the movie "The Song of Bernadette," I recalled all of these incidents with much joy.

In Paris we found our flight home delayed. Suddenly we had two days in Paris, and we used the time well. In the first evening we went to the Opera House to see Stravinsky's ballet, *The Firebird*. The following night we were told we would have a similar experience. But when our bus arrived at the theater, it wasn't the Opera House. We had very good seats in the front row of the balcony. Accompanied by the two Benedictine sisters, I led the group into the row and sat down next to a man who had a pair of binoculars; not opera glasses, but real racing binoculars. Finally, the house lights dimmed, the curtains parted, and there before us was, lo and behold, a tableau of statuesque beauties in various stages of undress. It was the Folies Bergere. As I looked over at the two sisters, all I could see were two veils flying through the door. The student next to me asked the question.

"Well, should we go, too?"

My response came quicker than I could imagine.

"Hell, no! We paid perfectly good money to come here."

The man next to me was glued to his binoculars the rest of the evening.

Finally, we took off from the Paris airport, thinking that our summer of studies abroad with a holy-year pilgrimage thrown in had been a well-rounded experience, our own *Canterbury Tales*.

12

Summer School in Holland

The following year at Assumption College, 1951, a scholarship to pursue an introduction to international law was offered by International University Services and would be held at the University of Leyden. I was urged to apply by some of my professors and, much to my surprise, I won. This time, instead of traveling with a group, I was all on my own. The scholarship would pay for major expenses. My father was delighted; he gave me his blessing and a check for the minor expenses.

I traveled to Europe on Holland American Line's *Waterman*. We left from the New Jersey port, traveled down the Hudson River, enjoying the Manhattan vista in all its glory, and out past the Statue of Liberty into the Atlantic. The crossing was uneventful with good food and interesting companions. My berth in the lower decks was somewhat suffocating, so I went up on the upper deck and spent most of the night wrapped in a blanket in a deck chair. When I arrived in Amsterdam, I took the train directly to Leyden where I registered and settled in.

I was assigned to live in the home of Admiral and Mrs. Rost van Tonnigen. It was a lovely place in Wassingnar. I discovered that there were two sons in the family, Nicholas and his older brother, who was away most of the time. As a result I became friends with Nicholas, who was younger than I, and his parents. The father was former head of the Dutch fleet in Indonesia before World War II; he returned to Holland just before the outbreak of the war. As I came to know them better, I was able to piece together this story.

The admiral's brother was the leading quisling who betrayed Holland to the Nazis. When the admiral, who'd become the naval aide–de–camp to the queen of Holland, was attempting to leave the country with the royal family just before the Nazis arrived; apparently, the two brothers looked a great deal alike, at least in the eyes of the would-be assassin. Severely wounded, the admiral was captured by the Germans and subsequently hospitalized. Later he was captured by the Soviet Army and sent to Siberia. The great wonder of it all was that he survived the whole ordeal.

When the war ended, he was able to make his way back through Asia to Egypt, where he contacted the Dutch embassy; the queen sent a plane to bring him back to Holland. When I arrived on the scene, he'd been reinstated as the naval aide–de–camp to Queen Juliana. Each day he commuted to and from the royal palace at Sussdyck in one of the royal cars, Rolls Royce, Bentley, Mercedes Benz. Naturally this got our attention. Being young students, Nicholas and I were wowed by them.

As a footnote to this story, I was told that the admiral's brother was tried for treason at the end of the war and executed for his role in helping betray Holland to the Nazis.

Classes at Leyden went well. My principal professor was the former Supreme Court Justice of India, Sir Bendigal Rahal. He was an erudite scholar, well versed in the history of international law as it originated from historical conflicts in Mexico. The issue: Were Indians slaves to the Spanish conquistadors or freemen in their own right? Historically, a Dominican priest-friar by the name of Francesco de Vittorio presented the case successfully in front of King Philip II of Spain. He argued that the Indians were human and, therefore, they were to be treated as humans with their own rights. It was no wonder that Vittorio became known as the founder of international law.

The main building of the University of Leyden had been a monastery belonging to the Carmelite Order. With the confiscation of Church property during reformation and post-reformation periods, the campus became the site for the University.

During my studies there, I came to know a young Indian student who lived not too far from the van Tonnigens. We oftentimes met and walked to school in the mornings, enjoying our university experiences. He was a friend and confidante of the Duke of Windsor.

When I was graduated, I invited my host and hostess to attend. However, the admiral said that he was too much on display all day and had to preserve his privacy whenever he could. He congratulated me on receiving my diploma in international law, and we celebrated with a little dinner at home.

13

Back to Assumption

On my return to Canada, and before resuming my academic life at Assumption, I attended the graduation of Jason McCallum. He'd been a good friend of Brian Laragh's and mine over the years. In fact, we oftentimes went to one another's homes for Christmas, New Year's, and Thanksgiving. At one point I even restored one of the pastoral paintings hanging in their living room. Looking back, I think I re-did the painting rather than restored it, but we had many happy occasions together, sometimes with unexpected results.

For example, on the day that Mr. McCallum died, we rushed over to the house to extend our condolences. He was a banker and had died suddenly of a heart attack. As we gathered in their front hall, Mrs. McCallum came down the stairs dressed in a beautiful grey gown with a white fox fur. She stopped on the landing and made the following statement.

"I want to thank you all for coming to express your condolences on the death of my dear husband. But I just want you to know that I feel as if chains have fallen from me."

That was the end of our condolences. Then we went in to dinner.

At this time, when Brian and I were going to Assumption, Jason went off to college for pre-law. After a couple of years he decided it wasn't for him. I asked him why he changed to psychology.

"I'm trying to figure out whether I'm crazy or my family is crazy."

When he'd finished his doctorate in psychology, I asked him if he'd ever solved the old question.

"Oh yes, I've decided we're all crazy."

When he did graduate, we all went over to the house to help; they were going to have a garden party. We arrived about an hour and a half early, but we couldn't find a soul. Finally we went to the basement. The McCallums were laid out on the floor. Apparently, they'd been mixing the cocktails without measuring and gotten drunk from the sipping. So we had to pick them up and literally throw them into showers. By the time the caterers arrived, they were all appropriately dressed, although we didn't get the hat on Mrs. McCallum quite straight.

Jackie, the daughter, insisted on helping the maids with the cocktails. She picked up a tray of glasses and, as she walked out onto the terrace, the inevitable happened. She fell flat on her face. We rushed over to help her.

"I knew I shouldn't have worn spiked heels!"

The last I heard from Jason was that he was happily married, living in Toronto, and enjoying his practice of psychology.

These social interludes in my regular academic studies added a great deal of zest and contrast to my regular study life.

When I returned to Assumption College, I finished off my B.A. and began work on my M.A. in philosophy under Professor Flood. For thesis topic I chose "The Philosophical Basis of Aesthetic Criticism." This gave me the opportunity to research the subject, focussing on an historical perspective on the question beginning with Plato and Aristotle going through the early Christians, especially Plotinus, Augustine, and Aquinas all the way up to Descartes, Kant, and Baumgartner.

I discovered that the philosophical basis of aesthetic criticism was rooted in an understanding of the ways that works of art came to be; it compared favorably with the ways that things in nature came to be. The end result was that there was a real relationship between the genesis of a work of art with inspiration as the soul of the work and how that inspiration worked its way through the expression of the particular art.

This study also renewed my awareness of the fact that all works of art had a beginning, middle, and end. They were subject to scrutiny, as one would scrutinize the life of another, with objective standards verifying the integrity, clarity and validity of the work of art.

Fortunately, I completed the thesis and passed the oral examination, *magna cum laude*.

There was one incident about my thesis work that I must tell; it epitomized the intellectual life. Three fifths of the way through my thesis, my mind went blank; I just felt I couldn't finish the work. When I told my father he advised me to come home and forget about the thesis.

"Your life isn't dependent on completing a thesis."

So I went home to London, forgot all about it for a week, enjoyed myself, relaxed, and went back to Windsor. I finished off the last two chapters with renewed interest and zest. In my oral exam, several of the board members wanted to know what happened to me in the fourth and fifth chapters.

"You're much more spontaneous and fluid in your writing style."

I told them the story of my father's advice. By distancing myself from my thesis, I was able to draw closer to its argument.

14

Monastery Crawling

Once I had completed my thesis, after I was graduated, I relaxed for a few weeks, or so I planned. But there emerged for immediate consideration the big question. "What are you going to do with the rest of your life?"

I reviewed my options. I had long thought of college teaching as well as the priesthood and religious life. It was time to make a decision. Growing up in London I had frequent contact with our parish priest, such members of the faculty of St. Peter's Seminary as Monsignors Wimple and Flannery. They were all most helpful. Alas, the choice was mine and mine alone!

First, I had to decide whether married life was appealing; it was, or so I concluded, but not necessarily for me.

Second, I decided to try the priesthood. Marriage would be a fall-back position.

Third, if I wanted to be a priest, I would have to decide between diocesan priest and religious order priest. With regard to the former, I had a reservation. Our former pastor, Father Phelan, influenced me in this regard. At the height of his career at St. Martin's he suffered a heart attack and had no one to care for him, except his sister who lived nearby. On future investigation, I learned that dioceses did have retirement homes for their elderly.

Fourth, because religious orders had infirmaries and communities for their elderly, *religious order priest* it had to be. Besides, I'd always wanted to give myself completely to the Lord.

I told my father and talked it over with some friends. The only thing left to do, said my friend Jack Farrell, was to have a "monastery-crawl."

I visited the Carmelites in upper New York State and the Benedictines at Mount Saviour, New York; the latter invited me to live their life for a week.

I accepted the invitation. While there I met an older man, a professor of the New Testament at the University of Chicago who specialized in St. John's Gospel. I was appalled to learn that, even though he knew his Greek and the Gospel of John very well, he didn't believe one sentence of it. He admired the simplicity and symmetry of the language but had no awareness or the intellectual and spiritual import. "How odd!" I thought to myself. He'd missed the point completely.

Next stop was the Trappists at St. Joseph's Abbey in Spencer, Massachusetts. Unfortunately, the buildings had burned to the ground a few years before. Restoration was in progress. One of the recent members had come from the Brooks Brothers family, the clothiers; he entered after finishing his architectural degree. Judging from the sad state that the old building had been in, I couldn't suppress the feeling that he'd burned it down so that he could build the new one.

Whatever the real circumstances were, he built a beautiful monastery. If I made my judgment solely on aesthetics, I'd have chosen to stay forever. The Trappists were definitely a live community with a great aesthetic sense and a deep contemplative lifestyle. Yet I found their emphasis on death and dying was too much for me as a young man. I left with a sense of relief and also of regret that I was leaving such a beautiful place.

Fortunately, my instincts were right. One didn't choose a vocation based upon aesthetics but on whether the charism of the order fitted one's personality. As St. Thomas Aquinas said in a discussion on vocations, the vocation should fit the personality "much like a glove fits a hand."

From the east I went to the central part of the United States, to Chicago to visit the Dominicans in River Forest and to Minnesota to visit the Benedictines.

In Chicago I went to visit the Dominican house of studies at the corner of Harlem and Division. It was a beautiful house designed by C. N. Anthony in Elizabethan-Gothic style. It had an aesthetic appeal, at least on the outside. There I met up with some Dominicans, all of whom were enthusiastic, vibrant, and very much alive. The following day I went to visit the vocations director, Father Gilbert Graham, O.P., at 1909 South Ashland Avenue, the Church of St. Pius V. Father Graham told me straight off that whatever my aspirations to become a Dominican might be, they would have to be the Lord's and not mine. I didn't quite comprehend what he was getting at. The good thing was I felt very much at home there.

Close by in Riverside, Illinois, lived one of the friends I made in Fribourg, Lorin Filmore. I visited with him and his mother for several days and reflected with them on what I was doing and the quest I was on.

Then, by train up the Mississippi River to St. Paul/Minneapolis and by bus to Collegeville, Minnesota, I arrived at the Benedictines. I was impressed by the size of the monastery and the recently completed chapel designed by Marcel Breuer. Again, it was a balance between the aesthetic and the academic. At that time the Benedictine community was one of the largest in the world. They were intellectually alive and had their own printing press; they obviously were *au courant* with regard to contemporary architecture and liturgical developments.

After all these visits and experiences I returned home to London where for the next month I pondered and prayed. Where was the Lord calling me? Where could I fulfill my aspirations? I remember clearly going into the cathedral in London and praying in front of the Shrine of Our Lady of Perpetual Help. When I left, I found I'd chosen the Dominicans. St. Dominic had always embodied for me the twin aspirations of preaching and teaching as well as the desire to give myself to the service of the Lord according to that ancient itinerant preaching charism.

After notifying the vocation director of my desire and filling out my application, it was not long before I was accepted and would be reporting to the novitiate in Winona, Minnesota.

15

Novice in Winona

It didn't take long for my good news to travel. Friends gave me farewell parties. My entrance into religious life, however, was delayed a number of months; it took longer to negotiate my residence visa to the United States than I anticipated. Hence, the inevitable. "What, are you still here?" Finally, in early November, the night came. A crowd saw me off. I said my good-byes, then boarded the CPR train in London for Chicago.

Once in my compartment I experienced two contradictory feelings. The first was that I was absolutely crazy. Here I was leaving my family and friends and an opportunity to teach at a university. The second was that I was absolutely right: "Don't give a care in the world about what you feel, just do it." With that thought I went to bed. Next morning I awoke in Chicago, changed trains, and arrived in Winona late in the afternoon.

As I left the train I put my luggage down on the platform. I was greatly appalled. I'd come to the middle of nowhere, and no one was there to welcome me. As the train pulled out, on the other side of the platform, there they were, the welcoming committee. Three thug-like creatures wearing black fedoras. Either they've come to greet me or to wipe me out.

"Milk shakes! We're dying for milk shakes! Take us to a soda fountain now!"

On the way there, they introduced themselves: Brother Mark Leuer, Brother Antoninus Kilroy, Brother Cajetan Fiori.

"Milk shakes all around for my new friends," I said, and I had to pay; they weren't carrying any money. When I asked if this was how all incoming novices were greeted, I don't think I got a straight answer. Perhaps it was a custom dating back to the Founder himself.

Between swigs of milkshake my new brothers in Christ took great delight in telling me, in painstaking detail, that my religious name would be that of a Dominican bishop martyr from Tonkin in present day Vietnam.

"Valentine de Barrio-Ochoa."

And I thought *Ambrose* was bad!

I discovered later that I was given this name because I was arriving at the novitiate on November 18th, which was just in time to celebrate the feast of the Dominican martyrs of Tonkin. In a year's time, on that very date, I made my first simple vows with the illustrious name of the first Roman Catholic Bishop of Tonkin, Valentine, to symbolize my new religious life.

After checking for white moustaches, they drove me through the high hills overlooking the Mississippi River toward the recently built Priory of St. Peter Martyr. Suddenly, I realized my luggage was still at the station. We hurried back down, collected the luggage, and sped back to the novitiate, arriving just in time for supper. We were greeted by the novice master.

"What took you so long?"

"I had to get a visa."

"Oh, I see!"

He smiled the smile of one who knew exactly what caused the delay; he'd once been a novice himself. He welcomed me warmly and introduced me to the community who were also glad to see me.

In my class we began with twenty-four novices; in four years our ranks were reduced to twelve. We became a community, praying morning, noon, and evening, the regular divine office as well as the office of the Blessed Virgin Mary. During that time I made discoveries about myself, the history of the Order of Preachers, the liturgy of the Order, and the spiritual life.

Our novice master was Father Nicholas Walsh, O.P., an Irishman with a blithe spirit who knew how to shape character and still leave room for personality.

Many incidents happened during those days, especially as winter came on and buried us in snow and temperatures that often went down to 15 degrees below zero. Our novice master directed that we walk with him for an hour each day. But after a dozen steps he was the first to return when the temperature was 16 below.

The formation program at the novitiate was basically designed so that Father Walsh and the senior community could judge whether we were suitable candidates imbibing the life and the spirit of the Order. At the same time the novices were judging the priests as suitable confreres and models.

Materially speaking, it could not have been a nicer house, recently built, well furnished, certainly well heated against the Minnesota winters, and well designed for the exercises of religious life. To make us contemplatives the schedule provided time for prayer and meditation, lots of reading, and classes in the history of the Order, its spirituality, and Latin classes for those who needed them. I needed them, but I never took them because I had all those years of Latin in my high school and college records.

We studied the Psalms. They were David's prayerful reflections on the Jewish people and their relationship with God; on the one hand, their willingness to serve; on the other hand, their unwillingness to serve, but to rebel. Thus the Church used these prayers to remind all God's people not to repeat the mistakes of the Jewish people, but to imitate their good qualities. One day we entered into a long and lively discussion on whether the psalms were good poetry. Literature wasn't the novice master's strong point; frustrated, he ended the class abruptly.

"Well, whether you think it's good poetry or not, it's all divinely inspired, and you'd better get used to it!"

In March of my novitiate year, my father came to visit. One of my classmates was Tony Kilroy, O.P., whom we affectionately referred to as "Conning Tower Kilroy"; he was always looking out the tower window to see who was driving up the long driveway to the top of the hill. This day, when my father arrived, he came rushing to my room to tell me. I made my way to the parlor. My father had already asked for me but unbeknownst to him, my name in religion was now Brother Valentine. Naturally, he asked for Brother Ambrose. We had such a brother in our class, and he answered the call to see my father.

"I'm Brother Ambrose," he said to my father.

"My, how you've changed!"

That's when I made my entrance.

In the spring, we were all assigned duties. My classmate, Brother Antoninus (Tony), and I were given the job of planting a line of gladioli at the entrance to the cemetery. We dug the row for the bulbs and dutifully planted the first half upside down. With no gardening experience, how were we to know which end was up? We replanted and waited. Some arrived a full three weeks before the others.

The more serious aspects of the novice year were the spiritual growth in our lives, the readings, regular confessions, the meditative walks in the beautiful countryside around the priory. I remember still, during Holy Week, walking around the graveyard thinking of the people who were buried there, although there weren't all that many. Nonetheless, the experience of knowing we all must die to ourselves in order to be reborn in Christ penetrated the inner being of my life. I was freed from my preoccupation with myself and the world. That uncovered the wellspring of God's Presence dwelling within me. The blood of Christ washing over me and my community each day in the Eucharist was indeed a purifying experience.

In our class we had diverse people from all parts of the United States and all strata of society. One of our student brothers was a graduate of Yale. He was a very intelligent and accomplished young man. At the same time living in our novitiate house in the senior community was a very famous French Dominican by the name of Pere Raymond L. Bruckberger. He'd been Charles de Gaulle's personal chaplain during the Second World War. When De Gaulle arrived back in Paris, he refused to be greeted by the archbishop; he considered him a collaborator with the Nazis. As a result, Bruckberger officially greeted De Gaulle when he entered Notre Dame Cathedral and reclaimed the city and the country for the Free French.

Bruckberger went on to become a celebrated writer. He wrote a famous work on Mary Magdalene and co-wrote the scenario for the opera, *Dialogs of the Carmelites*. He'd recently finished two books that became bestsellers in the United States, one entitled *One Sky to Share*, the other, *DeToqueville—A Hundred Years Later*.

One evening, our novice master invited Bruckberger to come talk to us. We gathered in our "rec" room. It was a simple talk about how, if we give ourselves to the Lord, all sorts of things will multiply in our lives, unfolding the theme of generosity. At the end of his talk, my classmate from Yale asked why he wasn't allowed to bring his books to the novitiate; he pointed out that another brother, myself, had been allowed to bring most of his library. He said he felt discriminated against. Bruckberger refused to get involved in the dispute.

"First seek the kingdom of heaven, and then all of these things will be added to you—including your books."

At the end of our novitiate, we took first simple vows, which would run for the next three years. In other words, after an initial commitment of one year, Canon Law granted us three more years to decide whether the religious life was for us. When our novitiate year ended, I didn't go down to Chicago with my class; I was required to stay three months longer in order to complete my full canonical year. Finally, when my time was completed, I took my first simple vows, packed my bags, and boarded the train for Chicago.

16

Philosophy in River Forest

Since I was the final novice of my class leaving Winona, the novice master gave me the complete file on my class; I was to turn it over to the student master in River Forest the next day.

En route, I sat on the observation deck of the Zephyr, enjoying the scenery. I was wearing my Roman collar for the first time. A lady approached.

"Are you a priest?"

"No, I'm a religious."

"I'm just coming home from my father's funeral, and I have all sorts of Mass stipends; I want to give them to you to have Masses said for him."

She gave me $600. What struck me was the obvious trust people had in the collar. To me as a young religious it was gratifying.

That evening I arrived in River Forest and was greeted by my classmates. The interior of the building, they alerted me, wasn't as modern as the novitiate, especially in the toilet and shower areas. I survived the shock. When they finally took me to my room, I was shocked again; someone had taken a statue of the Virgin Mary and put it in my bed. This was rather an adroit move since no one was allowed to enter another's room. Hence, it had to be done by a very big person with a very large reach.

Finally, I asked them to take me to the student master. When we went to his office he wasn't in. The following morning after Mass, prayers, and breakfast, I went to his office again; again he wasn't in.

"I'm over here!" came a voice across the corridor.

There was the student master sitting on his throne, taking care of his physical needs.

Just like home, I thought.

"Where are you from?"

"London, Ontario."

"How did you ever get interested in the Dominicans in London, Ontario?"

"The Dominicans were in London from 1850 to 1856."

"The Dominicans were never in London, Ontario."

"Do you have Father Bonniwell's *History of the Dominicans in the United States*?"

"Do I have the *History of the Dominicans in the United States*!" He almost had a catatonic fit! He got up and went to look up the *History of the Dominicans in the United States*, and there it was, the Dominicans in London from 1850 to 1856.

Later I learned that Father Bernard Walker, our student master, was one of the leading historians of the Order. No wonder I could do no wrong in his history class. But I feared he'd catch me on one of my many other deficiencies.

Father Walker was succeeded as student master by Father Raymond Scullion, O.P., an entirely different type of personality. He was preoccupied with the thought that too many students were overly dependent upon their mothers; he'd fix that. Since my mother died when I was very young, I didn't fall under his wrath. Nonetheless, I'd have problems with him.

On one occasion, in my second year of philosophy, in early December, I asked the master if my father, one of my brothers, Patrick, and my friend, Dr. Jack Farrell could come visit me during Holy Week. He gave permission. But when Holy Week rolled in, he called me up and demanded to know why I had the arrogance to invite my father, brother, and friend during Holy Week.

"What are you talking about? You yourself gave me permission in December to have them come."

Whereupon he demanded that I make a venia, a public confession when one has made a significant mistake or fault against the rule or the constitution; it required kneeling on the floor, throwing your scapula in front of you, and stretching out on top of it. I refused to do so.

"That was your mistake, not mine."

"Oh, oh, oh, I forgot."

When I asked where they were staying, he couldn't tell me.

"You mean to tell me they've come 600 miles to visit me and you can't tell me where they're staying?"

He said they'd be back to see me on Holy Saturday evening.

I went immediately to see my confessor and explained the problem. Fortunately, he was able to smooth things over. I'd get to see them, but not before Holy Saturday.

This crisis was a real test of my vocation. *What do you do with people who can't remember they gave you permission?* Did I really want to be subjected to people of that sort? Fortunately, with the help of classmates and priest friends, the incident blew over. I did get to see my visitors on Holy Saturday; they were able to stay over until Easter Monday. Eventually, I came to understand why the student master had acted that way; Cardinal Stritch had asked religious superiors in the archdiocese of Chicago to defer all visits until after Easter.

Tests like these are common in religious life; they give you opportunities to determine whether you'll allow your anger to upset you to the point you forget the real reason you're there. On a deeper spiritual level, however, there were experiences that helped us grow in our faith. For example, I can remember still going to confession one evening. Most of my classmates had little or no academic background, but I was feeling superior and condescending to them. I revealed this weakness, and the confessor replied.

"Brother Valentine, you can decide to do one of two things. You can choose to look at the brothers and concentrate on their defects; in this case you'll get depressed and probably leave religious life. Or you can choose to pick out the one quality that each brother seems to excel in. If you do that, you'll see the full spectrum of the virtuous life in front of you. You'll be grateful and humble that you've been brought into such a remarkable group of men."

When it came to studying philosophy in River Forest, I discovered two schools of Thomistic thought.

One school concentrated on the Thomistic revival with leadership coming from Gilson and Maritain as purveyed by the Basilians at the Mediaeval Institute of St. Michael's College at the University of Toronto. Gilson's approach was strictly historical, examining the traditions of Aristotle and Thomas and analyzing the contents of their works.

The Maritains entered Thomistic studies when they were students at the University of Paris. Traipsing through the corridors one day, they happened upon a lecture being given by Pere Antonin-Gilbert Sertillanges, O.P. They paused at the door to listen. By the time the lecture ended, they were enthralled with the Dominican's *elan* and insight. They forgot their depression and their inclination to suicide.

The Maritains began their ascent into the faith and mystical studies tutored by Sertillanges who favored the "intuition of being" approach.

This was the Thomism I'd been introduced to in college. Now in graduate school I was introduced to another, albeit complementary, Thomism.

The River Forest School of Thomism pursued a methodological approach based on the inductive method of Aristotle and Thomas. In this curriculum the beginning of Thomistic study was natural philosophy, ethics, politics; it then ascended into metaphysics, and from there into theodicy and theology.

Father Benedict Ashley and, in our second year, Father Athanasius Weisheipl were most helpful in showing how all these different facets fitted together. They weren't necessarily polemical, as Father Kane tended to emphasize; they were simply different approaches. Father John Thomas Bonee taught logic and the *Anterior and Posterior Analytics* of Aristotle.

In our philosophical courses, we followed the method of disputation laid out by Thomas in the *Summa Theologica*; it taught how to address a question from all sides, answer the objections, and conclude with the best resolution of the truth.

Studying philosophy in Latin demanded that we think with precision, beginning with simple apprehension, ending in judgment, and stringing judgments together in a reasoning process that enabled the mind to comprehend reality. Epistemology was a great help.

During these years there were other faculty members who made great impressions. Looking back, I find some of the stories concerning them are better than Ripley's "Believe It Or Not."

Father Ralph "Doc" Powell was a brilliant fellow with a doctorate in history from Louvain, Belgium. He belonged to a very clever family—they owned the Mayflower Hotel in Washington, D.C.—and had eccentricities of his own. He spoke in a high-pitched voice, punctuated with various intonations that were hard to describe. I still remember his first lecture on the history of Byzantium.

"On the morning of September 3 in the year 430, the emperor rose and found himself surrounded by people who were about to murder him...."

He captivated us for two weeks. The third week, things changed.

"Brothers, you're all too naive. Everything I've taught you so far has been false. You have to become critical, even of me."

From that moment on we were merciless.

When I did a major paper on the English Dominican, Father Victor White, and his well-known book on Carl Jung, *God and the Unconscious*, Fr. Powell was a great help.

Father Athanasius had taken his doctorate in philosophy at the Angelicum in Rome, followed by a D. Phil. in history at Oxford. When he came to River Forest during my second year, he was a breath of fresh air. He complemented our theoretical studies of St. Thomas with the practical historical milieu out of which St. Thomas' thinking arose. He had the great gift of putting everything in historical perspective. Besides, he was younger than most of the professors; we felt more at ease with him.

His parents were both deaf and dumb; they entrusted him to the Dominican Sisters in Racine, Wisconsin, who provided him with a splendid classical education. On graduating from high school his parents gave him a copy of Aristotle's works in Greek. He was an accomplished teacher and became a dear friend, along with Father Benedict, an equally gifted teacher and a universal genius. These two professors were particularly helpful and became our true brothers in religion.

After three years of studies, we finished up with a baccalaureate in philosophy and a licentiate in philosophy.

After three years of simple vows, we approached final vows; really one vow, obedience in which we'd pledge ourselves to the service of Christ in his Church under obedience to the pope, our master general, and the provincial, to serve until death. The following professed members of the community would decide who was invited in and who wasn't. The vote had to be unanimous; if it wasn't, the individual was invited to leave. All twelve of our class were voted in and took the final solemn vow. Next stop, Dubuque.

17

Theology in Dubuque

In Dubuque, Iowa, on the Mississippi, the Province of St. Albert the Great had built a large house of studies. Awed at first by the size of it, we came to think it wasn't all that beautiful, referring to it as "not home but much." Truth to tell, we developed an unflattering critique. If communists were to bomb Dubuque, they'd target the house of studies for sure, it looked so much like a major manufacturing center.

While there we immersed ourselves in theology. We began with courses in Sacred Scripture. Father "Chum" McDonnell, O.P., taught Old Testament; Father Richard T. A. Murphy, O.P., New Testament. The former was one of those people who could teach clearly and make you want to read more on the topic. The latter, on the other hand, was a distinguished scholar but not a gifted teacher, and he knew it. He'd lecture for fifty minutes, but by the five-minute mark he'd lost us completely; we turned to our homework.

One morning he came in to lecture but, before he began, he made an announcement.

"My Aunt Maud has died."

I was just about to start my homework.

"Brother Valentine, what do you think of that?"

I'd only heard half what he said, and so I gave him half an answer.

"Let's celebrate!"

"Celebrate?"

"Yes, let's celebrate a Mass for her."

His annoyance turned to pleasure.

Years later he told me that, after they had sent him to obtain a bundle of biblical degrees, he had no alternative but to teach. When we left his classes, we would go to the library to make up what he wasn't capable of communicating. In some ways, the two professors were foils to each other, but they both did communicate the fundamentals of Scripture by enabling us to build our own understanding of the Bible. He became one of my dear friends in the Order; and he was able to do what he'd always wanted to do, write books instead of teaching in a classroom.

Dogmatic theology was taught by Dominican Fathers Louis Bertrand Cunningham and Reginald Masterson; moral theology by Benie McDonnell. We dutifully attended all these courses and over a three-year period. worked our way through the *Summa* of St. Thomas

When Father McDonnell was made a Master of Sacred Theology (an honor given by the Master of the Order to distinguished professors), there was a Mass to celebrate the occasion. In our classroom we decided to have a celebration of our own, a mock liturgical celebration. We secured the bishop's chair and put it in the front. We persuaded Father McDonnell to wear his biretta with the red pompom symbolizing his new degree and status as a Master. We loaded the thurible with a mixture of incense and cotton batten, and incensed him three times, each time singing *Sic transit gloria mundi*. He got a great kick out of it, and we got something out of it too; we'd cut half an hour from our fifty-minute period. Needless to say, he enjoyed our guile as well as our wile.

For recreation during these strenuous studies, we had movies on weekends. During the summer months we went up to our camp in Menonomee, Michigan, where we often froze to death.

The culmination of all my studies was focused on a series of ordinations. The first was devoted to diaconate ordination: simple tonsure, acolyte, lector, subdeacon, and deacon; the second, to priesthood ordination.

Our class was ordained to the diaconate in Dubuque and a year later, on the third of June, 1961, we were ordained to the priesthood by Bishop George J. Biskup, auxiliary of Dubuque. In preparation for my ordination I asked my father if I could design a chalice and patin in memory of my mother as a perpetual tribute to her and my family for the gift of life and faith; he agreed and provided the funds. The design took almost a year.

Around the top of the cup was a reproduction of the last supper; I was following the design of an ancient Basque drawing. On the lower stem of the cup was the crucifixion surrounded on either side with St. Catherine of Siena, St. Dominic, St. Thomas Aquinas, and St. Albert the Great on the sides.

My father then commissioned the famous chalice makers of Hamer and

Brothers in New York City and Belgium to create the inlaid cloisonne chalice and patin. It bore the date of ordination and the inscription, "Pray for them." On the reverse side of the patin was the blue cloisonne star of St. Dominic. Fortunately, my father and two of my brothers, Jack and Patrick, were able to attend my ordination, along with one of my best friends, Claude Arnold, who by this time had become a Basilian priest and was studying at the University of Michigan for a doctorate in English.

My first Mass was in the Chapel of St. Rose Priory in Dubuque, Iowa. It was a glorious moment of celebration and represented the fulfillment of many years of preparation and aspiration.

Then our group returned home to London, Ontario, where I had my second "first Mass." It took place in St. Martin of Tours parish with my old friend Monsignor Flannery as the archpriest; four hundred people were present. On this unique occasion we were robed in a solemn set of vestments designed by Murray McCance, the Canadian liturgical vestment maker; they were a gift to the Order in memory of my family.

The "School of Christ" had paid off. Monsignor Flannery was very proud of his one-time student. After the Mass, he graciously insisted on hosting a formal banquet at a nearby restaurant.

18

Assignment in the Twin Cities

Following ordination was a "young dad's year" during which we finished up our studies, gained some pastoral experience by going out on weekends for Masses and preaching, and in general made plans for our first assignment. In my case, I was assigned in the summer of 1962 to the Priory of St. Albert the Great in Minneapolis and posted to the College of St. Thomas in St. Paul.

Fortunately, it was exactly what I wanted to do. Before I knew it, I was busy teaching courses in sacramental and moral theology. The college community was filled with energetic young students willing to challenge at every turn. This sparked a wonderful intellectual exchange and proved to be a very satisfying teaching experience.

Simultaneously I was in dialog with my provincial about the possibility of beginning the Order in English-speaking Canada. Much to my surprise, he notified me that I was to go to London, Ontario, and teach at Christ the King College (later King's College) in the University of Western Ontario. This was a wonderful opportunity.

When I arrived in London, Ontario, in the fall of 1965, I was back with the family again and back at the very university where I'd had been initially educated myself. Preceding me there was Father Richard Murphy, my Scripture professor; he'd been assigned as the Roman Catholic university chaplain. I was to take his place.

The College of Christ the King was a self-contained building with a residence for forty or fifty students; we lived in common, celebrating Mass in the morning, having our meals together in a common refectory, with a common library and study hall. It was like an enlarged community of religious, except that the students were Catholic laymen doing studies in the university of which the college was a part. I was appointed chair of the philosophy and theology departments and was in charge of the curriculum. I ended up teaching a course in ethics and a course in sacramental theology.

I'd been in London only a few months when one of my old school chums, Jack Chambers, appeared one day; he wanted to tell me about his life story since high school. We'd both shown promise in the arts, especially painting and sketching; we'd attended art classes at the London Public Library and Gallery. When I went off to Assumption College, he went to the University of Western Ontario but found it not to his liking. Next he went to Mexico and subsequently to Spain, where he met Pablo Picasso. He went to Madrid and entered the fine arts school Picasso had attended.

During the visit he told me he'd been recently diagnosed with cancer and wanted to renew his faith. He'd become a Roman Catholic in Spain, met a lovely Spanish girl, and brought her back to London; they were married and had two boys. My monograph on Jack Chambers entitled, *To Rise with the Light : The Spiritual Odyssey of Jack Chambers*, gives the details of this encounter, finishing with Jack's death and burial.

In the fall of 1965, Bishop G. Emmett Carter invited me to open the academic year at the cathedral; he asked me to preach to the Catholic students and the faculties of the colleges of Christ the King and Brescia Hall. The Second Vatican Council was newly convened. I thought it appropriate to speak briefly about the renewal of the Church; Pope John XXIII promised it would be a new age of the Holy Spirit renewing the face of the earth.

Later I was invited by the rector of the seminary, Monsignor Mahoney, to celebrate and preach the inaugural Mass to the seminarians at St. Peter's. I spoke in a more detailed way about the Council. I referred to the original *schema* presented by the Vatican Curia and how the gathered bishops had changed it. Instead of the hierarchical structure of the pyramid in which the pope was on top, then the cardinals and bishops, then priests and religious, with the laity on the bottom, the attending bishops decided to follow the reverse model with the people of God on top, with the priests and religious in the service of the people and the bishops, cardinals and pope in the service of the people of God.

It was energizing to meet and mingle with the students and faculty. I was off to a good start with the seminarians and the students.

My stay in London also provided the time and opportunity to finish my Ph.D. in aesthetics and the history of art. My thesis dealt with one aspect of American educator John Dewey's thought. The title of my thesis was, *"Consummatory Experience" in John Dewey's Philosophy*. The thesis described how Dewey's philosophy had systematically eliminated any reference to the role of contemplation in philosophy and the arts. Toward the end of his life he realized what he'd done and felt he should offer a correction in the work, *Art as Experience*. Referring to contemplation as "consummatory experience," he acknowledged that contemplation had to be a part of the educational experience; without it there could be no reflective enjoyment; that was to say, no contemplative rest or satisfaction.

Fortunately, I was able to finish the thesis in early fall of 1965 and defend it at our house of studies in River Forest. I was awarded my doctoral degree in philosophy from our Pontifical Faculty of Philosophy.

Regrettably, my stay in London was to be short-lived. I'd applied for a grant from the Canada Council to study Pere Joseph-Marie Coutourier, O.P., and the French liturgical revival after the Second World War. To my surprise and delight, I received the grant.

Almost at the same time I learned from my provincial that I'd unwittingly antagonized Bishop G. Emmett Carter. The rector of the seminary, Msgr. Mahoney, told me I'd caused some concern; the bishop was jealous of my presence. Apparently, he was afraid I was going to get into his prize herd and milk them before he had a chance himself. I was completely oblivious to this.

Later I learned that the provincial's account was true. The bishop was delighted to hear I'd received the grant and couldn't wait for me to leave for France. No doubt it was a relief to him and, I guess, to me as well.

My 1965-1966 academic year in London renewed old friendships, including the Chambers family, along with the Ivys, the Steers family, Sir Arthur Carty, his sister Olive, and their friend Babe McCabe. Of course my own immediate family enjoyed my return to London as I did myself. The year was successful both academically and socially speaking.

Unfortunately, the hope of establishing the Dominican Order in English-speaking Canada came to an abrupt end. The provincial came with our regent of studies, Father Ashley, and our director of campus ministry, Father Richard Butler. It became evident that we didn't have enough Dominicans to assign to Canada. We had to decline the invitation to take over King's College at the University of Western, Ontario, for the same reason. I was therefore informed that after my research grant was completed in France, I'd be assigned to Tulane University in New Orleans and the Catholic Center there.

19

Canada Council Grant

In 1966 I spent four months in France researching and writing the life and work of the famous Dominican artist, Pere Joseph-Marie Coutourier, O.P. As a young man he was wounded during the First World War and had to recuperate at his parents' home. He attended the "Beaux Arts" in Paris, where he met and befriended the leading painters of his day: Picasso, Rouault, Chagall, Masson, Leger, and many others.

But he recognized early on that his main talent was to become a priest and religious. He entered the Dominicans who urged him to pursue his artistic goals as well. Eventually, he did significant art work in Santa Sabina, Roman headquarters of the Dominican Order worldwide.

Coutourier's greatest contribution was to solicit the aid of the French architect Le Corbusier in designing and building the chapels at Assey, Audencourt, and Ronchamps. Once these were completed, Coutourier persuaded French artists to decorate them. These became models for the French liturgical art revival.

Fortunately, on my grant I was able to visit all these places. Unfortunately, Pere Coutourier died in 1954. Nonetheless, I wrote up my research and did a paper outlining the significant contributions he'd made to the French liturgical art revival.

LAVELLI AND MUSSOLINI

While I was in Europe doing research on Pere Coutourier, I met Mimi and Giovanni Lavelli from Como, Italy; they were the aunt and uncle of one of my Canadian students at King's College, London, Ontario. They were a most interesting family and played a significant part in shaping the conclusion of the Second World War in northern Italy.

In the summer of 1966, with one of my Dominican confreres I visited them; they lived in two houses: one outside of Como, their year-round home; the other on Lake Lugano, their summer villa.

We drove across the Alps from France and made our way to northern Italy. When we arrived at their residence outside of Como, we were told that the family had already gone to Lugano for the summer. With a minimum of directions and no wrong turns we made our way along the lake up to Lugano, where we pulled into the piazza of a small town. We asked for final directions to their address. It was dark by now but, lo and behold, the first door we knocked on was their home! They welcomed us with open arms, served an enjoyable dinner, brought us to our rooms on the second floor, and retired for the evening. We were exhausted!

In the morning I opened the shutters on my window to a magnificent view of Lake Lugano looking out toward the Alps. It was breathtaking!

We asked about saying Mass. They directed us to a small household chapel on their first floor. As I vested, I read a framed document establishing the chapel some four hundred years ago. It was signed by Carlos Cardinale Borromeo, archbishop of Milan and one of the leaders of the post-reformation movement in the Roman Catholic Church. Later, I found out he grew up in the lake district.

The Como home was a nineteenth-century, four-story country house with three wings. The main one contained the living quarters of the family and, like many Italian families, it literally housed everyone, including sons and daughters with their spouses and families. One wing was for the help and their families; another was a glorified barn with a courtyard in the center of the quad.

One night around one I was roused to witness the birth of a calf. The whole household gathered around to make sure everything came out well. It was an astonishing event!

There were two Lavelli sons and a daughter. Interestingly, one son married a communist girl. Everyone else in the household was a devout Roman Catholic. Each couple had their own separate quarters. We gathered for common meals and entertainment in the evening after dinner.

The drawing room was a great hall with a huge walk-in fireplace. When evenings were cool, everyone sat in a semicircle in front of the flames. At the other end the room extended out into the gardens on the front side of the building.

In such an enjoyable atmosphere, I came to know Mimi and Giovanni. At that time they were both in their late seventies, early eighties.

And herein lies a tale.

Mimi saw me reading a paperback book; I'd picked it up at the airport before flying to France. I thought it was about Mary Stuart, Queen of Scots; instead it contained Anglo-Saxon tales by Mary Stuart. "Mary Stuart was a classmate of mine at New College, Oxford," she said.

And herein lies a tale within the tale.

Mimi's father was the Italian ambassador to Great Britain for the first part of the period between the two world wars. Winston Churchill took a liking to him. I can't remember her maiden name, but while in England they often were guests of the Churchills for weekend parties at Blenheim. The palace was a mere dozen miles from Oxford, where she was specializing in Anglo-Saxon folklore.

On these weekends days were for hunting, and evenings for dancing. Apparently, Winston wasn't a good dancer, but he did enjoy dancing with Mimi and her mother. They, on the other hand, or perhaps I should say *other foot*, preferred to tuck their feet under and chat the charming man up on the sidelines.

Eventually, Mimi and her family went back to Italy where she married Giovanni. World War II broke out, and Winston became prime minister of England.

In the 1980s while in Italy working on the Vatican pavilion I dropped in on the Lavellis. Mimi wasn't feeling well; I said Mass for her in her sitting room; afterward I had breakfast with her and some of the family.

And herein lies a third tale, which began in this visit and continued during subsequent ones.

Mimi's husband, Giovanni, was one of Mussolini's generals. In 1945, near the end of the war, he was able to save much of northern Italy from the scorched earth policy practiced by the retreating German troops. He convinced them to stop the destruction and withdraw as quickly as possible. Mussolini arrived on the scene in Milan, having been rescued from the island of Ischia by German parachute troops. He was on his way to the residence of the archbishop where he planned to surrender; one condition, that he be protected from harm. Gunfire broke out in front of the residence, and Mussolini lost his nerve.

He decided to retreat to Como with a German escort; there he actually joined Mimi and Giovanni for part of a day. He put his private papers in the

Lavellis' hands. They finally agreed to accept them with the understanding that they'd take them secretly into Switzerland, where they would be held on condition that they not be released for a hundred years after Mussolini's death. After he left, Mimi and Giovanni took the papers and put them in the home of an adjoining friend, where they remained for several months.

In the meantime, Mussolini stayed in the Como area for a week or so, visiting Clara Petacci, one of his paramours, before deciding to make a dash for the Brenner Pass into Germany. As he was making his escape, the convoy—there were at least fifteen in the party—stopped at an inn for something to drink. Mussolini removed his helmet and was recognized. The people, most of whom were Italian partisans on the lookout for him, began to stone him. The German escort apparently deserted.

Mussolini and his girl friend were tied to the back of a truck and dragged into Milan. In the process they both died. Once in the city their bodies were strung up on a light post. Subsequent photographs were flashed around the world. Finally, an American general had them cut down and secretly buried.

Within a few days of these incidents, as Mimi related it to me decades later, Sir Winston Churchill flew into Milan and went directly to Como; he asked the Lavellis what happened to Mussolini's papers. Mimi was able to tell them that he had visited them, but there was not a paper belonging to Mussolini in her house. Besides, Mimi reminded Churchill, her mother was still alive living on the second floor and would be glad to see him, "She has never forgotten those days at Blenheim Palace when you went dancing on her feet."

Three months later, which was after the war was over, the Lavellis took Mussolini's private papers into Switzerland through a back mountainous route and deposited them in the National Archives of Switzerland.

That was the last of the family secrets told to me by Mimi on my last visit to the Lavellis in 1980. There were some loose threads to the stories, but that was how she remembered them. Particularly troublesome on the day Churchill arrived at Como were the conflicting loyalties. To whom did the Mussolini papers belong? The Germans, Italians, Americans, English? The passage of time resolved them all.

To this mini-memoir of Lavelli and Mussolini, I would add a remembrance of my own.

When I was in college at Assumption University, Windsor, I met Douglas Hamilton from Flint, Michigan; a former U.S. army lieutenant and intelligence officer studying on the GI Bill. On one mission toward the end of the war, he was dropped into the area of Lake Como. His job was to follow the steps of Mussolini as he made his escape-attempt from Italy. He told me about *Il Duce's* last hours; and he showed copies of his intelligence photographs taken while Mussolini and his mistress were being stoned.

There were loose ends in this story, but I've left them to others more expert to resolve.

20

Tulane Catholic Center

Upon return from France at the end of summer 1966, I left Canada for my new assignment. I'd never lived in the south, except the southern part of Canada. New Orleans turned out to be such a unique place with a cultural mix of French, Italian, Spanish, German, Irish, black, and white. I took up residence at St. Dominic Priory, where there was a community of ten Dominicans working at such places as the Dominican parish, St. Mary's Dominican High School, and the archdiocesan chancery. At the time I thought I'd enjoy a few years or so in the Crescent City and then move on.

I took up my assignment at the Catholic Center adjoining the Tulane campus. It was located in "The Tea House," a great old place bought by the archdiocese shortly after the Second World War, where one could get a cup of something or meet a friend. It was manned at first by diocesan priests. In 1966 Archbishop John Cody invited the Dominicans to take it over. By the time I arrived, Cody had moved on to Chicago, and Philip H. Hannan had arrived as the new archbishop; he welcomed the Dominicans with open arms.

Another Dominican was also assigned to the Catholic Center, Father Gilbert Roxborough. Together we began the formation of a new community at the center. The students were lovely, gifted young people, but something was not quite right. We called a meeting to discuss the situation with them. We simply said that the Catholic Center had the air of an exclusionary Catholic fraternity or sorority about it, which wasn't necessarily a bad thing; but we intended to open the center to all the students on campus, Catholic and otherwise. Some of the Catholic core would be disappointed and leave; others would stay and complain, but we would ask them to leave. The rest could help in bringing the change about. Fortunately, we received a marvelous response.

Within a relatively short time, we went from one to five Masses on a weekend and from a dribble of students to a packed house at each Mass. In that post-Vatican II period people wanted a more relaxed, informal environment for liturgy; the grand living room of the old Tea House proved to be the perfect setting; we set out a hundred chairs. Students, faculty, and administrative staff at the university came in droves, including many of our campus neighbors. We became so successful in a short time that Holy Name of Jesus, our geographical parish run by the Jesuits, was surprised and about to accuse us of priracy.

There were two liturgies at work at each weekend time slot. The liturgy of the Mass and the liturgy of coffee and doughnuts. We simply turned the chairs around to face the counter offering nourishment of a different sort. It took time for the Jesuits of Holy Name to become doughnut-friendly after their Sunday Mass. A number of factors contributed to our success. There was our preaching, which was directly aimed at the students; our liturgies, which were now in English and accompanied with guitar or flute or whatever instrument happened to be in attendance. After consultation with the students on Tuesday evening we met with various student groups to read the scriptural passages for the following Sunday, pick out the main theme, and choose music that not only reflected that theme but also was "sing-able." As I reminded the musicians, they weren't there to perform but to facilitate the liturgy. These were all very dedicated young men and women and it was very inspiring to work with them. There was a decent library with books for Catholics and reference works for all; chairs and tables for study. Finally, there was luncheon after the midday Mass. Once a month we put on a barbecue; we charged a pittance; students volunteered to work; hundreds came.

One evening I can remember having my hamburger with a group of girls; one of them spoke out.

"Father, whatever you do, keep up the barbecues. It's the only place on campus we can go and meet new people without feeling we're intruding. We don't belong to a sorority, and this is the only place we can sit and enjoy ourselves, have a good meal, and meet a lot of new people."

Not only was there food; there was good food from our cook, Myrtle Johnson; she prepared the lunch after daily Mass in the chapel on the second floor; a dollar a plate. Sixty to seventy-five students showed up every day, eating lunch with us and enjoying the informal atmosphere of a home. In fact, it was a home away from home for many of us.

Another factor improved our presence on the campus: a series of public lectures in the evening to fill the gaps in university life. Students helped; they were for the most part in late adolescence and early adulthood, falling in love, figuring out sex, and trying to learn how to love well. The topic for the first lecture series had to be "Love, Friendship, and Sex."

The title was clear enough but, apparently, not all that clear. One evening I got a phone call.

"What's this program, 'Love, Friendship and Sex,' about?"

"It's an informative talk explaining the role of sex in one's life."

"That's not the type of sex I'm looking for."

"Sorry!"

Many others did seem to be looking for answers, and we had no trouble filling the place. Programming of this sort greatly appealed to students and brought them out.

Still another factor was a series of luncheons for medical students. For this we had benefactors. The Catholic Doctors Guild in the medical school, chaired by Dr. William ("Billy") Harris, was able to raise enough money to sponsor six luncheons each semester. The students chose the professors and asked them to talk about timely topics like "What's it like to be married to a doctor?"

Fortunately, these sessions developed into an elective in the medical curriculum, "Human Values and Decision Making in Medicine." These lectures were the inspiration for the Chair of Medical Ethics named for my dear friend, Dr. James Knight, a former Presbyterian minister who subsequently became a psychiatrist and assistant dean of the Tulane Medical School. Dr. Knight, who died after he returned from establishing the School of Medicine at Texas A&M at College Station, was a gifted and charming man whom the students loved. Together with his wife, Sally, and their son, I had the pleasure of helping to care for him in his last days.

For law school students we had buffet luncheons cum talk at the Catholic Center. We solicited Catholic lawyers among others to help support the program. It too was a great success.

During this time, as an adjunct professor in the University College I taught courses like "Introduction to Sacred Scripture, "Teilhard de Chardin,"

"Thomas Merton," and "The Second Vatican Council." The teaching opened the doors to many students and faculty that would otherwise never have met me.

RELIGIOUS STAFF ASSOCIATION

When Father Gilbert and I arrived on campus, there were, counting us, ten full time chaplains. Two Roman Catholics, two Episcopalians, one Methodist, one Presbyterian, one Baptist, two Jewish, and one Lutheran. Not long after, we organized ourselves into the Religious Staff Association (RSA); we met every Monday morning. At these meetings we coordinated programs in the service of the community and figured out ways we could be of assistance to them as a whole. These efforts made the administration aware that we were really in the service of the university. In recognition they began to assign us to various committees, and we gained a certain power and influence within the university.

One evening I went to the university student center for a dinner meeting with a group of Catholic student officers. In the cafeteria line I found myself behind a young man.

"Hello," I said to him.

"Who are you?" he asked me hesitantly.

"I'm Father Val McInnes."

"What's that mean?"

"What religious background are you?"

"I'm Jewish."

"I'm like the rabbi."

"What's a rabbi?"

"Hmmm."

Ours was a brief encounter, not lasting more than a minute; then I said goodbye. After my meeting with the Catholic students, I found the young Jewish student waiting for me at the door of the cafeteria.

"Father, can I join you?"

"Sure, walk along with me."

He'd been a freshman at the university for more than two weeks, and I was the first person to say hello.

"As a matter of fact," I said, "I deliberately carry on what I call an *apostolate of the hello* in order to engage young people and recognize them."

By this time we'd reached the Catholic Center. I told him he was welcome to visit us any time; we had a great lunch program for a dollar. And so he had lunch with us every day. The Jewish chaplain got wind of this. At the next Monday meeting of the chaplains, the rabbi expressed his displeasure.

"What's this business of you proselytizing a Jewish student?"

I laughed.

"What are you laughing at?"

I told him the story. "And you're damn lucky I said hello to him. I'm just helping him to become a good Jew. You can pick him up any time you want."

21

Chair of Judeo-Christian Studies

At one Monday meeting the chaplains concluded that religion on the campus should have more academic presence. We conceded that students in the philosophy department could major in religion by visiting other departments and taking courses like Early Christian History, Christian Art, Latin, History of the Middle Ages, and the Church of the Renaissance; nonetheless, academic religion had no real presence on the campus.

Since I was the one pushing it, the RSA asked me to head up a committee to explore the possibility of establishing a Chair of Judeo-Christian Studies at Tulane. We approached President Sheldon Hackney who was just ending his stay at Tulane; we were in transition to President Eamon Kelly; the bridge in the administration was the provost, Professor Frank Birtel. After negotiations, it was agreed and approved by the president and the faculty senate that we could have a Chair of Judeo-Christian Studies. There was one condition; we had to raise the funds ourselves. This was the challenge given to the RSA in general and to me in particular.

Parenthetically, in the late 1970s and early 1980s the oil market was at its height. One day I went to a luncheon from which I came away with a quarter of a million dollars. Our two benefactors were Alden J. Laborde, commonly referred to as "Doc," and our other good friend, John Bricker. At the end of luncheon, as we were departing, I couldn't resist.

"Four more luncheons, and we're home free!"

We did raise another half million dollars, giving us $750,000 in all; the rest was matched by the State of Louisiana. In the course of time we received major funding, including $500,000 from Mrs. Catherine Gaisman, widow of Mr. Henry J. Gaisman, a Gillette Corporation executive.

At the same time we were in construction. A well-known New Orleans lawyer, James Mitchell Rogers, left funds to the university to build a non-denominational chapel in memory of his late sister, Myra Clare Rogers, who'd been head of the classics department at Newcomb. It was designed by the Louisiana architect John Desmond from Hammond in two stages.

The first stage was the erection of the chapel area for denominational and ecumenical worship services and the reception area with offices to house the Chair of Judeo-Christian Studies (one for the director, one for his assistant/secretary, and seminar rooms for the visiting professors for the chair).

The second stage included the Center for World Religions with office space for the Chair of Muslim Studies, and a Chair of Japanese, Buddhistic, Shintoist Studies. Included also was office space for assistants and secretaries as well as apartment accomodations for visiting professors, three seminar rooms, a large religious library with space for computer stations. (The original drawing is in my office.)

Right in the middle of the schedule construction was halted. Some heirs of the Rogers family brought a lawsuit against Tulane/Newcomb, claiming that the original intent was to build a chapel only for worship; it couldn't be used for anything else. I was called to court as an expert witness. From the Middle Ages on, I argued, university chapels were multi-purpose buildings in which, besides the liturgical celebrations, there were public lectures, dramas, concerts, and other functions germane to the university community. That testimony and others persuaded the judge to throw out the suit; construction resumed, and the chapel was completed on time.

After we finished our fund-raising campaign for the chapel, and after I finished two terms as pastor of the university parish of St. Thomas More, which we'd founded in 1970, I was able to go on a sabbatical to Europe.

I spent three months scouring for professors of reputation to come to Tulane and lecture for our Chair. Perhaps the most distinguished I visited was W. D. Davies, a New Testament scholar at Duke University. He accepted our invitation; he was accompanied by his dear wife; he gave a brilliant inaugural lecture on the role of land in Jewish tradition. The turnout was superb; all 120 seats were filled; and the Chair was proudly launched.

Initially, I was appointed executive secretary for the Chair and later director and finally chair. Professor Frank Birtel has always fulfilled the role as special

Chair of Judeo-Christian Studies 63

faculty adviser to the Chair; we've worked congenially and fruitfully over the years; I'm grateful for his admirable advice and constant support.

By a lovely coincidence the first public lecture for the Chair of Judeo-Christian Studies was delivered when the chapel was completed and inaugurated with liturgical celebrations in April 1980. All subsequent lectures have been held in the chapel; a list of them may be found in Appendix C.

22

Dominican Teaching and Pastoral Life

Next to celebrating Mass, I think preaching is the most rewarding activity of the priesthood. Pere Yves Congar, Dominican theologian at the Second Vatican Council, put it this way. If you ever had to choose between preaching and saying Mass, you would ultimately have to choose preaching; without it there can be no intellectual communication of the Word and therefore there could be no sacramental life in the Church. Preaching is the door to salvation, and without a preacher, as St. Paul reminds us, how can people hear the Word? If they cannot hear the Word, how can they believe?

PREACHING AND TEACHING

My teaching experiences began in Minneapolis; I was at the College of St. Thomas from 1962 to 1965. While there I was in residence at our priory of St. Albert the Great where I'd help out pastorally. One day I got a call; a lady was dying; this would be my first sick call. She was relatively young and suffering from cancer; she didn't have much time left. I heard her confession, anointed her, and gave her communion. And then, unexpectedly, I witnessed a death in total peacefulness, not only for herself but for her husband and family. It was a revelation to me.

While teaching at the college I'd occasionally have Mass with the community of students and priests in residence. It brought the community together in worship. It was a source of great joy for me.

In spring 1965 my provincial came for visitation. He notified me that in the fall I'd be re-assigned to Christ the King College at the University of Western Ontario located in London, my home town. Besides academic duties I'd assume the campus ministry as well. When I arrived, I established the chapel in a nearby high-rise. My father and some of his friends furnished the new site with a liturgical altar and all the appropriate appurtenances. Within a short time, it was a very popular place for weekend Masses. The students, as did I, enjoyed the informality.

HENRY EDWARD DORMER

One evening Mass I preached about Henry Edward Dormer, a young English Army officer who came to London, Ontario, in 1865; he was a part of the British Army assignment to counteract Fenian raids coming up from the United States. He spent a year in London taking care not only of his regiment (King's Own Rifles) but also the poor and the alcoholic in the area. When I concluded the Mass, a man come up to me.

"I'm Ted Schmeck, head of the 4th degree Knights of Columbus. Our chapter is named for Henry Edward Dormer, the person you were just talking about."

Immediately we sat and talked for some time. Since the hundredth anniversary of Dormer's death would be the following year, 1966, and since Dormer planned to become a Dominican at the end of his military service, we decided to do something about it. We would form a committee. It would include such local luminaries as Mrs. John S. Labatt (Bessie), Ted Schmeck, Bishop G. Emmett Carter, Dr. John K. A. Farrell, and me. Dormer's cause for being declared venerable was up for consideration by Bishop Carter.

Time was short, at least for the celebration we planned. The centenary birthday was October 22, 1966. It was a Tuesday; we set the celebration for the weekend that followed.

Through Bessie Labatt we notified Governor General and Mrs. Vanier; he'd been a former Canadian Army General and former Canadian Ambassador to France. His interest was aroused.

"I know personally how difficult it is to practice any form of religion in the military, and if this Dormer soldier obtained any form of holiness, that is indeed something worth celebrating."

Vanier arranged for a battalion of troops from Dormer's own regiment with honor guard to come from London, England, for the occasion. As for him and his wife, they made an official visit to London to celebrate the weekend.

Once Gordon Jeffreys, a leading musician and well known lawyer as well as a friend of mine, got wind of the Dormer story, he commissioned a one-act opera. Another mutual friend from the London Little Theatre,

Martin O'Meara, agreed to sing the title role. Before we knew it, the London Symphony Orchestra volunteered to play.

We were able to track down some Dormer descendants both in England and Australia. That summer I visited some of the Dormer family in London, England, and at their country place near Broadway. I invited them to come participate in this celebration in honor of one of their ancestors. Much to our delight, several accepted.

Finally, capping the celebration, the Bishop of London agreed to a solemn Mass in the cathedral followed by a banquet at the Hotel London. Unfortunately, Bishop Carter wasn't able to attend; Bishop Nelligan was able to take his place.

The details of this celebration are found in the book, *A Thousand Arrows*, edited by Arthur Carty, published by the University of Windsor Press.

When I preached about Henry Dormer, the students were amazed to think that such a young man—Dormer died at the age of twenty-one—could obtain a remarkable degree of holiness. Following the homily, eight students came to me and wanted to know more. One of them invited the rest of us to his home for brunch; his mother was intrigued by the conversation; I continued the story of Dormer, I told them he was buried in the cemetery of London, Ontario.

"Let's go out and visit the grave!" shouted the students.

"What? It's February!" I replied. "There's a foot and a half of snow on the ground!"

The host's mother took a bouquet of red roses on her mantelpiece and gave them to her son.

"Lay them on his grave from me."

Thus on a sunny afternoon in the middle of winter, we went to St. Peter's, found Henry Dormer's grave, laid the roses, and said a prayer for his cause.

Some time later when I was telling the story to my artist friend Jack Chambers, he said spontaneously,

"Isn't it amazing that young people one hundred years after the death of another young person would be so moved to pay a tribute like that? You've just given me the idea for a new painting. I'm going to do a new work, and I'll call it the Henry Edward Dormer tribute."

Further details of the weekend and the tribute can be read in my work, *To Rise with the Light: The Spiritual Odyssey of Jack Chambers*.

TULANE CATHOLIC CENTER

The Sunday morning liturgies provided great opportunities for preaching. Many people complimented on our homilies, but not all.

FOLK & JAZZ MASSES

A student musician gave every appearance of enjoying his role as coordinator of the music for the main 10:30 Sunday Mass. He was charismatic and reliable. But one Sunday he didn't appear. Much to my chagrin, I had to lead the singing, but we managed to survive. Immediately following the Mass I called him to find out what happened.

"Well, you know, Father, I was coming out of the dorm this morning, and I noticed that some of the students were having a jam session in our common room. I decided that I might be able to do more good there than going to Mass."

I was appalled by this comment.

"Didn't you tell me you were a graduate of a Catholic high school in Florida?"

"Yes."

"Didn't they teach you about the real presence of Christ in the Eucharist?"

"What do you mean?"

I suggested he come over right away to have a little talk.

Shortly he appeared in my office; we had a discussion about his so-called religious education. I couldn't believe what he said, namely, that in no time in his four years in his Catholic education did anyone teach him about the real presence of Christ in the Eucharist and the need to receive the Eucharist to keep himself spiritually alive.

It suddenly dawned on me that we were passing through that period of so-called renewal called Vatican II; it dumped many doctrinal issues and assumed that it was just sufficient to love one another in order to survive. He was a perfect example of the latter, and we immediately went to work informing him of his deficiencies. He was delighted to receive the instructions and began to grow more in his faith.

This experience revealed to me the need for a whole new series of homilies and talks based on the sacramental life of the church for the benefit of the spiritual renewal of the students and faculty.

ON THE BRINK

Another Sunday I celebrated Mass and gave a homily that struck one of the students in a very profound way. Of course I can't remember what I said. In any case, he came up to me after Mass.

"May I talk to you for a few minutes?"

We went into the downstairs office and sat down.

"Father, you may not know it, but you've just saved my life. I was on my way to commit suicide."

He said he'd gotten up that morning, despondent for a number of reasons, and felt the only solution was to commit suicide. He came to Mass to say goodbye to the Lord and was absolutely amazed to hear my homily; he felt I was talking directly to him and his problem. He then told me the problem. I heard his confession and sent him over to the university clinic to receive some psychological counseling.

That incident was a perfect example of how the Lord wrote straight with crooked lines. It has happened many times in my preaching life. Today that young man is a successful businessman in New Orleans.

NON-CATHOLIC PARENTS

One morning there was an overflow crowd; some of the community had to take refuge on the front porch. I wasn't saying that Mass, so I went out to say hello. Two of the men were Preston Wales and Henry Schlesinger. They were talking about how ironic it was that they were sitting outside a Catholic service when one was Episcopalian and the other was Jewish. Preston said that his mother, who was a very devout and somewhat inflexible Episcopalian would have dropped dead if she knew that her three grandchildren were attending a Roman Catholic Mass.

"Well," added Henry, "how do you think my mother must feel since she's a good Jewish lady?"

Both of them were married to Catholics and were dutifully taking care of their children's spiritual needs.

RUBRICS READ

I'd just received the new transitional liturgical books in English. The directions about the sequence of the Mass were usually in red print; the prayers, in black. But because these were temporary books, all was printed in black.

I was halfway through my reading when my associate, Father Brian Donovan, who was in his office, began to scream with laughter. I realized what I was doing, made a few on-the-spot substitutions, and concluded with the real prayers in black. Fortunately, the people in the congregation didn't really know what was happening.

HEAVENLY BODIES

Preaching on the Feast of the Assumption one year, I was trying to make the point that at the present moment there were two glorified bodies in heaven. One is Our Lord's; the other, his virgin mother's. If Mary shared in the passion and death of her son, she should also share in his victory over death. From there I wanted to make the point that we too would share in the bodily resurrection, not in the moment of our death but in the moment of the general resurrection. Suddenly I realized that some of the people didn't really believe in the bodily resurrection and ascension of Mary. So I backtracked and in a moment of inspiration reminded them of what St. Paul said.

"If you do not believe in the Risen Christ, then you do not believe that He is the first born from the dead. But if He is risen from the dead, He is the first born from the dead and He is our hope and our aspiration and Mary who stood by Him in His Passion and death now sits with Him in glory calling us home to the great victory that they want us to celebrate for all eternity."

WHEN MOTHERS AREN'T MODELS

Once again I was preaching about Mary as the mother of us all; as indeed our own mothers have taken care of us physically, so Mary will take care of us spiritually. When I finished my little homily, a rather irate young lady came up to me.

"Father, don't always presume that mothers are wonderful. My mother was a first-class bitch, and she was never a model to me in any way, shape, or form. So please don't suppose all of us have good mothers."

That's known as feedback!

It was always a balancing act to keep the Catholic Students' center in a dynamic relationship with the neighboring Catholic churches. That was to say, people from Holy Name threatened to overwhelm the student center. On one occasion we had to remind some parishioners that the Catholic Center was open mainly to students and faculty; that Saturday Masses at 9:30 and 5:30 were open to everyone; including parishioners; and that Sunday Masses at 11:30 and 5:30 were for the students and faculty only. Out-of-town parents and grandparents could tilt the number of chairs available to the students. Whatever happened, the mix was always interesting.

GRANDMOTHER WITH A STRING OF PEARLS

On one occasion an elegantly dressed grandmother appeared with her grandson. She was wearing black dress, black hat, black gloves, and a string of pearls. She didn't know it, but it was commonplace for students to drop a tenner into the collection and take out nine dollars. And so her grandson did just that. She took her black umbrella and swatted his hand.

"Just leave the money in the basket and don't worry about the change!"

GENTLEMAN WITH THE JAUNTY HAT

On weekday evenings students and neighbors would come to the 4:30 Mass. When I first arrived, I noticed a very elegantly dressed gentleman wearing a fedora and a cravat with a sports jacket and generally looking jaunty. His name was James Donnelly.

His appearance confirmed his profession as a former American diplomat; he finished his career as the American high commissioner to West Germany right after the Second World War. In fact, he'd been one of President Roosevelt's favorites.

As I got to know him, I learned that he'd fallen in love with a lady from Bogota, Maria-Helena Sampar, when he was first secretary to the embassy in Colombia; they were married in the chapel of the cathedral. She belonged to the famous Sampar family who originally brought electricity to Colombia through her grandfather who'd studied in Germany.

As Donnelly's diplomatic career blossomed, they traveled to many different postings around the world, ending up in West Germany. One charge was interesting: the restoration to their rightful owners of paintings stolen by Hitler and Herman Goering from private and public collections. It was a monumental task requiring a huge staff of curators and art experts.

When I visited them for dinner one evening, I was impressed with their beautiful collection of paintings. They were gifts, he told me, from the curators whose galleries benefited from the restorations. A special Act of Congress had to be passed in order for him and his wife to retain them. They weren't first-class masterpieces, but on the walls of their home on Palmer Avenue they were stunning.

Later on I discovered he had a heart condition. When his youngest daughter was scheduled to be married in Bogota, he naturally made plans to go with his wife to give the bride away. Doctors, however, warned him not to go; because of Bogota's high altitude he'd run the risk of a heart attack.

"Look, I have to go to give away my daughter."

The wedding went as scheduled, but on the following day he had a massive heart attack. As he lay dying the same priest who married the two of them forty years before came to administer the sacrament of the sick and dying. When Marie-Helena returned to New Orleans, she told me of the providence of the occasion; she felt a providential incident had taken place. So much for the gentleman with the jaunty hat and cravat.

UNIVERSITY PARISH

The Dominicans took over the Tulane Catholic Center in 1966. On our staff we had two Dominican priests, Gilbert Roxbourgh and myself, and Dominican Sister Mary Ellen Wolfe. Subsequently we had Frs. R. B. Williams, Brian Donovan, Thomas M. Condon, Scott O'Brien, John Markey, John Lydon, and others. My tenure as pastor extended from 1966 to 1979. In 1970 we established the university parish of St. Thomas More and continued as a thriving parish until Hurricane Katrina in 2005. The parish was one of the fatalities; it was reduced to the status of a campus ministry in 2008.

During the period I like to refer to as the "golden age of campus ministry at Tulane," the university parish flourished. It was one of the spiritual centers for the Archdiocese of New Orleans and certainly for the university section and uptown area.

Of course, marriages were the number one success story. We sponsored retreats each semester. Many of the young people enjoyed getting away for a weekend in the country and getting to know one another better. Out of these relationships developed lasting friendships culminating in some instances in marriage. At least one incident deserves remembering.

We secured Young House in Bay St. Louis; it was Y-shaped with a wing for boys and a wing for girls. On the particular weekend we had three Karens, Karen No. 1, Karen No. 2 and Karen No. 3. During the retreat the discussion centered around marriage and marriage customs. We also had with us a young man from Egypt, where marriage customs were different from ours. His parents' marriage was arranged, and so was the marriage of a Chinese retreatant. In both cases the parents didn't know their spouses until the deals were made. The American retreatants expressed wonderment that such customs still existed. Others pointed out that many arranged marriages turned out to be happy ones.

The American students wanted none of that, especially Karen No. 3; she said she was never going to get married. I advised her that she should never use the word *never* because the nevers were usually the first married. As it turned out, Karen No. 1 and Karen No. 2 later married fellows who'd been on the same retreat. Karen No. 3, Miss Never, eventually met and married a retired nuclear submarine commander. All three are happily married and prospering with their families.

VOCATIONS

There were a number of very fine vocations to the priesthood and religious life as well. Looking back upon this period from the perspective of the present, I realize that the Lord sowed his seeds in many different ways.

We're particularly proud of a number of priests and religious vocations. These included Thomas J. Rodi, who took his law degree at Tulane and entered Notre Dame Seminary; he'd frequently attend noon Mass and join us for lunch afterward. He lived in New Orleans and is presently Archbishop of Mobile, Alabama.

Also we were graced with the presence of Father Francis George of the Oblates of Mary Immaculate; he came to Tulane in the late 1960s and early 1970s to take a doctorate in philosophy, specializing in the works of Josiah Royce. An engaging personality he too was a frequent participant in our noon Masses and lunches. He lived just down Audubon Street from us in Oblate House.

After he completed his doctoral studies, he was elected provincial of the Oblates in the central part of the United States; a short time later he attended their general chapter in Rome and was appointed the vicar general of the Oblates throughout the world. It's the largest male missionary religious society in the Roman Catholic Church. On several different occasions when I was in Rome on business, I had the pleasure of visiting with him, having dinner with the Oblates, and traveling around Italy with him.

Once his term as vicar general was completed, he wrote a theology doctoral thesis on the works of Pope John Paul II, stressing the themes of communion in the Church and the world. When the pope read it, or so it was reported, he had one comment.

"It's a better expression of my thought than my own."

A short time later he was appointed bishop of Yakima, Washington. After serving there for nine years, he was made archbishop of Portland, Oregon;

within six months he was named the new archbishop of Chicago after the death of Cardinal Bernadin.

Subsequently a whole group of friends accompanied him to Rome for his elevation as Cardinal. It was a grand experience to follow his career and to share in the fruits of his labor. As I told him on a number of occasions, we will never let him forget that he's a graduate of Tulane and the Tulane Catholic Center.

There were other vocations as well, one to the Dominican sisterhood and one to the Dominican priesthood. Stephen Goetz was an accomplished and gifted young man who went to Loyola University. He'd come to Mass at the Tulane Catholic Center and ask the age-old question.

"How come they don't have a Catholic Center at Loyola?"

And I'd give the age-old answer.

"Since Loyola was a Catholic university, it didn't need a Catholic center."

He was a bright young scientist. When he obtained his first degree, he went off to Florida to teach, then entered our Southern Dominican Province and was ordained a priest. When he took the graduate record exam, he had the highest score of anyone on record; he subsequently was given a full doctoral scholarship to the Yale Divinity School.

When he arrived in New Haven, he was assigned to our Dominican Priory there. He immediately became part of the community and celebrated weekend Masses.

One weekend he didn't turn up for his assigned Mass at 5 p.m.; that was very unlike him since he was a very reliable fellow. When the prior inquired of one of the faculty what they should do, he said, call the morgue. Evidently, Father Goetz died of a heart attack during an early morning run; he'd left his identification behind. It was a tragic loss for his family and for the Order. When an autopsy was done, it showed that he had the vascular system of an 85-year-old man. His family was immediately warned to avoid strenuous activity.

Our vocations also included Father Hampton Davis of the diocese of Lafayette, Louisiana, and our own Roger Morin, presently the bishop of Biloxi, Mississippi.

All these are in some measure a sign of the fruitfulness of the Spirit working at the Tulane Catholic Center. I'm sure there are many other religious vocations of which I'm not aware. However, the majority of vocations were to the married life. We performed many weddings for many wonderful people while serving at Tulane. In many ways, the community produced these vocations by the distinct spirit and example of faith that was given by the members of the university community of St. Thomas More.

There is another vocation from Tulane, from our Law School. He had taken his first doctorate in English and then his law doctoral degree. A bright and gifted man, he entered our diocesan seminary of Notre Dame. Subsequently he was sent to Rome to take a doctorate in canon law. Once when I was in Rome, I thought of him, making a mental note to myself. "I must call him." As I was walking out of St. Peter's, whom did I run slam bang into but Father Karl Peterson. He had a promising career in the chancery office of the archdiocese of New Orleans, especially in the marriage tribunal, but unfortunately that career was cut short. He was murdered one evening as he was attending to pastoral duties in the French Quarter.

Finally, a surprising religious vocation was that of Lee Martin Martiny. He did undergraduate studies at Tulane's Navy ROTC Program; he went on to become instructor and professor of English at the Naval Academy in Annapolis; while there, he pursued a law degree in Marylnd. Later in his career he became Naval Attaché to General, later Ambassador ,Vernon A. "Dick" Walters. Lee ended his career as Chief of staff at the US Mission to the United Nations when Walters was there. After twenty years of service, Commander Martiny retired from the Navy; after long and prayerful deliberation, he entered the Eastern Division Province of St. Joseph where he was ordained. He's presently superior of our Dominican House in Kisumu, near the shores of Lake Victoria in Kenya, shepherding 250 orphans, all of whose parents were victims of the HIV epidemic.

23

The Vatican Pavilion

When I first came to Louisiana in 1966 as the Roman Catholic Chaplain at Tulane, and since I was a Canadian citizen, I was invited by the Canadian Council General in New Orleans, Dr. Robert MacNeill, to a dinner party at his home. It came about by my father's friendship with the Honorable Paul Martin, who was at that time the Canadian Minister for External Affairs. The MacNeills were obviously alerted; they meant it as a welcome to the Crescent City and an introduction to some of its outstanding citizens.

The guest list read like a *Who's Who* and included such local luminaries as Mrs. Edith Stern, granddaughter of the founder of Sears Roebuck; Mrs. Lucile Blum, president of the Louisiana Council for Music and the Performing Arts; Mr. Beau Dextra, a native of Holland, the Shell Oil engineer who discovered oil in the Gulf of Mexico; and of course the MacNeills, Bob and his wife Edith and their daughter Marjorie, and myself.

In the course of the conversation, I mentioned that I was interested in the arts; in fact, I had a doctorate in aesthetics and the history of art. Before I knew it, I was chairman of the fine arts section of the Louisiana Council for Music and the Performing Arts (LCMPA).

Little did I know that evening, that I'd develop a long and enduring friendship with Lucile Blum and her family. She knew how to get things done; she was totally dedicated to the arts; she deservedly earned the title "First Lady of the Arts" in Louisiana. We went to Washington often to visit the offices of Senator Russell B. Long and Congresswoman Corinne "Lindy" Boggs to secure funds for LCMPA, which provided the basis for the Louisiana State Arts Council and Endowment for the Arts. I consider this her greatest accomplishment.

Besides loving the arts, Lucile loved her family and friends, and especially her grandchildren.

"Once when we were traveling, she told me a story of her grandson, Jeff. As a little boy he often spent weekends at her house. On one occasion in early November, he came over for a visit, went to his room, unpacked his bag, then called out.

"Grandma, come on in here. I want to talk to you."

Lucile came and sat down on the bed beside him.

"You're growing old, aren't you?"

"Yes, we all have to grow old."

"Why?"

"Well, it's like the trees in springtime. The leaves come out as little buds, then in the spring, the rains come and the leaves grow and they mature and then in the fall, they fall off. That's what life is like."

"Do you think you're going to last till Christmas?"

"Yes," she assured him, "and you'll have your Christmas gifts."

One day while sitting at my desk at the Tulane Catholic Center, an idea popped into my head. *Not everybody could go to Rome to see the Vatican. Perhaps the Vatican could come to us.*

I arranged an appointment with Archbishop Hannan. He was enthusiastic and cooperative. We agreed that the best way to pursue this idea was to petition the Holy Father for such an exhibition. It would have to be signed by a group of the American cardinals and archbishops. I drafted a letter for the archbishop; it was sent to various prelates; we got a positive response from everyone except the archbishop of New York.

The next step was to make an appointment to see the Holy Father. The archbishop gladly arranged such a meeting in the fall of 1981. The pope was shot in May of that year; we were among the first private audiences he granted when he resumed his daily schedule.

In preparation we drew up our wish list, the things we'd like to have. Initially it included three great pieces: the Michelangelo statue of *Cristo Resorto* in the Church of *Santa Maria Supra Minerva*, the *Shroud of Turin*, and the famous painting by Caravaggio of the *Deposition of Christ from the Cross*. This last incorporated the shroud as burial cloth in the painting.

Arriving in Rome in early December, we stayed at the Hotel Michelangelo near the Vatican. The following morning we had breakfast with Ambassador and Mrs. William Wilson, the first U.S. Ambassador to the Holy See in a hundred years. Our audience with the pope was scheduled at ten o'clock in the Apostolic Palace. Initially, Archbishop Hannan went in to see the pope; then the pope's private secretary, Monsignor Stanislaw Dziwisz, invited me to join. We had an energetic conversation about the possibilities of having a Vatican Pavilion at the New Orleans World Exposition in 1984. When we mentioned the theme of the pavilion—"Jesus Christ the Redeemer, the Source of Living Water"— the pope's face lit up.

"That's a good theme!"

Actually, it was part of the title of his first encyclical.

At the side of the papal desk there was a large globe of the world.

"Where is New Orleans again on the map?"

We pointed it out on the Mississippi.

"I must go there someday."

He concluded the meeting with the following declaration.

"I give you permission to have the exhibition as long as the curators agree to the loan of the various works of art."

He gave us his apostolic blessing and a souvenir of the occasion, the yearly papal gold medal struck in his honor.

Archbishop Hannan and I were jubilant as we left the audience.

KARSH AND THE CANADIAN PARTICIPATION

In preparation for the Vatican Pavilion, I had the occasion to visit Ottawa and the famous Canadian photographer, Yousuf Karsh in 1982. I had to obtain permission from him to use his Pope John Paul II beautiful photograph. He was delighted we had chosen it and graciously gave his permission for us to display it and use it for postcard photographs and sale during the Vatican Pavilion.

Also, while I was in Ottawa, I had to visit the Canadian Secretary of State, M. Serge Joyal, who was in charge of all the public museums in Canada. I was particularly interested in securing works of art from the Musee de Quebec. As our vision for the Vatican Pavilion grew, we wanted to include works of art not only from the Vatican but from those major countries which helped develop Louisiana, such as Spain, France, England, Ireland, Italy, and Canada. So I proposed a meeting with the Secretary of State.

Our wish list included some early Canadian religious masterpieces, especially silver chalices and other liturgical vessels, and a gold leaf wood carving of the pelican feeding its young, an ancient symbol of the Eucharist and at the same time a symbol of the State of Louisiana.

M. Joyal was most accommodating; he gave us his permission to have them on loan.

A few weeks later the Secretary of State called and informed me that the Prince and Princess of Wales were scheduled to make a state visit to Canada later that year. He inquired if I'd be interested in meeting them and attending an official state dinner. Naturally, I accepted with gratitude and was off to Ottawa. I thought it would be a reasonably small dinner of forty or fifty guests. When I arrived in Ottawa, I was greeted by the protocol people and put into M. Joyal's party. We were driven to the country residence of McKenzie King, a former prime minister who willed his estate to the government. To my surprise, there was a great tent accommodating at least four hundred guests.

Fortunately, the secretary of state's party was stationed right inside the entrance; it included the governor general and his wife, followed by the prime minister and his wife, and the members of the cabinet, their spouses, M. Joyal, and myself.

When the royals arrived they were greeted with suitable fanfare. They came immediately to greet the Governor General and the rest of the dignitaries before they went for a walk-around.

Princess Diana was a hit, along with the Prince of Wales; everyone was delighted with their presence. However, it was noticeable that the princess went off one way to greet the people, and the prince went another.

Later that evening, at the formal dinner party, M. Joyal mentioned that one of his responsibilities was to issue invitations on behalf of Canada to visiting heads of state. Then he invited me to meet Princess Diana. As we rose and approached her table, which was next to ours. Immediately, we were challenged by British Security Services; the Mounties filled them in; they gladly admitted us. She could not have been more welcoming. I told her very briefly that we were having the Louisiana World's Fair in 1984 and that we would like to invite her to come to visit the Vatican Pavilion. She was enthusiastic about the idea and asked that I send a letter to Kensington Palace. As we returned to our table, M. Joyal wished me luck.

As it turned out, the princess declined; she was expecting her second child and had to curtail her traveling. Naturally, I was disappointed, but we did have a consolation prize.

M. Joyal, Canadian Secretary of State, and his party represented Canada at the opening of the Vatican Pavilion.

FINALIZING THE PLANS

By mid-January, 1982, we had documents from the Vatican secretary of state confirming the pope's permission and the tentative list of the art we wanted to borrow.

In the meantime, I was in contact with Dr. Walter Persegati, who was the acting director of the Vatican Museums. He confided to me that Cardinal Archbishop Medeiras of Boston had persuaded the Holy Father to loan works of art to the states. Then we discovered that Cardinal Cooke, Archbishop of New York, had made a similar request to ours. In any case Dr. Persegati told me, the permissions were granted. He told me to call on Monsignor Clark; he reassured me that the exhibit would go to New Orleans. I hurried back to the archbishop at the Michelangelo Hotel. He too told me definitely to see the monsignor as I passed through New York on my way home to New Orleans.

When I arrived in New York, I made an appointment and acquainted the monsignor with our part in this whole scheme of things. At first he pretended to know nothing about it. I wondered whether I was speaking to the right Monsignor Clark. When I was assured there wasn't another, I told him that the day before in Rome Dr. Persegati told me the permissions had been granted and that he, Clark, was to be the coordinator with Cardinal Cooke for the planned exhibition to come to the United States. When he realized I obviously knew what I was talking about, he acknowledged that the permissions had been granted but it was to be kept completely confidential. I found this a bit odd, since neither the pope nor Dr. Persegati had mentioned anything about confidentiality. Coincidentally, the day I met with Monsignor Clark was the same day Archbishop Fulton Sheen was being buried from St. Patrick's Cathedral. After our meeting, we shared a cab to St. Patrick's Cathedral to be present at that historic occasion.

Once home in New Orleans, I began to feel a little uneasy about the rather odd meeting in New York. I shared my feelings with the archbishop; his advice was to wait and see. Walter Persegati told me that the official press release concerning this great Vatican exhibition to be placed on loan to the United States would be made on a certain date. One of my Jesuit historian friends, Father James O'Neil, S.J., who was in Rome, served as my observer and confidant and kept me posted. He called to tell me he'd seen the unofficial list of the cities to which the exhibit would go: New York, Chicago, San Francisco. New Orleans was singularly absent from the list. I called Archbishop Hannan to express my concern; he told me to call Monsignor Clark; he'd told me that the exhibit would go to New Orleans as well. Two days later, the release appeared in the *New York Times*; New Orleans wasn't on the list. Finally, Archbishop Hannan himself got on the phone and called Cardinal Cooke to ask what was going on.

Whatever transpired in the conversation clarified the situation; the exhibit at least in part would come to New Orleans, whether it was on the press release or not. Archbishop Hannan and I returned to Rome to make sure that all lines of communication were saying the same thing. Fortunately, the confusion was resolved, and we confirmed the works of art we wanted in New Orleans.

ENTER ANN MILLER

One day I was sitting at my desk at the university when I received a most interesting telephone call. A woman's voice was at the other end of the line.

"I'm Mrs. Richard K. Miller of San Francisco. I'm in charge with my friend Ginny Milner of the Vatican Exhibition when it comes to San Francisco. We hear that you're in charge of the Vatican Pavilion at the New Orleans World's Fair. We want to invite you to come to the opening of our exhibition if you will agree to invite us to the opening of your exhibition."

I inquired about the particulars.

"Well, you can come and stay at our house. I have ten children, and we have lots of room."

"I don't know if I want to stay in a house with ten children."

"Oh no, you don't have to worry about that. They're all grown up. I meant to say, you have the pick of those rooms."

I agreed to the deal, and before I knew it I was winging my way to San Francisco for the opening of the Vatican Exhibition. Of course it had opened initially in New York at the Metropolitan and then in Chicago at the Chicago Art Museum to rave reviews, and we were to have the same reviews for the opening in San Francisco.

Mrs. Miller, commonly referred to as Ann, was a vivacious, beautiful, and energetic socialite who was the leading lady of San Francisco society. Her friend Ginny Milner was her counterpart from Los Angeles. They both, along with Archbishop Quinn of San Francisco and Cardinal Caseroli, hosted the opening of the exhibition with Dr. Persegati.

I was billeted in a lovely Miller guest room. On the sofa were a variety of pillows with beautifully petit-pointed messages. "You are leaving this weekend, aren't you?" "Guests like fish smell after three days."

When I returned to New Orleans, I told Archbishop Hannan about the experience and warned him of the impending visit of Ann Miller and company at the opening of our Vatican Pavilion. He really didn't realize what I meant until he met her on opening night.

OPENING NIGHT

Unlike the other three exhibitions, ours was smaller and more focused on "Jesus Christ, Our Redeemer in Art—Source of Living Waters." The building was built from scratch, adhering to specifications and standards set by the Vatican Museums. As the building progressed, the architect who won the competition, Nathaniel "Buster" Curtis, had to be replaced by another architect, Ron Blitch. This alteration took place because of an overrun on budget that threatened to delay the arrival of the works of art. Fortunately, it was resolved. A collaboration with the New Orleans Museum of Art and its director John Bullard, his assistant Jackie Sullivan, and their curators enabled us to receive the works of art and store them until the pavilion was complete.

More details concerning the Vatican Pavilion may be found in my book, *Treasures of the Vatican* (1987), and in my essay, "The Making of the Vatican Pavilion," which appeared in the anthology, *Cross, Crozier and Crucible: A Volume Celebrating the Bicentennial of a Catholic Diocese in Louisiana* (1992).

The Vatican Pavilion was opened by the Apostolic Nuncio, Archbishop Pio Laghi, the papal representative, Ambassador Vernon A. Walters representing the President of the United States, Congresswoman Lindy Boggs, and Ambassador Clare Boothe Luce. Our dear friend Matilda Stream gave the pre-opening party in her lovely Esplanade Avenue mansion. She invited some of her friends from California, including Ann Miller and a host of others, among them movie star Betty Grable.

The exhibition was a tremendous success, in fact probably the greatest success of the Louisiana World Exhibition. We had almost a million visitors in a six-month period; everyone was awe-struck by the layout of the exhibition, climaxing with the famous Raphael tapestry of the Risen Christ and the theme of "Living Waters" expressed by Mestrovic's famous sculpture, *The Woman at the Well*. The latter is presently located on the front lawn of Notre Dame Seminary in New Orleans.

At the end Archbishop Hannan said a Mass of Thanksgiving at St. Dominic's Church to thank the two thousand volunteers.

"It was a great experience, but I'm glad we had to do it only once!"

24

Backstage at the Vatican Pavilion

Out front the Vatican Pavilion looked elegant, but backstage it was hellzapoppin. Some of the odd stories deserve recording for posterity's sake.

LOST MUSIC

Spanish tenor Placido Domingo planned to come with an orchestra and do at least a half-hour program highlighting the Vatican Pavilion. Of course we were all delighted with the prospect; it would give us national and international visibility and prompt more people to come see our wonderful exhibition.

When he arrived, we decided to close the pavilion for the day, allowing him and his entourage to prepare leisurely for a concert in a suitable place. He would sing *Ave Maria*, the *Our Father* and *O Salutaris* and other classic spiritual works; they would record the concert for television.

There was only one problem. The sheet music and musical arrangements couldn't be found; apparently, they were never shipped. The musicians rooted around trying to find substitute music sheets. We urged him to do something spontaneous; he demurred on the basis that it would be too risky. As a result, the concert sputtered out; Domingo and his entourage left; we opened the pavilion to the public in the early afternoon. One good thing came out of it; his apology was sincere and heartfelt.

GIRL KIDNAPPED

A well-known Texas family arrived at the pavilion with their young daughter; she was five or six years old and looked like a doll. Her hair was blonde; her dress, blue with pink ribbons; her shoes, a unique shade of blue. The family asked for a VIP tour; I was happy to oblige. They were delighted with the exhibition and afterward thanked us warmly.

They headed for the Italian Plaza and some Italian ice cream when the parents noticed that their girl was nowhere to be seen. Mother and father looked around quietly, then searched frantically. They returned to the Vatican Pavilion, thinking perhaps she might have made her way back to us. Would that she had! We immediately called both exits to the fair and notified them that a young girl was missing. The mother went to one exit; the father, to the other. The police arrived and began a methodical search. For an hour there was no sign of her.

The father, who was posted at the main entrance/exit saw a man carrying a little girl over his shoulder. She was exhausted and needed to get home as soon as possible, said the stranger. The father looked the girl over as she passed. She was the right size, but she was a redhead; her dress was baggy, and it wasn't blue. But her shoes, they were that special shade of blue.

The father grabbed the girl from the stranger and discovered that the red hair was a wig and that a blue dress lay under the baggy one. The stranger attempted to run away, but the police nailed him and held him down.

It turned out that the little girl was heiress to a huge oil fortune in Texas. Her parents were appalled at the attempt to kidnap her, but decided the press shouldn't be informed. The police took the kidnapper away, but the parents refused to bring charges against him. To this day the mystery remains unsolved.

FLUFF AT THE GATE

During preparation for the Vatican Pavilion, we secured the good services of Stuart Silver, former member of the Metropolitan Museum staff in New York; he was famous for the installation of major exhibitions. He designed the layout of the Vatican Pavilion exhibition and collaborated with John Bullard, Jackie Sullivan, and me, the curators of the New Orleans Museum of Art for the installation.

Since the theme of the fair was "water" and the exhibition title was "Jesus Christ, Our Redeemer in Art: The Source of Living Waters," my mind turned toward the famous sculpture, "The Woman at the Well" by Croatian sculptor, Ivan Mestrovic. Through a rare stroke of providence, I was able to contact his widow and told her the sculpture would make the perfect centerpiece for the Vatican Pavilion. What did she think? She was elated and immediately gave me permission to have the mold struck in bronze one more time. She gave it to us for the simple cost of the casting. This was a tremendous gift since the work of art was worth half a million dollars. The original foundry in New York did the job again. Stuart Silver with the architect helped design the well; Frank Stewart Enterprises kindly constructed the well and gave it to us.

Subsequently, I received a note from Mrs. Mestrovic telling me that her daughter would be returning from Europe via New Orleans en route to South America; she would like her to see the installation. We were delighted to make the arrangements; admissions people at the main gate were notified; they were to call us immediately so we could go to the gate and escort her to the pavilion. When the appointed day and time arrived, she didn't turn up.

Later that day I received a phone call from her. She had indeed come to the entrance but was turned away. She returned to the airport and was about to make her connection to South America. What else could I do? I apologized profusely for the misunderstanding and unfortunate miscommunication. However, I told her that I'd send her and her mother photographs showing the centrality of the sculpture to the exhibition.

FEE VERSUS FREE

In the initial planning for the Vatican Pavilion, we asked for and received permission to charge a fee of $10 for admission to the pavilion itself; that was in addition to the ticket fee to enter the Louisiana Exhibition as a whole. We also developed a special section of the pavilion that could be viewed by the public for no fee.

This public display was basically an exhibition that included beautiful photographs of Pope John Paul II by Karsh, the well known Canadian photographer. There were also some other photographs of the pope's first visit to the United States.

As I mentioned above, when I negotiated the arrangements with Mr. Karsh, I had to go to Ottawa. He was delighted that we'd chosen his famous photograph of the pope.

In passing Karsh told me of two famous sittings of famous men, the pope and the prime minister.

When he took photographs of John Paul II, he found the pope very agreeable and willing to do whatever he suggested. He wanted him in a contemplative mood, sitting on his throne or a large chair with a tapestry of the Holy Family nearby. They arranged these elements very quickly and took the photographs in no time. The result? A masterpiece.

When he photographed Winston Churchill, he put the prime minister through a variety of poses; none of them worked. One problem was that Churchill had a lit cigar in his mouth and wouldn't take it out. Karsh reset his camera for one final shot. Then he yanked the cigar out of Churchill's mouth, leaving behind on the film the tenacious and pugnacious bulldog look that became famous around the world.

SIGNAGE NEEDED

Another item in the free section of the Vatican Pavilion was the Shroud of Turin. It was a perfect colored reproduction. In fact, it was so perfect that many people thought it was the real thing. The signage people had a remedy for that. A sign saying, *"Photographic Reproduction of the Shroud."*

Parenthetically, we started off hoping to have the actual Shroud of Turin. We even had permission of the former King of Italy to have the Shroud on loan from Turin. However, it had recently been deeded to the Holy See; Cardinal Anastasio Ballestrero of Turin didn't want to risk the loan for fear it might complicate the transfer of the Shroud's ownership into the hands of the papacy.

RENEGING ON A MAJOR AGREEMENT

The Vatican Pavilion provided many crushing disappointments. A better word would be excruciating. Perhaps the worst came from the Italian government; they rescinded permission for the loan of the famous Michelangelo statue, *"Cristo Resorto* (Christ Risen)." Archbishop Hannan and I had negotiated that loan three years before; a special circular room or rotunda was built to display it in the pavilion. I was disappointed beyond words.

Why did the government wait until the last minute to cancel the permission? Newspapers had great fun printing photographs of the boxed statue inside Santa Maria Supra Minerva (Dominican church built over a pagan shrine). The inevitable caption? "Will Jesus Christ rise again after three days on the steps of the Minerva?" But it was not to be, and that was all there was to that. The archbishop asked me to stay in Rome for a few days to see if we could negotiate a compromise. At the same time he was worried about my mental health; he thought I might have a nervous breakdown. When he told me that, I reassured him.

"I wouldn't give those Italians the satisfaction of having a nervous breakdown!"

Fortunately, American Archbishop Paul Marcinkus, president of the Vatican Bank, and Dr. Walter Persegati of the Vatican Museums came to my rescue. They negotiated the loan of the famous Raphael tapestry, *The Risen Christ*.

Alas, the solution to one monstrous problem begat another. When the curators learned the tapestry would be hung on a circular wall, they cried out; that would destroy the warp and the woof of the work.

After last minute negotiations we agreed to a compromise. We invited two tapestry experts to come with the tapestry and help hang it in the rotunda. That seemed to satisfy everyone. When the great tapestry was hung, it occupied almost three quarters of the circular wall. That meant, as one entered the room, it was like entering into the tomb with Christ.

The disappointment at not having the Michelangelo statue lingered for a long while. Nonetheless the Raphael tapestry proved to be a lifesaver; perhaps it added a greater dimension than the statue.

MAYORAL FOLDEROL

Two weeks after the exhibition opened, Mayor Dutch Morial announced that he would withhold payment to the city employees involved in the fair, thus canceling what everybody else thought was a firm agreement. I had gone to Oklahoma for a wedding. When I arrived at the hotel, I turned on the television set to see and hear the news; the whole Louisiana Exposition was going to close because of the Mayor's decision. I couldn't believe my ears. This unfortunate news release was wrong; it deterred thousands, perhaps tens of thousands of Americans, from coming to the fair. The Vatican Pavilion felt the pinch.

DEATH COMES TO THE SCULPTOR

In the fall of 1981 when we were making preparations for the Vatican Pavilion, I read a Henry Moore book on sculpture. In it he expressed a desire, like many other artists, to do a Crucifixion before he died.

"As one grows older, one sees the necessity of wrestling with the idea of death, and what better way of doing that, for an artist, than to ponder the mystery of Christ's death on the Cross and to give expression to that in some artistic form."

It struck me that, even though Moore didn't accept commissions, perhaps he could be persuaded to do a Crucifixion, especially in light of the fact that we'd have a Michelangelo; over and above that, Moore considered the Italian sculptor his mentor. That afternoon I was playing tennis with one of my good friends, Richard C. Colton, Jr. His grandmother, Mrs. Joseph

T. Lykes, and his own mother, Mrs. Richard C. Colton (Howell), had both been collectors of Moore's works. In the course of our match I told Dick my thoughts on a Moore Crucifixion. Would he and his family be interested in commissioning such a work? We discussed the matter briefly; he promised to look into it. A few weeks later he responded in the affirmative.

How would we go about extending the invitation to the sculptor? We both sat down and drafted a letter.

"Recently we were reading one of your works in which you expressed a desire to do a Crucifixion. Presently I'm the director of the Vatican Pavilion for the Louisiana Exposition scheduled to open in early May of 1984. Michelangelo's *Cristo Resorto* will be the main sculpture represented. We have received permission to have it on loan.

"Your frequently expressed affinity and gratitude to Michelangelo moves us to make the following proposal. Would you be willing to consider doing a Crucifixion which would complement Michelangelo's statue? This would provide a great opportunity for you to express your artistic talents on this important subject.

"Mr. Richard Colton and I are planning a trip to England in early February of next year. We would be delighted to meet with you to pursue this possibility if it is of interest to you. We expect to be in London from the 1st to the 8th of February. We would be honored to meet with you at your convenience...."

A few weeks later, we received a positive response. In spite of his many commitments, Moore said he'd be willing to meet with us on the first Tuesday of February. We flew to London, stayed overnight to rest; the following day we drove up to Much Hadham. Evidently, during the Second World War he'd bought this country house as a place of refuge for him and his family; it subsequently became his home and studio. When we arrived, we were directed to a Quonset hut; Moore greeted us warmly. He was enthusiastic about the project; in fact, he'd already done three sketches; he asked his secretary to fetch them. They were small; the first two were conventional in style.

"Quite frankly, when dealing with such a venerable subject as the Crucifixion," he said, "one cannot take as many liberties as one would be inclined to do. There are certain restraints which the subject itself places upon you."

We agreed.

"Nonetheless, in this third sketch I have done something which I feel reflects my own insight into the mystery of the death of Christ. I have taken the liberty of showing his one arm nailed to the cross, but the other one freely embraces it. This implies to me that he freely submitted to the cross and his own death."

Quite spontaneously, all three of us agreed; the third sketch was the one for the Vatican Pavilion. One of his collaborators reminded him that he was already over-committed. Moore, however, felt that he could at least produce a *maquette* (model). On this elevated note we left with great expectations; we'd have a Henry Moore for our pavilion.

Unfortunately, this was not to be. He really didn't have the time or the energy. He died in 1986; he was eighty-eight years old.

Dick Colton continued to show interest in obtaining the third sketch. At that time the Henry Moore Foundation had a policy of not selling the master's works; that policy changed in 1987. Dick and I made a second pilgrimage to Much Hadham; he was able to buy the sketch; it's now housed in his private art collection in New Orleans.

Three sketches are published for the first time and may be found in the pictorial insert of this book.

HINDSIGHT

Such were the surprises arising from our work on the Vatican Pavilion. The Moore involvement would have made the pavilion more attractive and twice as successful. But on the whole, the pavilion was the crown in the Louisiana Exhibition and a favorite of the locals who came time and time again.

Alas, the exposition as a whole was a financial flop, but the Vatican Pavilion, under the chairmanship of Alden J. "Doc" Laborde and the Board, broke even.

25

Promoter of Development

Many who have looked at me as a religious and as a Dominican have expressed surprise that I've been stationed in one place for so long, from September 1966 to the present, 2009. This is indeed unusual, but I've fulfilled many different functions and enjoyed them all. But let me concentrate on one.

The great legacy Dominic left to the Dominicans was the governance of the Order. In his own lifetime he decided that superiors should be elected by the community, serve for a limited period of time, then give way to the next wave of elected officials.

The Order was structured in such a way that most local houses elected priors as their own superiors; then these priors, along with community-elected representatives, went to provincial chapters every fourth year; there, the priors elected a major superior called the provincial. Then, in turn, the provincial in each province, together with an elected member from the province, gathered in general chapters every nine years to elect a master of the Order. St. Dominic himself resigned as major superior to make way for his successor.

In my case, I've enjoyed the opportunity of serving my fellow Dominicans as prior on four different occasions; I've served on the provincial council at least five terms. In addition to these positions, I've also served on a number of commissions, such as admissions board, finance board, director of development, and vocations board.

Long ago when I entered the Order, my father, who was an astute businessman, paved my way with this bit of wisdom.

"Just because you're entering a religious order doesn't mean you won't be concerned with money. Everything runs on money!"

Promoter of Development

He'd prepared me well for jobs concerning finance and administration; he insisted on my making a budget for everything, especially before each year of college.

Besides elective offices in the Order, there were appointed jobs. For example, I was appointed director of development or promoter of development for the Southern Dominican province. I served in this capacity for nine years, during which time I developed the annual Southern Dominican Gala honoring distinguished men and women with the St. Martin de Porres Award. These honorees reflected the qualities of our provincial patron, St. Martin, who is the patron of social justice for the universal church; he also represents a bridge between blacks and whites and all other racial groups. Over the years, in Houston, Memphis, Miami, and New Orleans, we've had the pleasure of honoring many gifted people and friends who have contributed to the well-being of society, the Church, and our Order.

For a list of honorees, please see Appendix E.

GALA HONORS McINNES

The Houston advisory board had every reason to bestow the 2000 St. Martin de Porres Award on Rose and Harry H. Cullen. The Cullens have been outstanding citizens of Houston, famous for their generosity to and support of the Dominicans and many others as well. Also the board decided to honor me as well on this occasion. They wished to thank me for my role in establishing the Annual Southern Dominican Galas.

Our gala evenings were well supported by our many friends and benefactors; this evening was no exception. My brother Angus, his wife Ann, and their daughter Carol Ann with my niece, Maureen, came down from London, Ontario. It was also a celebration for them as well; my sister-in-law and brother were celebrating their thirty-seventh wedding anniversary.

In my acceptance remarks I expressed gratitude to my Dominican family and the Houston Dominican advisory board for their kindness in pairing me with the distinguished Cullens since they represented all that was best in Houston. If I recall correctly, the only other Dominicans to receive the award were Fr. Timothy Radcliffe, our former master of the Order of Preachers, Sister Edna Ann Hebert of the Houston Dominicans, Father Joe Konkel, and Father Victor Brown.

I reminded them all of that old Dominican saying. "The shorter the homily, the bigger the collection." However, since the collection, as it were, had already been taken up, I plunged ahead with my remarks.

Over the years, not only in Houston but also in Memphis, Miami, and New Orleans we had the pleasure of honoring many gifted people.

FUND-RAISING

I told this story to the Houston crowd.

"My sabbatical year was crowded. I made a long retreat, wrote a book on my artist friend Jack Chambers, and made notes on another work. *Relieving People of Their Undue Burdens: The Art of Fund-raising.* Basically, it was what I learned from my own experiences. I was hoping it would become a best-seller if, for no other reason, than it would tattle tales about most of the people in attendance, and I just knew they'd like to read about themselves.

"Seriously, though, here's what I found out about fund-raising.

"First, people are waiting to be asked to help.

"Second, if you don't ask, you don't get.

"Third, nine times out of ten, people respond with great generosity. Of course, it helps to have a good cause like that of the Southern Dominicans—to educate young men for the priesthood and religious life and to care for the elderly. In fact, we have one of the best causes, since we promote the kingdom of God in our midst and in the families we serve.

"To me the best fund-raising story of all belongs to St. Ignatius of Loyola. He wrote to one of his confreres, asking him to interview a certain noble lady in Madrid with a view to her funding a project. The young Jesuit responded.

"'I will have nothing to do with the mammon of iniquity.'

"'There must be some misunderstanding,' responded Loyola; 'this wasn't an invitation; it was an order.'"

Dominicans may not get away with such a direct approach, but the thought is there nonetheless!

At our tables that evening were rosaries that were specially commissioned for the Southern Dominicans; they'd been designed by the papal artist Manfrini and blessed by the Holy Father himself. The cross was modeled on the pope's crozier; the joiner showed a pregnant Madonna. On the reverse side was a Dominican shield. *A.D. 2000-Anno Domino 2000*, celebrating the 2,000th anniversary of the birth of Christianity. My smart-aleck classmate, Fr. Neil McDermott, insisted that it really meant, "Add $2,000 to your annual subscription."

The evening ended with dancing to the wonderful music of Ned Bittista a la carte.

Fund-raising became an intimate part of my daily life in the Order; some people think that's all I'm interested in. Over the years there have been many interesting adages ascribed to me or about me. "Where there's a will, there's a way." I prefer the one that says, "Where there's a will, the Dominicans want to be in it."

People often ask, "How can you ask people for money?" My response? "Why not? Everybody else asks people for money. Why shouldn't we?"

We are by definition professional beggars. The service we give in preaching and teaching deserves compensation. No one is more indebted to us than the people we serve in the pastoral life of our ministry. But we don't ask to be paid.

However, in fund-raising, a fundamental principle is that if you don't ask, you don't get. People will only give you funds to support your projects when they honestly see that it emerges from your ministry by way of helping others. Oftentimes we sit around wondering why people don't support us; the simple truth is, we haven't asked them. We need to communicate our needs to others. When we do so, people are more than generous; they're selfless to the point of embarrassing us.

I'm reminded of an old story. We Dominicans are like the guy who winks at his girlfriend in the dark; he knows what he's doing, but nobody else does. Usually people will respond positively to a request for funds. If they can't do so then, they often help later, if you have patience.

Once I accompanied Rabbi Julian B. Feibelman of Temple Sinai on a fund-raising call for the Chair of Judeo-Christian Studies. We approached an important benefactor of the university, who will remain nameless. This benefactor gave us $100. The rabbi was outraged.

"Father, give that money back! That's an insult."

"Rabbi, there's a principle in fund-raising you never break. You never give money back. What you do is write a little note thanking them for the first installment on their pledge."

"Well, you learn something every day."

I've come to learn that the best way to raise funds is not to ask people for money at all. Talk enthusiastically to them about the needs and the work of the Order, and they will spontaneously offer to help. If they don't, then you ask them.

Over the years our fund-raising for the Southern Dominicans has grown through the cooperation of all our brothers. The need for each one to reach out to those they serve and ask for help is growing. These principles have been institutionalized through our annual 1216 campaign named for the year the Order of Preachers was founded It appeals for help to educate our young students for the priesthood and take care of our elderly. In fact, there is in our Southern Dominican province a McInnes scholarship fund named in my honor. It's one of the closest things to my heart. If we want to have Dominicans around, we have to invite people to help support our students' education. After all, we're preparing a new generation of religious and priests to serve the children of those who have helped us.

Our Southern Dominican Province also raises funds internally through a taxation system of all the houses of the province. Each house gives a percentage of each year's income to the provincial office for the running of the provincial government. Individuals in each house must personally make out a budget every year and abide by it. (Shades of my father reappearing years later!)

When our province was founded in 1979, we received a percentage of the patrimony of the parent provinces from which each member came, namely the central province of St. Albert the Great and the Eastern province of St. Joseph. These funds helped us launch our province and gave us the funds we needed until we could establish our own financial footing and have our own development office.

We chose our fellow Dominican St. Martin de Porres as overall patron for our Southern Dominicans. We did so with a great deal of reflection and intent. He was himself the illegitimate son of a Spanish grandee and a freed mulatto slave. He epitomizes the mission of the Dominicans in the South, which is to build bridges between rich and poor, black and white, as Martin did in his own day in Lima, Peru. He has proven to be a wonderful patron and provider for the Southern Dominicans, for which we are very grateful.

Nothing breeds success better than success. One of the best things our fledgling province did after the founding of our province was that we decided to buy into Medicare. While it was initially a great expense and somewhat of a hardship, it nevertheless proved in the long run to be the best thing we ever did.

Fortunately, over the years the development office has grown with a staff of Dominicans and lay people alike; it has become a stable and necessary part of our financial underpinning. Mrs. Jenny Block particularly helped organize our development, especially our Annual 1216 Campaign.

YEAR OF AWARDS

The year 2000, the millennial year of Christ's birth, was also the year in which I received another award based upon my interest in and service to the arts and artists' lives. Ever since I had done my initial research into the life of Pere Joseph-Marie Couturier and the French liturgical art revival immediately after the Second World War, I was interested in promoting religion in the arts. During my long association with the Louisiana Council of Music and the Performing Arts, I commissioned local artists for art work in places of worship as well as in their usual haunts and habitats.

All of the above culminated in a project called *Louisiana Renaissance: Religion and the Arts*, about which I produced a monograph entitled "Taste and See: Religion and the Arts." Some people thought it was a cookbook, but it was really an attempt to reconnect the arts with the many facets of worship that enrich the relation between God and man. In it we catalogued a list of artists who would be available for such commissions and consultations. This project was launched in Natchitoches, Louisiana, in the early 1970s and proved a great success.

Over the years I've met and encouraged many artists; some have been associated with me at the Newcomb School of Fine Arts, the Tulane School of Architecture, and in a wide variety of local theatrical and musical locales. In fact, only recently one of my dear friends was dying and his former wife called up one of our local artists, George Schmidt, for help.

"Call the artists' priest, Father Val McInnes! He'll be able to help you."

Through that kindness and referral I was able to take care of my dear friend and long time associate from the Newcomb School of Art, Franklin Adams, as he died. Coincidentally, I'd baptized Franklin's two sons as infants; they were George Schmidt's godsons.

I'm grateful for the many associations I've had with distinguished artists like Franklin, Lynn Emery, Jana Napoli, Angela Gregory, Nathaniel "Buster" Curtis, Jean Seidenberg, Dean John Lawrence of the Tulane School of Architecture, Bernie Lemann, Ron Blitch, Verna Arbour, Tim Trapolin, Ida Kohlmeyer, Dr. Arthur Silverman, Hal Kearney, Karen Laborde,

Karen Edmonds, and Henry Casselli. All of them and many other artists contributed to the richness of my life. They revealed the infinite creativity that God has placed within us to help recreate the world in which we live, especially when we're tired and depressed.

I'm sure it was for these and many other reasons that my Dominican confreres decided that I should receive the Fra Angelico Art and Spirituality Award at the New Orleans Museum of Art on May 16, 2000. During that enjoyable evening, I was presented with a very beautiful replica of a Fra Angelico angel holding a palette and a paintbrush. Much to my delight, I was informed that the award would be named the McInnes-Fra Angelico Art and Spirituality Award.

May I share the remarks I made that evening?

"From my earliest years, questions of art, beauty, truth, and God have intrigued me. I have been deeply and even passionately concerned about their relation. They all have to do with the good care of our soul and the well springs of our spirituality. The question is, how do we go about integrating all of them?

"While I'm an amateur painter and artist myself, my formal academic training led me into the philosophy of aesthetics and the history of art. At the same time, my studies in the theology of spirituality helped to give me insights into what makes us whole and holy. What makes us resplendent in God's sight as his beloved sons and daughters?

"Somewhere along my journey, my family gave me a copy of Skira's beautiful publication of Fra Angelico's works. This volume told the story of his spiritual life and illustrated his principal works in brilliant color. Thus, through Fra Angelico's life and works and those of other great artists such as El Greco, I have learned that if you really want to grow, there must be a fundamental reorientation and transformation in our lives. In religious terms this metamorphosis of dying in order to be reborn in God and Christ is a condition of cultivating the contemplative aspects of our personalities.

"We need to learn to be still and to discover the sense of mystery and awe-inspiring presence of God in our midst, and yes, even dwelling within us. As we discover that, it gradually dawns on us that we really are the beloved sons and daughters of the living God. Then, we learned to develop a real sense of our personal worth made in the image and likeness of God.

"Furthermore, the artistic muses under the inspiration of the Holy Spirit are constantly calling us to deeper levels of being, to ever new challenges, urging us to let go of the past and even our present comfortable identities and to welcome new visions, in the unfolding drama of our journey home to the Lord.

"C. S. Lewis once said that beauty inspires within us a desire for 'our own far off country, the home for which we long and have never seen.' Others, like Simone Weil, have written, 'The beauty in the world is God's tender smile for us coming through matter. It is God dwelling in our souls, and it goes out to God, present in the universe.' This experience is much like that of a sacrament, much like the experience of seeing a great Rembrandt and catching a glimpse of his genius in his work.

"These subtle links between art, spirituality and sacramentality were perhaps best expressed by the French artist Henri Matisse when he confided to Pere Joseph-Marie Couturier that every time he created a work of art, he tried to recapture the joy he experienced on the day he made his first communion.

"This is an extraordinary statement by one of the great French artists. Instinctively, he saw art and spirituality as linked in the deepest levels of our soul.

"Unfortunately, we live in a world in which spirituality is neglected. Also, beauty is often placed last on our list of priorities. The unfortunate implication is we can do without spirituality and the arts. They are, in fact, dispensable and non-existent for many people.

"But we cannot live without beauty, art and spirituality, any more than we can live without air. Therefore, we cannot live without the arts. We need to make room for the spirituality of the soul, by making room for the arts and beauty in our daily life. A living spirituality enthusiastically embraces the need for artistic beauty in the deepest recesses of our soul.

"Fra Angelico knew this and lived it. Beauty and truth met in his soul and produced some of the greatest religious works of art.

"Perhaps this new Fra Angelico Award, which I have the pleasure of receiving this evening as the first recipient, and which is named for me, will trigger a new rebirth of the relatedness between art and the vital needs of our spirituality today, much like Matisse intuitively perceived it and Fra Angelico lived it.

"There is an old Chinese saying, 'Remember that all the seeds planted today contain all the flowers of tomorrow.' Let's hope that this new Fra Angelico Award will bear much fruit in your lives and in the lives of many artists and holy people yet to come."

INTERNATIONAL DOMINICAN FOUNDATION

With the successful establishment of the development office, my term came to an end in the year 2000. I was still a development consultant for our own provincial office, but I was enjoying a respite.

One day I received a call from Rome asking me if I'd be interested in serving as the President/Director of the International Dominican Foundation (IDF). I wasn't sure what this would involve. Trying to stall a bit for time, I said I'd consult my provincial and they should send me a detailed job description. The stall didn't work. They'd already consulted the provincial and received his permission.

Well, the job description wasn't in the mail, and before I knew it, I was euchred into accepting the job. All I knew was that it involved fund-raising for the international projects of the Order. Other religious orders have prospered financially, but the Dominicans have never been famous as fund-raisers; their specialists have been philosophers, theologians, canon lawyers, and saints. However, I discovered that these aren't incompatible needs; all these had to have been fund-raisers at one time or another. No one can get by without funding.

Later, I discovered that the recommendation for an IDF had been made at the Bologna Chapter of the Order in 1998. It was revisited at our elective chapter in Providence in 2001. As it turned out, I'd been elected a socius to my provincial to attend that chapter; I also had to prepare a document for the approval of our chapter. I traveled to Rome to consult with Father Timothy Radcliffe, O.P., then the current master of the Order and the treasurer of the Order, Father Edmund Nantes.

As I read the documents it gradually became clear this new organization was commissioned by the Dominican chapters to raise funds for the following Dominican centers of learning: The University of St. Thomas in Rome, commonly called the Angelicum. The Oriental Institute for Moslem and Christian Dialog in Cairo. The Kiev Institute for Higher Education in Christian Theology. The Dominican Center in Brussels connected with the European community.

Promoter of Development 99

At the 2001 chapter I made a presentation, describing briefly the purpose of IDF and the kind of financial support it would need to be properly launched. After discussion from the floor, IDF was approved with assurances of financial backing from the Order.

I was approved as coordinator and president and charged with the responsibility of establishing an American office, a board to include the four provincials in the United States, members of the United States hierarchy, and others.

The chapter encouraged us to hire Community Counseling Services (CCS) as a fund-raising organization; it had been recommended by Father Joseph Fox, O.P., former development officer for the Angelicum. CCS would assist us in the establishment of our new office in New Orleans and facilitate our initial fund-raising activities.

In many ways CCS people were very helpful, especially in organizing the IDF office. Mrs. Judy Comeau-Hart was assigned to be administrative assistant and fund-raising coordinator. Fortunately, our good friend, Joe Canizaro, was kind enough to offer offices in his recently acquired Galleria Building in Metairie, a suburb of New Orleans. The first few months were pre-occupied with refurbishing some old desks the Galleria had in storage, acquiring computers, taking care of telephone lines, etc.

After consultation with the master and curia in Rome, we decided first to obtain a 501(c)3 Federal ID number as a duly established nonprofit charitable organization. After consulting our legal people, we made the necessary applications. This required having articles of incorporation and a board with officers. Within a year we had all the official documents.

Again through consultation with the curia and the four Dominican provincials of the U.S., we met in New York at the offices of the provincial of the St. Joseph province. Father Chrys Finn, O.P., the vicar of the Order, presided at the meeting. We determined the membership of the board and the proposed chairman. From the beginning it was affirmed that Dominican provincials would be *ex officio* members together with the president who would be recommended by the master and approved and confirmed by the board.

Over a period of time, these details were worked out, including the role of the chairman of the board; additional board members were appointed. These included members of the U.S. hierarchy and other members of the

Dominican family, such as our Dominican Sisters and members of the Dominican laity.

For original and present board members, consult Appendix A and the illustrated booklets entitled, "Support the International Campaign for Global Priorities and Giving Opportunities for International Dominican Foundation."

The board would meet once a year in conjunction with the National Catholic Conference of Bishops' (NCCB) annual meeting. Our first meeting was held in St. Louis, Missouri in 2003, immediately before the NCCB.

To write up the Dominican projects I had to travel abroad.

First destination was our University of St. Thomas Aquinas / Angelicum in Rome; our major intellectual center, it provided an indispensable service to the universal church by training canon lawyers, philosophers, dogmatic and moral theologians as well those in the social sciences. I made a detailed analysis of their needs.

I moved on to visit the Oriental Institute in Cairo. There our Dominicans had established, at the urging of the Holy See, an institute for a dialog with Muslims and Christians. Their library is one of the best in the world for source material on Muslim-Christian relations. Our brothers there were very welcoming. We toured their facilities, especially the beautiful new library and adjacent residence for visiting professors.

From there I flew to Israel and had the pleasure of visiting my French Dominican confreres at the *Ecole Biblique*. The school was founded in 1890 by Pere Joseph-Marie Lagrange, a leading biblical scholar. In the late 1950s it produced the famous Jerusalem Bible, which has a reputation as one of the best translations in Christian history.

On this trip I learned that they were planning an innovative edition of the Bible. It was to be called *The Bible in Its Traditions*. It would incorporate for the first time all known biblical sources, including variant readings; marginal notes would include commentaries from both the Jewish Talmud and the Fathers of the Church; included also would be significant literary, artistic, and musical references.

Of course, all this was made possible because of the computer enabling scholars to work on different books at the same time, then referring the new translations to the editorial board headquartered at the Ecole. For the first time in biblical history, Catholic, Protestant, Jewish, and Muslim scholars were working collaboratively together on texts in their various fields of specialty.

An electronic cyberspace translation that would be available on the Internet captured the imagination of many scholars. It's a monumental task involving expenditures into millions of dollars, probably in the neighborhood of $18 million. It would be and still is an ideal project for one of the great computer companies; without computers the project would be impossible.

I met with the faculty to hear them describe in detail how this new project was coming and what their expectations were. The new fund-raising arm would enable the scholarly work to proceed. It has given the Ecole an additional focus besides their regular academic work with graduate students and biblical scholars.

I rounded off my 2004 visit by celebrating Midnight Mass with the Latin Patriarch, Archbishop Sabat, and many other prelates and priests at the Church of the Nativity in Bethlehem over the place where Christ was reputedly born. It was certainly the high point of my visit, renewing me in my own faith and joy.

En route home I spent a few days in Brussels staying with the Dominicans. There they have a religious center for the members of the European community right in the heart of the downtown buildings. The grand priory had recently been remodeled along with some aspects of the church and the meeting rooms. They'd conceived this center as a common meeting place of the different religions of the European communities, including all Christians, Jewish, and Muslim believers. The plan is that it will be a cultural and artistic center for the mounting of exhibitions and the celebration of concerts as well as providing meeting facilities to discuss the interface of religion with politics.

Later in the year, after one of the curial meetings in Rome, I visited the Institute for Higher Studies at Kiev in the Ukraine. There the Dominicans, principally from Poland, established a center affiliated with the University of St. Thomas Aquinas in Rome; it would provide degrees in philosophy and theology for young people who'd been deprived of any sort of religious and theological education during the Soviet regime. It was edifying to see young men and women coming out after their workday to take classes beginning at 6:30 in the evening and ending around 11:00. They were so dedicated and grateful for the opportunity to learn something about God and morality.

While there we visited an old derelict military building from Tsarist times, subsequently used by the Soviets until the collapse of the Soviet empire. It was available. The Dominicans were able to buy it and renovate it. Our charge was to assist in the fund-raising for the renovation. This we did for the chapel and the living quarters.

As you can see from this brief overview, we were already involved in the need to raise millions of dollars. Fortunately, many of our friends came to our assistance; we've been able to raise substantial funds for these various projects. The demand is still very great, even more so when the world economy takes a downturn.

At our Dominican chapter in Krakow in 2006, it was decided that we should add one additional project to IDF: the Dominican Sisters House in Southern France, the place near Fanjeaux called Prouilhe where St. Dominic founded the Order in 1216.

Each year at the annual IDF board meetings, reports are submitted on the progress of these various projects and funds approved according to the 501(c)3 requirements. Because of my recent illness, I was obliged to resign as president of IDF in 2006. We were fortunate enough to find my replacement in the person of Father Mark Edney, O.P., who has capably and enthusiastically assumed the responsibilities of president.

1. Ambrose fishing in the Thames River outside of London, Ontario in 1933 – "The Foreshadowing of a Future Vocation—Fishers of Men."

2. Father Val's parents, Angus J. McInnes, Sr., and Genevieve Rodgers McInnes.

3. 1954 graduation with M.A. in philosophy from Assumption College, University of Western Ontario.

4. Photo of the author and his brothers during their time in London. Left to right, Angus J. McInnes, James A. McInnes, the author, Patrick R. McInnes, John Charles McInnes.

5. The author's Dominican class of 1955 for the Province of St. Albert the Great, St. Peter Martyr Priory, Winona, MN. The photo is the simple profession of vows on August 31, 1955. Father Val is left front (in white since he was not professed until November.)

6. Seated after his simple profession of vows and reception of the Dominican black and white habit, November 18, 1955, at St. Peter Martyr Priory, Winona, MN. He was given the religious name of Valentine after the Dominican Basque martyr, Bishop Valentine de Barrio Occoha.

7. The Genevieve Rodgers McInnes Memorial Chalice designed by Fr. Val and executed by Hamers Chalice Company of Belgium celebrating Fr. Val's ordination day, 3rd of June 1961. It was a gift of his father to the Dominicans.

8a. Angus J. McInnes, Sr., at the time of his son's ordination, 1961.

8b. Ordination class of 1961 with the author in the front row on the right hand side.

8c. Governor General Georges P. Vanier of Canada laying a wreath in honor of Ensign Henry Edward Dormer at the War Memorial, Victoria Park, London, Ontario during the Centenary Celebration of Dormer's death, October 1966."

9. Professor W. D. Davies, opening lecture for the Chair of Judeo-Christian Studies at Tulane University, April 14, 1980.

10. President Herbert Longenecker of Tulane University greeting Professor W. D. Davies with Fr. McInnes at the conclusion of the inaugural lecture.

11. Mr. John Bricker, one of the major benefactors for the Chair of Judeo-Christian Studies, speaking to Evelyn Gaudin, a Southern Dominican patron.

12. Sir John Haught, the first recipient of the St. Thomas Aquinas Environmental Award

13. H.R.H. The Prince of Wales receiving the second St. Thomas Aquinas Environmental Award from Fr. McInnes at his official residence of Clarence House in London, September 9, 2008.

14. Award designed by the Dominican sculptor, Fr. Thomas McGlynn.

15. The photograph of His Holiness John Paul II by Karsh of Ottawa granted with his special permission for the Vatican Pavilion at the 1984 Louisiana World Exposition.

16. *The Vatican Pavilion at night.*

17. *The tapestry of the Risen Christ, Vatican Pavilion.*

18. A series of six photographs of Henry Moore's preliminary sketches for the Crucifixion study ending with the finished sketch. The photographs reveal the evolution of his inspiration and, as he said, "I must respect the sacred moment of sacrifice without taking too many liberties from the conventional portrayal of Christ's death." Unfortunately, he did not find time to execute a maquette for the Vatican Pavilion. (With permission of the Henry Moore Foundation.)

19. HE Archbishop Philip M. Hannan, his Holiness Pope John Paul II, Fr. Val A. McInnes *following the meeting for the arrangements for the Vatican Pavilion at the Louisiana World Exposition, December 2, 1981.*

20. *The Woman at the Well, the centerpiece of the Vatican Pavilion, created by the internationally famous Croatian sculptor, Ivan Mestrovic.*

21. Very Rev. Valentine Ambrose McInnes, O.P., EGCLJ, GCMLJ, SMLJ, PhD. Senior Chaplain for the Military and Hospitaller Order of St. Lazarus of Jerusalem at the St. Lazarus National Shrine in the Old Ursuline Convent in New Orleans.

22. Fr. Val McInnes presenting Chevalier Dr. Hans von Leden, Grand Prior of the Military and Hospitaller Order of St. Lazarus of Jerusalem, to His Holiness, Pope John Paul II, 1992.

23. The solemn profession of Lee Martin Martiny, August 15, 1993. Left to right: Fr. Val A McInnes, O.P., Fr. Lee Martin Martiny, Fr. Timothy Radcliffe, Master of the Order of Preachers, Ambassador Vernon A. "Dick" Walters.

24. First recipient of the St. Martin de Porres Award Loretta Young and Fr. Val A. McInnes, 1986.

25. Houston 2000 St. Martin de Porres honoree Mrs. Rose Cullen with Fr. Val A. McInnes.

26. Some of Fr. Val's family celebrating at the 2000 Houston Dominican Gala. Left to right: his brother, Angus J. McInnes, Jr., his niece, Maureen McInnes, Angus' wife, Ann McInnes, their daughter, Carol Ann, and Fr. Val McInnes.

27. Father Roberto Rodriguez, Southern Dominican Provincial, presenting Fr. McInnes with the 2000 Fra Angelico Award on behalf of his Southern Dominican Friars for his work with the arts and spirituality. The citation reads, "A visionary, transforming the world through art and spirituality."

28. New Orleans Southern Dominican Gala 2008. Father Val with his niece, Marilyn Coles Calderone.

29. Harry Connick, Jr. accepting the 2008 St. Martin de Porres Award in recognition of his help in the recovery of New Orleans after Hurricane Katrina.

30. 2001 General Chapter, Providence College. Southern Dominicans gathered with the Master, Carlos Azpiroz Costa, in the center. Fr. Val is on his immediate right and Fr. Rodriguez on his immediate left.

31. The 2009 members of the IDF Board. Left to right: Dr. Gene Stark, the Very Rev. Fr. Michael J. Mascari, O.P., Dr. Patrick Jordan, Mrs. Lou Jordan, Very Rev Fr. Marty Gleeson, O.P., Fr. Val A. McInnes, O.P., President Emeritus, Rev. Msgr. James F. Checchio, Bishop Kevin W. Vann, Archbishop Robert J.Carlson, Archbishop Thomas J. Rodi. Seated: Father Mark Edney, O.P., President, Archbishop Donald W. Wuerl, Chairman, and Francis Cardinal George, OMI, honorary member.

32. The original members of the IDF Board of Directors. Front row: Most Rev. Robert J. Carlson, Very Rev. Fr Roberto Corral, O.P., HE Francis Cardinal George (honorary member), Very Rev. Fr Martin J. Gleeson, O.P.. Back row: Very Rev. Fr. Edmond C. Nantes, O.P., Rev. Mon. James F. Checchio, Very Rev. Fr. Val A. McInnes, O.P. , President, Most Rev. Donald W. Wuerl, O.P., Most Rev. Timothy M. Dolan, Chairman, Most Rev. Thomas C. Kelly, O.P., Most Rev. Edward F. O'Brien, O.P., and Very Rev. Fr. D. Dominic Izzo, O.P. Missing from the photo HE Theodore Cardinal McCarrick, Ms. Donna Miller, KC, Very Rev Fr. Neal W. McDermott, O.P., Sr. Rose Marie Masserano, O.P., and Most Rev. Michael J. Sheridan.

33. The International Dominican Foundation Advisory Board and Associates greeting Christoph Cardinal Schonborn at his residence in Vienna.

34. Wolfgang and Judith Feuchtmuller, former Tulane students of Fr. Val's from Vienna, in Christoph Cardinal Schonborn's study, Vienna 2008, showing the bullet holes shot into the painting by the Nazis when they stormed into the building in 1938.

35. Father Val McInnes presenting his monograph, To Rise with the Light, to Pope John Paul II.

36. Fr. Val presents Jack Chambers' Dormer Tribute to the Vatican Museums. Receiving the serigraph is Dr. Walter Persegati on behalf of the museums with Helen Boehm looking on.

37. The "sporty" Father Val in Capri.

38. Father Val in front of Dolores and Bob Hope's new home in Palm Springs.

39. Portofino photograph. On the famous yacht trip, Mrs. Louise Russell (mother of Sr. Mary Joseph) and Fr. Val at Portofino, Italy with Valentino's yacht in the background —similar to the one they were on.

40. A general view of the futuristic Hope home.

41. Dolores Hope and Father Val.

42. Father Val, Bob Hope, and Ann Miller's son, Donald.

43. Ann Miller with Father Val and her mother, Mrs. Louise Russell with an interloper.

44. Ann Miller, Father Val, and Walter Annenberg.

45. Ann Miller, now Sister Mary Joseph of the Most Holy Trinity, on the day of her simple profession of vows. As one of our mutual friends on hearing of her new religious name said, "Only Ann Miller could manage to include all the principles of salvation in her religious name."

46. Jo and Bob Ponds' Ponderosa estate in Palm Springs where the annual retreats are held.

47. Dolores Hope, the widow of legendary comedian Bob Hope, looking on as guests sing "Happy Birthday" at her 100th birthday party in Los Angeles, with Fr Val helping hold up the cake, May 27, 2009 (AP Chris Pizzello).

48. Fr. Benedict Groeschel, CFR, Fr. Val and one of Fr. Groeschel's good friends, Fr. John Lynch at Dolores Hope's birthday party.

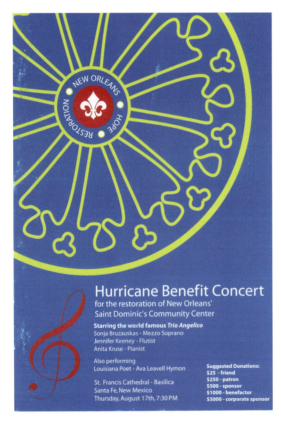

49. Cover for the program of the Hurricane Katrina Benefit Concert in Santa Fe, New Mexico, designed by Brett Landry of San Francisco.

50-1 *Two sketches by the author: "The Tree of Life" and "Mount Vesuvius from Capri." (1999)*

52. *The official photograph of the members of the International Dominican Foundation Advisory Board and Associates with the Latin Patriarch, His Beatitude Archbishop Michael Sabbat, in Jerusalem, April 18, 2008.*

53. *Father Val, with Dick Colton, at his 80th birthday party.*

54. Portrait of Fr. Val A. McInnes, O.P., by the American artist Verna Arbour. (Note the Cross and Star of David in the upper left of the canvas.)

55. *"Madonna and Child" watercolor created by Henry Casselli for Our Lady of Hope Chapel in St. Dominic's Church, New Orleans. Photo courtesy of the artist.*

26

Vatican Museums and Medjugorje Visions

In 1964 Pope Paul issued invitations to many in the art world to meet with him; he wanted to renew the centuries-old dialog between Church and art. On May 7th they gathered in the Sistine Chapel, a mini art museum in itself. He expressed the hope that the close and fruitful links of the past could be revived. On his part he was initiating a Twentieth-Century Art Museum in the Vatican Collections. As a direct result of this meeting, and thanks to the generosity of artists, collectors, and public and private benefactors, a number of works of art were donated.

VATICAN MUSEUMS

In 1970, with the approval of Pope Paul IV, Paul Marcinkus, American archbishop and Vatican banker, sent an invitation to a group of artists, agents, and art patrons in the New York area. On behalf of the pope he urged them to attend the opening of the new museum in the Vatican Museum complex, the Museum for Modern Religious Art, inaugurated in 1973. The archbishop particularly invited them to consider giving works of art from such contemporary painters as Rouault, Matisse, Chagall, Masson, Leger, Picasso, and other leading artists for the opening exhibition.

Many responded generously and came to Rome to celebrate the opening. The museum was magnificent, they agreed, but their contributions, generous though they were, appeared paltry in the spacious halls housing the new collection. What happened next was a happy unintended consequence. Almost to a person, they decided to give much larger and more important works of art.

With these people as a base, joined by the Kennedy Galleries of New York City and individual connoisseurs of art, a group of patrons arose.

Shortly thereafter, the Vatican, as I've mentioned previously, agreed to a major exhibition of Vatican art to travel to New York, Chicago, San Francisco, and New Orleans. Each city had its own supporters and subsequent to its exhibition decided to establish support groups for the Vatican Museums under the name of *Patrons of the Arts in the Vatican Museums*.

Monsignor Clark was the leader in the New York area. Chicago was under the leadership of Archbishop Bernardin. San Francisco and Los Angeles were represented by Mrs. Ann Miller and Mrs. Ginny Milner. I headed up the group from the New Orleans area with Archbishop Philip Hannan in strong support.

These various leaders were given the Canova Medal named for the famous Italian sculptor who at one point in his life was the director of the Vatican Museums. The medals were presented by the Director General of the Vatican Museums, Professor Carlo Pietrangeli, and Dr. Walter Persegati in recognition of their support of the Vatican Museums. The presentation was made in one of the smaller salons of the Vatican Palace.

At a general meeting in Rome in April 1988, the various groups agreed on an annual membership fee of $500 per person. The groups flourished and expanded. They would sponsor trips to Rome to explore the Vatican Museums; they would be entertained with luncheons and formal dinner parties. Each group would support the restoration of a major work of art. These groups were partly responsible for such excellent exhibitions coming out of the Vatican in recent years such as "The Legacy of the Vatican Museums" and "The Papacy and the Vatican Museums"; other exhibitions have been placed on loan to various parts of the United States and Canada. Such was the beginning of the *Patrons of the Arts*; it continues to flourish to this day. The Canadian Patrons Group was founded by Carol and Paul Hill and has enjoyed a success of its own.

Recently, the twenty-fifth anniversary of the founding of the Patrons was celebrated in San Francisco with an emphasis on the role of the California chapter. Leaders from the rest of the United States were invited; I had the pleasure of representing the southern chapter. A beautifully illustrated book was published, recounting the history and the contributions the Patrons had made.

At the time a New Yorker remarked to me that New York seemed to have been omitted. I remarked to her that I couldn't find New Orleans. Evidently, the historian compiling the book neglected to get in touch with either New York or New Orleans chapters.

BURST OF HOPE

Over the years, Bob and Dolores Hope were generous hosts for the Patrons of the Arts in the Vatican Museums. On a number of occasions after they completed their beautiful new home on the side of a mountain, they sponsored successful dinner parties for the members of the Patrons and included some of their Hollywood friends, such as Loretta Young, John Wayne and his wife, including the Sinatras and others. Through these associations and giving retreats, I often found myself as their guest.

One of the most memorable experiences was dinner with the Hopes. It was an evening affair at their Toluca Lake home in West Hollywood. I celebrated Mass for them, and afterward we went into the dining room. Dolores had placed me next to Bob on his left-hand side, which was his good ear. We fell into a conversation about his early years in vaudeville. I asked how he started in his hometown of Akron, Ohio, after the family had settled there from England. He was delighted with the opportunity to reminisce. He broke into vaudeville as a dancer. He loved to dance, but he had to admit there was a limit to his ability. He had to rest from time to time. And during the rest periods he told stories. And the rest was history.

As he went on, his stories became more famous than his dancing. Other vaudevillians began to tell his stories as though they were their own. Bob's mother put a stop to that. She attended his competitors' acts. When she heard a comedian begin to tell one of Bob's jokes, she waited until the punch line, then pounced.

"That's my son, Bob Hope's, story!"

ANOTHER BURST OF HOPE

One of the most proud days of Bob's life, he told me, was the christening of the *USNS Bob Hope* on March 17, 1997, with his wife, Dolores, as the sponsor at the Avondale Shipyard on the Mississippi River in New Orleans. I had the impression that it was the crowning point of his recognition as a great American patriot and supporter of the Armed Forces over the years. I had the privilege of joining them with the Honorable Corinne "Lindy" Boggs, along with thousands of others.

MEDJUGORJE VISIONS

Back to the Patrons.

All of this is preamble to a very significant post-patrons trip in 1998. We'd completed our annual visit to the Vatican. Some of our group, wanting to push on to Medjugorje, persuaded me to lead a pilgrimage there. On the day of our departure we were invited to attend Pope John Paul II's private Mass. Afterward he approached us. I had the pleasure of introducing him to each of our group.

"Where are you going from here?"

"We're going on a pilgrimage to Medjugorje," I responded.

"Pray for me while you are there."

To say the least, we were overjoyed by the experience of being with him.

Our party included Colleen Ingraffia and her son Roy, Cherie Banos, Billy and Susie Glennon, Beth Cary, Marilyn Rusovich, Ruth Northrup, and Susan Stall.

The following day we left for Split. We spent the early part of the day visiting the palace remains of the last Roman emperor. Then we toured the rest of the city before leaving for the mountains. On the outskirts we visited the magnificent home of Yugoslav sculptor Ivan Mestrovic. It was a Grecian style villa with Doric pillars. Today it functions as a museum housing many of Mestrovic's masterpieces.

From there we made our way to Medjugorje, arriving in the late afternoon. The small town was filled with people, mostly young students from every part of the world. The government, though communist, had allowed additional housing to be built for the pilgrims. Fortunately, we were all cared for in one large house. We settled in and had our evening dinner. Immediately after, we visited the local church where some of the purported apparitions had taken place. The church was some distance away, but we had our bus to bring us back and forth.

At the church we were amazed at the number of people going to confession. There were at least twelve priests hearing confessions in different languages; the same was true the following morning when we went to Mass. Built in 1937, the building accommodated perhaps six hundred people, but there had to have been eight hundred there that morning.

Father Philip was the current pastor, succeeding Father Jozo who'd been there for the first apparitions. Fortunately, I was able to concelebrate with many different priests. I had the pleasure of reading the epistle in English and listening to Father Philip give the homily in English as well. It was about the parable of Christ being the vine and us being the branches. It was particularly striking because it was early spring; pruned bushes were sprouting again. When it came time for Communion, I extended my hand with the Host, at least a dozen hands reached out for it. Fortunately, with many priests we were able to give Communion quickly and efficiently. But the multitude of communicants certainly personified the gospel fruitfulness of those who remained in union with the vine.

After Mass we went back to our home where we had an enjoyable breakfast; then we were off to visit Vicka, one of the two surviving visionaries who were still in town. We met her briefly at the entrance to her home, and exchanged a few greetings. No doubt she would have spent more time with us if she hadn't burned herself while cooking.

We decided to climb the nearby mountain named Krizevac where the huge cross was located; reportedly, it often glowed at night. Praying the rosary appeared to be the favorite devotion of those visiting the site.

The second day we walked around the countryside, meditating, and praying and enjoying the ambiance. Some nearby groups told us they'd seen the "the miracle of the sun," but none of our group did.

The third day of our visit we gathered at the parish church around five o'clock; I heard confessions and celebrated Mass. Immediately following Mass, the recitation of the rosary began. But almost from the beginning there was a noise in the choir loft. It seemed that the other visionary, Ivan, a young man in his mid-twenties, began experiencing an apparition; the minor commotion lasted until the end of the rosary.

The fourth day, we said goodbye to our host family, boarded our little van, and made off. En route we said Mass and thanked God for the unique opportunity of visiting the holy place. The countryside was mountainous, and when we came up over the last mountain range, we looked down into the Adriatic Sea and the walled city of Dubrovnik, sheathed in white marble looking like a rich pearl on a turquoise sea. It was a splendid sight and caused us to catch our breath.

After getting settled at the hotel, we immediately went to the city to explore this ancient walled place constructed of white marble with paved marble streets.

We visited the Dominican Priory; it was established in the year 1221, the year St. Dominic died, and has been in continual existence ever since. For me it was a unique personal experience of Dominic's place in world history.

Our small pilgrim group, although reveling in the spiritual joy, expressed some regret. None of us had experienced the so-called "miracle of the sun." I tried to assure them that you couldn't have everything in life, and that we were just lucky to be there.

We returned to our hotel and had an afternoon siesta. Around five o'clock I got up and showered, and just as I was getting dressed, the couple in the next room went out on the balcony.

"Father Val, come out and look at the sun!"

"Don't look directly at the sun, it will blind you," I said rather emphatically.

"Come on out and see the sun, it's spinning!" So I finished dressing and went out on my balcony. The following is the account I began on the plane the next day.

MIRACLE OF THE SUN

Dubrovnik, Yugoslavia, 2nd of May, 1988 – 6:10 to 6:30 PM

After four days of pilgrimage to Medjugorje with a group of friends from New Orleans, we left that serene and enchanted valley to return to New Orleans by way of Dubrovnik. Since we departed early in the morning, we decided we would celebrate Mass en route. I pointed out in my homily that we had all had some extraordinary experiences visiting in the church and meeting the people on pilgrimage to Medjugorje. It was perhaps a bit arrogant on our part, I suggested, to have expected the Virgin to give us any extraordinary signs while we were visiting there, but in fact, extraordinary signs of faith had occurred all around us during our visit—for example, in the many young people praying, in the atmosphere of reconciliation found in the sacrament of Penance, in the serenity and peace of the place, and especially in our meeting with Fr. Jozo, the pastor of Medjugorje when the apparitions first started.

We had visited Fr. Jozo in his parish some 15 miles away. He explained why he thought Our Lady was appearing in Medjugorje: It was an invitation on her part to return to the simple messages of love and peace which her Son came to give the world. Mary loves each of us with a unique love, he said. He felt that the apparitions were Mary's way of sharing her concern over the erosion of faith and love in her Son, Jesus Christ. He used the simple image of shepherds in a valley who are all very much at home with their sheep as long as they stay under the mountain peaks which they call home. If, however, the sheep and the shepherds wandered beyond that territory, they would lose themselves and have to be brought back home.

Mary's invitation to the world in these apparitions is to bring people back home to her Son. The Good Shepherd promises that if we remain loyal to him we shall not wander too far from his path. Mary calls us to renew our love and to pray the Rosary, which is nothing other than a brief and salutary review of the life, death and Resurrection of Jesus. Mary energetically recalls all men and women to the simplicity of Christ's way to eternal life. This way involves prayer, a conversion of heart, confession, praying for peace and serenity, and fasting. For this reason she identified herself as the Holy Mother of Peace, and this is the special message and unique sign of Medjugorje.

Our experience alone with Fr. Jozo was enough sign to satisfy us. As pastor in Medjugorje when the apparitions first began, he was unimpressed by the five children claiming that they were seeing Mary. However, while he was praying one day, he heard a voice from within telling him to get up to save the children; they were being arrested by the police. From that moment, he had no doubts about the truth of the apparitions. He would suffer, subsequently, for protecting the children by taking them into his rectory. He was later accused of conspiracy for hiding them, and was sent to prison for three years. During this time, his prison door was often found unlocked in the morning. After other incidents of this sort, the authorities allowed him to go free with the understanding he would never again preach in Medjugorje.

Our visit with Fr. Jozo was indeed a privilege, an extraordinary sign of Our Lady's love for each of us. Maria, our guide, was kind enough to have arranged that meeting, and acted as the interpreter during our visit. Fr. Jozo's personality was that of a man full of joy and at peace with himself and the world around him.

The following day we attended the English-speaking Mass at ten o'clock. Fr. Philip asked me to read the first reading, and I did so gladly. Father's homily was based upon the Gospel reading of the vine and the branches. He spoke of the pruning which must take place in order to make the vine more fruitful. It was a most appropriate Gospel reading, because the valley in which Medjugorje is located is filled with vineyards. At that time of the year all the vines are beginning to sprout. The dead branches had been pruned from the vine so that new life might spring forth. He asked us simply to meditate, as we walked about the countryside, on that mystery of our being joined to Christ as the vine and we as the fruitful branches.

Sunday evening, the first of May, we left early to attend the Croatian Mass. We arrived an hour and a half early so that our group could find good seats in the church. I went out to hear some confessions, and then meditated in the church. At the beginning of the Rosary around six o'clock, young Ivan, the only member of the group of visionaries who attended the evening Rosary, arrived. He went immediately to the balcony of the church with two Franciscans, an elderly lady, and a young boy. There, we learned later, during the recitation of the Rosary, Mary once again appeared to him. The church was filled to overflowing. Never in my life as a priest have I given out so many Communions to so many people. They were so eager to receive the Bread of Life that they almost "snatched" the host from my hand. The singing of the Croatians was like waves of sound washing over the congregation, renewing and refreshing everyone there.

Mass preceded the recitation of the Rosary. Ivan, now a very handsome young man in his mid-twenties, was dressed in a light trench coat. After Mass and the apparitions, he simply walked off into a nearby field with no one following him.

All the members of our group were deeply moved by the friendliness of the people, and especially of our hostess Yaya and her family. Unlike most pilgrims to Medjugorje who originally had to live in rather cramped quarters of people's homes, we had the privilege of staying on the third floor of a recently constructed house, which was more than adequate and very pleasant. The intense faith of the local people is moving. Our hope and prayers are that they will be able to survive the inundation of the thousands of people coming each day to experience the extraordinary events going on in this little Croatian town.

As we left the next morning on our bus, I reminded our group that extraordinary signs had indeed been given to us in a myriad of little experiences: climbing the two mountains, meeting and conversing with people from all over the world—Canada, Australia, the United States, Ireland, the Philippines. People are being drawn to Medjugorje like a magnet. We too had been drawn there, experienced the power and presence of Christ and of his Mother, manifesting her concern that all people renew themselves at the deepest level of their faith, so that they may be touched and indeed renewed.

Jesus had some rather harsh words for people who are always looking for extraordinary signs. He said to the Pharisees, "You are an idolatrous generation, always looking for signs." Putting our visit in perspective, I suggested that we should be more than content with what we had experienced. Mary had connected with each one of us in a special way and had given her special love to us by bringing us together in our small group from New Orleans.

We then drove on to Dubrovnik and to an afternoon of sightseeing in the beautiful medieval town that is still well preserved inside the walls of the city. After visiting the citadel and the city walls containing the old Franciscan and Dominican convents and the beautiful cathedral of Our Lady, we returned to the Villa Dubrovnik to rest up and prepare for dinner.

I went out onto the balcony of my room, which overlooked the Adriatic. A beautiful island lay in the background. As I gazed at the green cypresses and pines with the cool air strongly scented with the perfume of orange blossoms, I couldn't help but think that we were as close to Paradise as we could expect on earth. I decided to sit down in the white wicker chair there to say the Rosary. My heart was full of gratitude for our wonderful visit in Rome where I had the unique privilege of concelebrating Mass with the Holy Father in the Matilda Chapel for our little group. Also I expressed our equal gratitude for the invitation of Our Lady to come to Medjugorje to receive the benefits of her hospitality.

Following a siesta, I decided to take a shower. As I finished I heard Billy Glennon and his wife Susan calling me to come out on the balcony. I finished dressing and walked over to the balcony. "Look at the sun," he told me. He insisted that I look, and as I did, I saw the most extraordinary sight of my life. As I gazed at the sun, it appeared as if a small eclipse was taking place. Something blotted out the center of the sun, leaving a periphery of light on the edge of the sun. The sun began to spin, much like a circular firecracker, leaving brilliant colors of yellow, crimson, red, blue in its wake. The sun, with the eclipse, began to pulsate and undulate back and forth. I blinked again, and asked Billy Glennon and his wife Susan if they were seeing the same thing I was seeing; they said they were, and described the same phenomenon of the sun spinning with brilliant colors leaping out from the sun. On the balcony beyond the Glennons, Colleen Ingraffia and her young son Roy were also witnessing the same event. I asked them also, "Are you seeing the same thing I'm seeing?" They said, "Yes."

As we stared in continued awe at the phenomenon of the sun partially eclipsed and twirling, the center of the blackened disc in front of the sun began to reveal various images. One image I saw was the face of Christ, indistinct but there in outline. Colleen and Roy Ingraffia saw the Image of the Virgin with the Christ Child. Whether these images were the product of our imaginations is something for others to decide, but there was no doubt in our minds that we were seeing and witnessing the Miracle of the Sun—an experience which many pilgrims have, either in Medjugorje, on their way home, or after they have arrived home from pilgrimage.

After the initial surprise and awe passed, I said we should say the Rosary. As we said the Joyful Mysteries together, the undulation and colorful outcroppings of the sun around the disc continued to move in a counter-clockwise direction, leaving a trail of colors. As we progressed in our prayer, the sun slowly began to set, and as we finished the Mystery of finding Jesus in the Temple, the sun fell below the horizon.

Later, while discussing these extraordinary events, Susan Glennon felt that Our Lady had given us a gesture of her love after we had resigned ourselves not to expect anything extraordinary, and that in turn we spontaneously offered her back the gesture of her Rosary as our thanksgiving.

Another member of our group, Beth Cary, reminded me that our Miracle of the Sun took place immediately above the area of Dubrovnik where our Dominican convent was located. We had just visited that convent and said a prayer to St. Dominic, our founder, to whom we owe the devotion of the Rosary in the first place. Tradition tells us it was to St. Dominic that Mary herself presented the Rosary at the beginning of the 13th century. Mary couldn't have surprised us more and planned our little Miracle of the Sun better. Later I was to discover in conversation that Beth Cary had been the one to suggest we look at the sun, since it was about the time of the saying of the Rosary in Medjugorje.

If someone had told me two weeks ago that I'd be telling a story like this, I'd have had to say that he was out of his mind or hallucinating. Now, however, having been to Medjugorje and experienced the peace and serenity of that lovely valley, I'm writing these few words to verify the facts of our experience of the Miracle of the Sun, and how this in turn adds validity in some small way to the extraordinary apparitions of Medjugorje. We indeed feel very deeply that the events of Medjugorje and Our Lady's apparitions there are true and that this final gesture of kindness to us of the Miracle of the Sun supports these events. Of course, all of this we recognize as our own personal experiences. We await the official Church pronouncement concerning the overall apparitions and their significance for the whole of the Church.

Fr. Val A. McInnes, O.P.
Chair of Judeo-Christian Studies, Tulane University
New Orleans, Louisiana, May 4, 1988

Such was the wonderful experience of our pilgrimage to Medjugorje. I sent a copy to the Apostolic Nuncio and asked him to forward it to the Secretary of State for the Vatican as a verified witness of what eleven people saw. It was something I wanted to put on record since I'm not usually given such extraordinary experiences.

Please see Appendix B for an account by one of our pilgrims, Mrs. Cherie Banos Schneider. It's a more detailed and concrete expression of our whole experience in Medjugorje.

One day after my return I received a call from my friend, the author Walker Percy. He heard I'd been to Medjugorje and written an account of the so-called Miracle of the Sun. He was interested in reading it; I sent him a copy. Later we got together at his home outside Covington, Louisiana. He wanted to know more about the incident, especially the way the sun twirled counter-clockwise and the wisps of variegated colors that floated around the sun as it twirled. He knew that something profound had happened and was delighted to hear my account.

27

The Pope Visits New Orleans

During the first visit that Archbishop Hannan and I had with Pope John Paul II concerning arrangements for the Vatican Pavilion, the Holy Father indicated his desire to come to New Orleans. In fact, this had been contemplated as a possibility during the Vatican Pavilion itself, but as I mentioned elsewhere he would be visiting Canada at the same time. Two years later, however, he did come to the Crescent City.

By this time in his reign his charismatic personality had made him a superstar. Wherever he went he was greeted by hundreds of thousands of people. It brought home the ancient Roman axiom that where Peter was, there the Church was. So for three days in 1987, from the 10th to the 12th of September, the Church was in New Orleans.

From the first instant of the Holy Father's arrival by plane, the spontaneous, outgoing, and enthusiastic welcome was literally overwhelming. Southern hospitality reached out with its usual energy and warmth. The pope did his part; he learned how to pronounce "N'Awlins." At the end of his visit he told the archbishop that he especially enjoyed the rich cultural life, the good food, the great music, and the Mississippi River, which he'd dreamed of seeing since he was a boy.

In preparation for the papal visit I wrote an article for the *Times-Picayune* highlighting his interest in drama. Little did he know when he gave up the desire to be an actor that the Lord was calling him to a much greater stage, one that was the envy of any great actor or producer. Any Cecil B. DeMille production would be dwarfed by a papal Mass in a field or stadium. His clear, blue eyes and warm, affectionate smile seemed to touch everybody; he greeted everyone like a long-lost grandson or granddaughter.

I wasn't among the welcoming party at the airport, but I did meet him personally on many other occasions in Rome with our Patrons groups and concelebrations, which was always a deeply moving spiritual experience. He was a man full of love who communicated the love of Christ to all around him.

I was present in the packed Cathedral of St. Louis in New Orleans. He greeted the priests and religious of the archdiocese as the Vicar of Christ and in the name of the Father, the Son, and the Holy Spirit. To him the Holy Trinity was indeed the ultimate community to which the Church was called and was in itself the visible sign of the Holy Trinity in time.

As head of the universal Church the pope was relating to the local church in New Orleans, as Archbishop Hannan pointed out in his opening remarks.

"In Louisiana the political subdivisions of the state are called parishes and not counties. Thus the whole of Louisiana today becomes your parish."

This sense of community we all experienced at the cathedral that day provided a thrilling experience of the oneness with Christ in all of God's people.

As the pope moved out of the cathedral, we stood on the pews to get a better view. As one of the priests said, "He likes working the crowd."

The pope moved out into Jackson Square where he dedicated the Pope John Paul II Plaza as a memorial of his visit.

In the Superdome he greeted the national black leadership group with the reassuring words that the Church needed the blacks as much as the blacks needed the Church.

The high point of his visit came with the youth rally. In typical New Orleans style the pope was greeted by young people showing their love for him. In true Mardi Gras fashion, there were marching bands, especially the mighty one from St. Aug's (St. Augustine High School), and Mardi Gras floats to express their enthusiasm through the practice of their own faith. The centerpiece of the pope's address to the students was St. Paul's words: "Do not allow the world to deceive you, but remain loyal to the truth of Jesus Christ, which alone frees us and keeps us young." With a record crowd of nearly 80,000 people, the Superdome was filled with enthusiastic cheers. In summing up the papal visit the archbishop would say, this moment was the highlight! The openness of the young people was truly astounding.

Later in spite of torrential rains that fell on the thousands of people waiting for his outdoor Mass, the clouds suddenly opened and the sun poured through at the time the Mass began. Next day's cartoon in the *Times Picayune* captured the moment with an umbrella being held by God over the Mass site. Musicians Al Hirt and Pete Fountain and a special choir contributed to the celebration with God at the center of it all.

I and Professor Frank Birtel were asked by Tulane University President Eamon Kelly to represent him at the pope's last public appearance. It took place at Xavier University of Louisiana during the academic convocation for presidents of universities and the National Catholic Education Association. Here he stressed the relationship of the mission of the Church with the mission of the academic world especially in the areas of philosophy, theology, and morality. Catholic education must be the authentic reflecting board for the pursuit of truth in the context of religious belief and academic freedom. Only by this complementary role can the Catholic university remain authentically Catholic and the Church remain present to the university, Catholic or otherwise.

His closing remarks were spontaneous and most touching. He thanked the universities for being present and represented; without their presence his presence wouldn't have been possible. He assured them of the importance of the prophetic role they must play as members of the Church of Christ, proclaiming the teaching mission to the students who are the life's blood of every university. He urged everyone to recall the prophetic role that makes them participants in the prophetic role of the universal church, and not to forget it.

His visit to New Orleans was a great success. It renewed the faith of many, and everyone was delighted by him.

28

California Retreats

In the early 1980s, even before the Vatican Pavilion event, I had been invited by Ann Miller and her good friend Dolores Hope to give annual retreats either at the St. Clare retreat center south of San Francisco near Monterrey or at Dolores and Bob Hope's home in the valley in Palm Springs. The Hopes had maintained their old house in the valley after having built the new great house with the bonnet roof on the side of one of the mountains overlooking Palm Springs. These retreats were for two different groups.

The first was an annual retreat under the auspices of the Miller family; they invited their friends to come and renew themselves each year. They used a variety of retreat masters; I enjoyed being one of them. The retreats usually took place in February or March and were attended by young and old alike. To maintain the interest of such a mixed group was always a challenge for a retreat master.

The second was Ann and Dick Miller's immediate family and for Bob and Dolores Hope with her sister Mildred and whatever children were available along with their friends. These always took place during Holy Week. On that weekend Bob Hope had an Easter television show. These shows were pre-recorded; Bob and his many friends would come in for an early buffet dinner, and then we'd watch his Easter show. All sorts of distinguished people, known and unknown to me, would appear, and meeting them was great fun.

Ann introduced me to General and Mrs. Westmoreland, the Honorable and Mrs. Walter Annenberg, and a host of others. At one point I went up and introduced myself as Father Val McInnes to a gentleman who looked very familiar.

"I'm Michael."

"How are you, Michael?" Then it dawned on me who he was, King-Prince Michael of Romania with his wife Anne, Princess of Bourbon-Parma. One of her uncles at the time was the Grand Master of the Military and Hospitaller Order of St. Lazarus of Jerusalem.

"We usually refer to him as *the double Bourbon*."

"Yes, that's what they all say," his wife said with a laugh.

After we finished dinner and watched the Easter show, we went up to the new, magnificently modern house overlooking Palm Springs. It was like having a Buck Rogers edifice come to life in front of your eyes with swirling circles and great sweeping balconies overlooking a carpet-green terrace with a swimming pool in the center. The local parish priest joined us for the Easter Vigil liturgy; we blessed the great new fire—Christ as the light of the world. The candle was lit from the new fire that symbolizes Christ overcoming the darkness of the world. It was always a very moving experience and helped us relive the Easter mystery of the death and Resurrection of Christ living on in all of his members. The following day, Easter Sunday, the Hopes welcomed fifty of us for brunch in the new house. We enjoyed the camaraderie of the moment.

That Easter Sunday Ann Miller was the spokesperson expressing our thanks for the brunch and the hospitality. Within minutes she had everyone in hysterics. Then Bob got up.

"I'll be damned. Here I'm in my own house, and this dame gets up and gives a five-minute talk and gets more laughs than I do, and she doesn't even have a speech writer."

Ann was in many ways a natural born comic with a sterling sense of humor. She was always ready to respond with a good gibe or a very insightful comment.

Walter Annenberg was standing next to me.

"We ought to run her as the next woman ambassador to the Holy See."

"No, no," she said. "I'm going to become a Carmelite nun, and that's all there is to that."

"Ann, don't bury your talents in a monastery."

"I'm not going to bury my talents. I'm liberating them." Mr. Annenberg wanted to know how our most recent retreat had been. I told him that people seemed to enjoy it very much. Once in the following years the Annenbergs were invited to a retreat but begged off because of a visiting house guest by the name of Margaret Thatcher. Later I wrote them a note.

"I wish you'd come with Mrs. Thatcher. I'd have liked to help make you as successful spiritually as you have been financially and politically."

No response!

These retreats continued in a modified form after Ann left for the Carmelites. Instead of hosting them at the Hopes', we moved on to the beautiful home of Jo and Bob Pond on the outskirts of Palm Springs. That was 1990, and this is how it happened. One morning we were exercising in a club with my friends, Clare and Bill Burgess, when a lovely lady came in and sat down on the exercise bike next to us. She knew my friends very well and immediately we were engaged in conversation. After we finished, she asked what we were planning to do for lunch; nothing, we said. "You must come to my house for lunch."

This is how we met Jo Pond. Her home was spectacular. The lunch was enjoyable. We also had the good fortune of meeting her husband Bob. Halfway through the conversation, Jo introduced a new topic.

"Father, you have to come out here and give us a retreat. Everybody out here has lots of money, but there's not too much spirituality."

"Well, you state the time, and I'll come and give the retreat."

Thus began the tradition of annual retreats at the Jo and Bob Pond estate on the outskirts of Palm Springs. We've had them every year for the last twenty years. These have been spiritual renewals for all of us, and they've been ecumenical, including other Christians and Jewish friends as well.

The only problem I have in giving retreats in Palm Springs is that everybody feels they've already died and gone to heaven. However, I try to remind them that in every garden there's a snake, and that brings us back to reality.

Bob Hope died seven years ago, two months short of being one hundred. Dolores just recently celebrated her hundredth birthday at Our Lady of Hope Chapel in her parish church, Toluca Lake. Celebrating with her were Cardinal Archbishop of Los Angeles Roger Mahony, who actually grew up in the parish with Dolores's sons and daughters; Cardinal Archbishop Emeritus McCarrick of Washington, D.C.; Michael J. Branfield, presently the Bishop of Wheeling-Charleston, West Virginia, but formerly the rector of the Shrine of the Immaculate Conception in Washington, D.C.; the well-known Father Groeschel; the pastor of the local parish; and myself. A small group of her immediate family and friends were also present. The altar of Our

Lady of Hope was banked in flowers like a grotto, and the flower arrangements flowed down around the altar.

Later in the afternoon at her home Dolores and her sister Mildred greeted everyone enthusiastically. Even though Dolores spent most of her time in a wheelchair, she still had that marvelous spark. Her daughter Linda and son Kelly made all the arrangements for her one-hundredth birthday party. The climax of the celebration came with a three-tiered birthday cake. In her beautiful rose garden there were ten kiosks, each one celebrating ten years of her hundred years. Also further out in the garage area there were ten vintage cars representing every ten years of her hundred–year life. It was a real Bob Hope Special choreographed by her children and grandchildren. What a wonderful way to celebrate a hundred years of a life filled with faith, hope, and lots of love.

29

From Socialite to Carmelite

On the opening day of the Vatican Pavilion, as I have mentioned already, Ann Miller (not the dancer but the socialite from San Francisco) took me aside to tell me that her husband Dick had been recently diagnosed with melanoma and wasn't expected to live. This was in early May of 1984; by early September he'd died. Unfortunately, I wasn't able to attend the funeral at St. Dominic's in San Francisco. A short time later, though, I was able to visit the family and extend my personal sympathy to each of them.

Ann continued to live in the great home on Divisidero near Broadway, which was on top of one of the hills of the city. She was still very much the center of San Francisco society and was being wined and dined by one of her old boyfriends, the one who'd missed out in marrying her in the first place, George "Corky" Bowles. He was a wealthy Californian, a friend of the Miller family for many years. He was pressing the point that he wanted to marry her; she, however, announced that in two-and-a-half years' time, when she was sixty-one, she was going to become a Carmelite nun.

Ann had already chosen the Carmelite community in Des Plaines, Illinois, a Discalced Carmelite community, which she and her husband had helped build. The sisters would jokingly say they were saving a room for her when she was ready. Little did anyone know at the time that that would actually come to pass.

The *San Francisco Chronicle* got wind of her decision and ran with it in a society column entitled, "Will Ann Miller become a Carmelite nun?" the column became a series. Far from scaring Corky off, the news made him more ardent in his pursuit.

Ann further announced she was going to visit all the major Marian shrines of the world. Of course, in all these various places she had friends.

I was invited as chaplain to Hawaii, South America, and Punta del Este in Uruguay (near the place where the Nazi pocket battleship *Graf Spee* was scuttled).

South Americans tell the story that if you want to go on a nice trip, you go to the United States. If you want to go on a better trip, you go to Europe. But if you really want to go to the most first-class place in the world, you go to Punta del Este; it had one of the most beautiful beaches in the world and very hospitable people.

At home in San Francisco Ann's family and friends thought she was daft about becoming a Carmelite. She'd done everything else, she said; she'd had a husband and five boys and five girls, traveled around the world, and was the center of the social, cultural, and religious life of San Francisco. Some of her children were concerned whether, with two years of travel preceding her entrance to the religious life, there'd be anything left of the family finances. These were a few of the reactions to her decision.

Finally, Corky realized her decision to enter Carmel was firm. He therefore offered a farewell gift to her, her family, and some of her friends. He chartered a yacht that would cruise the central Mediterranean. Everybody who heard about it thought it was a grand idea, including Ann. Corky invited me as chaplain for the cruise.

Twelve of us flew to Nice, then drove to San Remo on the Italian Riviera. The yacht looked as though it had just cruised out of a James Bond episode; in fact it had been used just a month earlier for that purpose. It was built in Perth, Australia, at a cost of $75 million for a family in Hartford, CT; when they weren't using it, it was available for charter. There was a crew of nine, among whom was a Cordon Bleu chef to take care of our culinary needs and wants.

As I was boarding the yacht, I met Ann's mother, Louise Russell; she immediately took me to a salon, sat me down, and spoke point blank.

"You know the reason for this trip, don't you?"

"Why, yes. It's a going-away present for your daughter."

"That's not the reason. The real reason is to get Corky Bowles to propose to Ann."

Evidently the ladies on board were conspiring to change Ann's mind.

Our "once in a lifetime cruise" began a modest run from San Remo to Monaco. Viewing the Riviera and the hills and mountains from the vantage point of a yacht turned the whole experience into a kind of fairy

From Socialite to Carmelite

tale. The following day we dropped anchor in the yacht basin of Monaco. Unfortunately, Princess Grace, whom Ginny Milner (one of Corky's guests) knew very well, was away, so we had to content ourselves with a tour of the principality.

I neglected to mention that when I arrived in Nice, my bags weren't on board the plane; they were promised next day in Cap Ferrat. Next day, no bags; we left word to forward them to Portofino. Next day, still no bags.

"Well, then," said Ann; "it's time for us to go shopping."

So I went with her and bought some clothes to hold me over.

The voyage was a delight; we just enjoyed relaxing on board this beautiful vessel. The food was a culinary delight and decidedly healthy; everything was fresh, the salads, fish, chicken, meat, fruit.

While in Portofino another beautiful yacht dropped anchor next to us. It belonged to the famous couturier, Valentino. It was slightly larger than ours. We mutually gawked at each other. Our own yacht was beautifully appointed with an apparatus at the back that enabled us to swim off the rear of the vessel at water level and to shove off on little water jet boats.

Finally my luggage arrived. We took off once again and cruised along the coast to Porto Vennari, where we visited the Italian naval base. Rough weather delayed our departure to Corsica. We kept close to the bay until the sky cleared. We cruised overnight to Corsica, where we eased into a slip surrounded with striking architecture under the auspices of Prince Aly Khan, new structures made to look old.

We explored the little chapel and were delighted with the interior. There was only one painting, and that was above the altar; it was El Greco's *Holy Family*. That evening we had dinner at a nearby restaurant. The next day we visited the widow of famous English conductor, Sir Henry Walden; she was one of Ann's many friends.

Finally, we departed and cruised overnight to Sardinia and dropped anchor in the main harbor area not far from Napoleon's home. We enjoyed the environs of the place and after an enjoyable tour, we were glad to get back to the yacht to relax and have dinner. Later that evening we left for Capri. Fortunately, most of these were overnight trips; each morning we woke up at a new destination.

Capri was a jewel sitting in the midst of the turquoise sea. One reason why Roman emperors loved the place was its one harbor, which made it a safe haven; attack from above was impossible; the cliffs were too sheer to climb; it was now the yacht basin. We went up to Capri and enjoyed the beautiful villas and hotels, then took the bus to Anacapri. Later we took the lift to the very top of Anacapri where we had a superb view of the Bay of Naples with Mount Vesuvius in the background.

As we toured the island, the ladies met a variety of friends who were traveling and invited them back to the yacht for dinner. The next day we took off through the Bay of Naples for the Amalfi coast down to San Pietro Soula and visited some of the hotels there.

The very last night, we returned to the Bay of Naples and dropped anchor off the coast of the island of Ischia, where Mussolini after his fall was held captive by the King of Italy; that was before he was rescued by Nazi paratroopers. There we celebrated our farewell dinner. The great circular table in the dining room was appropriately set with flowers and marvelous food. After dinner, we all began to get up and thank Corky for his marvelous generosity in inviting us on such a never-to-be- forgotten trip. Finally, he got up himself.

"I'm going to do something I've never done before in my life." He turned to me. "Father Val, I'm willing to take a crash course in Catholicism and become a Roman Catholic if Ann Miller will marry me."

Everybody jumped to their feet and began to clap except Ann. She just sat there blinking and smiling. Finally everyone sat down, and she rose.

"Corky, I've loved you from the first day I set eyes on you in grade six. I hope to love you all the days of my life right into eternity. But you don't seem to understand, and certain other people here present don't seem to realize, that I'm going to become a Carmelite nun, and that's all there is to it."

She sat down. Ginny Milner who was sitting next to me leaned over.

"Can you imagine any dame being so dumb? Just think what she could have done with his money!"

"Ginny, you don't seem to understand. There are more things in life than money."

"Well, I certainly do understand that very well, but it's a shame that she's so dumb."

That night, before going to bed (I shared the master two-bedroom suite with Corky), I reminded him that just because someone announced she was becoming a Carmelite nun didn't necessarily mean that she'd stay. Corky perked up.

From Socialite to Carmelite 125

"You mean there's still hope for me?"

A short time after this marvelous cruise, I went to Ann's country place south of San Francisco near Half Moon Bay up in the mountains around San Gregorio, where I gave the farewell retreat in a Shangri La setting; it was a house in the center of a small island, surrounded with a lake, which was surrounded with great redwoods.

At this retreat Ann had a chance to say goodbye to her mother, her immediate friends, and her children. Of course, they were no longer children but grown adults, many with their own families. But this gave them the opportunity to speak their mind about her decision. There were lots of discussions and a number of Masses; the air was cleared, and some objections resolved.

Following the retreat there were a number of farewell parties. Ann appeared at these wearing her nicest gowns and boas. Some of her friends were rejoicing, others were crying, that she was about to leave their midst.

On October 30, 1989, at St. Mary's Cathedral of San Francisco, Archbishop John Quinn concelebrated a Mass with several bishops and forty priests along with the San Francisco Symphony Orchestra performing Mozart's Mass in D Minor with some of the stars from the San Francisco Opera. They were joined by a congregation of six hundred people.

In his homily Archbishop Quinn was brief and to the point.

"As you know, recently we've had our severe earthquakes with many aftershocks. But I think the greatest of the aftershocks has been the news that Ann Miller is going to become a Carmelite nun. All I can say is that we wish her well, and we will pray for her as we hope she will pray for us."

Once the Mass was over, we all went to the undercroft of the cathedral for luncheon. There among the many people I met more of Ann's family, including her mother-in-law, who was from the Folger coffee family.

That evening at the Hilton Hotel, she had her own farewell party with eight hundred guests. She was in the center of it all with a balloon tied to her right arm. Written on the balloon were the words, "I'm here," with an arrow pointing downward. Right in the middle of this I had an unholy thought. If this were a fund raiser, all the doors would be locked; and I could raise enough money for the next ten years.

Many notables were there from all over the United States, from the richest to the poorest. A lady at my table had an unholy thought of her own.

"Just think of all the money she's spending on this farewell party. Isn't that scandalous? She could have given the money to the poor."

Recalling a similar comment made by the perfidious apostle, I couldn't resist a retort.

"Well, what are you doing here then?"

Shortly after, she left our table, but I noticed she didn't leave the party.

A large foxtrot orchestra played during the party. Toward the end Ann got up and expressed her thanks to everyone, especially to her family and in particular to Corky Bowles, and simply bade them farewell, asking them to pray for her. Suddenly the evening was over and everyone went home.

We stayed at the hotel that night. The following morning around eight o'clock I celebrated a farewell Mass with just the immediate family. I gave a brief homily on saying goodbye. After that Ann, wearing a white blouse with brown sweater and skirt, expressed her thanks once again for the understanding of her family and distributed her jewelry to her daughters and daughters-in-law. She refused to allow anyone to come to the airport except her driver who was a Vietnamese minister from the Baptist tradition. A short time later, carrying only a handbag, she took off for her new life.

The family just sat there at the hotel; it was as if their mother had just died and would no longer be in their midst.

Three years later in the Monastery of Carmel in Des Plaines, she made her final vows as a Carmelite nun.

In April 2009 she celebrated her eightieth birthday, and is still flourishing, learning obedience and humility.

The family eventually became reconciled to her new vocation. Her own dear mother actually was inclined to join the Sisters but, on second thought, she declined.

30

Order of St. Lazarus

In 1976 Ernest Carrere, a well known lawyer, together with Harold Stream, a distinguished member of the New Orleans social circle, invited me to attend a liturgy at St. Louis Cathedral, Archbishop Hannan presiding. New members of the Military and Hospitaller Order of St. Lazarus of Jerusalem were being installed. Afterward we had dinner at the Plimsoll Club, a restaurant high atop the World Trade Center.

I inquired what the order was all about.

The order had three purposes.

First, to care for and offer hospitality to those who had leprosy and similar contagious diseases. According to Church tradition, the Order of St. Lazarus was founded by St. Basil the Great around 379 to take care of the lepers of Jerusalem; they weren't allowed to live within the walls. Outside the walls of the city, for many centuries, small hostelries were established where lepers could reside and where the charitable could drop off clothing, food, and other supplies. Hence, members of the Order was known as hospitallers.

Second, in 1098, the order broadened its scope by adding a military component; these were the times crusaders commuted to and from Jerusalem, attempting to preserve Jerusalem from its enemies. They joined forces with other religious/military groups such as the Sovereign Order of St. John of Malta and the Order of the Holy Sepulcher to defend the sacred places in the Holy Land.

Third, it was an order for Christians. After the crusades many members returned to their homes in Europe and established priories where one or another aspect of the Order was fulfilled. Members of the French royal family became the grand masters. In Paris on the present site of la Gare St. Lazar, there was previously a great hospital where the Order cared for Parisians, poor and afflicted alike, for centuries.

When the French Revolution occurred at the end of the eighteenth century, these religious orders were suppressed in France; the French monarchy, and the Church were restored in 1820. Some Bourbons had become Protestants; others remained Catholics. As a result the Order took on an ecumenical dimension and was placed under the spiritual protection of the Melkite patriarchs; Melkite is one of the many rites in union with Rome; it descends, not from the apostolic tradition of Peter and Paul, but James and Mark. Since the end of the Second Vatican Council, it has become the major order concerned with promoting ecumenism in Eastern Europe and elsewhere.

So much for the background. Mr. Carrere and Mr. Stream invited me to become a chaplain member of the Order. I accepted and ordered dessert.

Today the Order of St. Lazarus is a world-wide organization promoting Christian unity and concentrating on leadership members in the various Christian denominations. It promotes preservation of the sacred places in the Holy Land and supports leprosaria; in Mexico alone we have two clinics taking care of lepers; leprosy is still a major disease in India, Africa, and some parts of South America.

The Order is presided over by its spiritual protector, the Melkite patriarch, His Beatitude Gregorios III; the Grand Master is His Excellency Don Carlos Gereda de Borbon, the Marquis de Almazan, a member of the Royal House of Spain. Of late, grand masters have included the Duke of Seville, Francesco de Borbon, and the Duke of Brissac, Francois de Crosse.

The Order is divided into jurisdictions based on national lines; the Grand Priory of America, the Grand Priory of Canada, the Grand Priory of France, etc. Membership is limited in each priory and is by invitation only. Certain qualifications have to be met, of which the most important is that prospective candidates are baptized, practicing members of their own churches, involved in the leadership of their churches and civic societies, and are willing to serve and promote the three purposes of the ecumenical order; support of hospitals and clinics taking care of the young and leprous; preservation of the holy sites in the Holy Land; promotion of ecumenical relations among the major Christian churches.

The *Green Book*, published by the order, lists active members in the Commanderies of the United States and the delegations of Mexico and Puerto Rico. Chevalier Bruce M. Herrington is the current Grand Prior of America.

Since the Second World War the Order has flourished in the United States, having Grand Commanderies in the Washington-New York area, Chicago, San Francisco-Los Angeles, Atlanta, Puerto Rico, Mexico, and New Orleans. The order attempts to deepen the spirituality of each member based on our common baptism in Jesus Christ so that each member might be a leaven in his or her particular church and also a leader in promoting ecumenism among the other Christian churches. Associated/affiliated members of the Order may include Jews, Muslims, and adherents to other religions who are in good standing in their respective faiths.

Every second year there are international meetings held in one or another of the jurisdictions with the spiritual leadership coming from the respective religious leaders of the Episcopal, Lutheran, Methodist, Presbyterian, and Roman Catholic Churches. These have been held at Oxford and Manchester in England, Anger in France, Vienna, Munich, Rome, Washington, Chicago, New Orleans, Sidney Australia, and Mexico City.

In 1998 the most impressive of these meetings was our pilgrimage to Jerusalem to celebrate the 900th anniversary of the military component of the Order in 1098. On that occasion we had the unique experience of walking in the footsteps of Jesus Christ from the place of his birth to where he grew up and preached and taught, from the shores of the Sea of Galilee to the City of Jerusalem. In 2008, the Order of St. Lazarus published my "Homilies of the Holy Land" with a DVD of the pilgrimage itself.

The bi-annual international meetings made new friendships and extended ecumenical connections. For a chaplain like me they provided opportunities to preach and to teach people the basics of ecumenism and the growing need for its influence in the twenty-first century. The Order is in many ways a paradigm for the unity of all the churches.

As I have mentioned, in 1970 I had the honor and pleasure of being one of the Catholic representatives to the World Conference on Religion and Peace along with Cardinal Wright and Bishop Dozier from Memphis, TN. When we were discussing the need for Christian unity, Dom Helder Camara, Archbishop of Recife and Belinde, rose to make a statement, which I quote again.

"Until all Christians get together and resolve their various differences, we will never have any impact upon the rest of the world religions because we are to them a sign of contradiction."

It was his way of saying that we as Christians must come to a new level of ecumenical unity and solidarity.

31

Displeasure and Dysplasia

Throughout my life I've enjoyed good health. It therefore came as a great shock in the beginning of 2005 to discover I was suffering from a rare blood disease.

I was giving a retreat to the members of the Southern Commandery of the Order of St. Lazarus at the home of Grace and Ken Newberger. Toward the end a bloody nose appeared. I held my nose for a couple of minutes, but it continued to bleed. After a half hour it stopped. I finished the retreat; we gathered around for the luncheon, then I made my way home with a Dominican Sister friend. That was on a Saturday.

The following Monday I made an appointment to see Dr. Ron French, my ENT man. He took one look up my nose.

"You know, there's something radically wrong with your blood."

He immediately sent me over to a hematologist for tests. The results were sent to Dr. Salvador Caputto at Touro; he diagnosed the disease as myelodysplasia, a rare blood disease caused by a malfunction of the bone marrow; it wasn't producing enough blood platelets. My blood platelet count had plunged to 5,000 which made me critically ill, suffering from what might be called a kind of hemophilia.

Immediately Dr. Caputto ordered transfusions of blood platelets and blood. Fortunately, they were the right things for the right moment. However, I expressed a desire to have the diagnosis confirmed by another consult; I asked about the possibility of going to the Mayo Clinic in Rochester, Minnesota, immediately. Unfortunately, we didn't have enough connections to get in. In spite of our lack of contacts Providence was at work. Dr. Richard Levy, a former neurosurgeon from Touro and a good friend of mine, had somehow found out that I was ill. He called me out of the blue, asking immediately if I'd gone to Mayo. I told him I couldn't get in.

"I'll call you back in ten minutes," he said.

When he called back, he had good news. Be at Mayo the following Monday; he'd meet me at the hotel, accompany me through the check-up, and be present at the review.

I asked him how he'd been able to get me in so quickly.

"I told them that over the years I'd recommended 150 patients, and if they didn't take you immediately, I wouldn't send another patient there!"

Now, that's what I call chutzpah!

Fortunately, my good friends, Sue Ellen and Joe Canizaro offered me their plane. I flew directly from New Orleans to Rochester. Richard was waiting for me at the hotel; he helped me check in and gave me a tour of the facilities. In the lobby we met up with Jane and Paul Nalty; he'd come up from New Orleans to have a knee replacement. We enjoyed the brief visit and had dinner with them that evening

Next day we had an appointment with the hematologist. At first he thought I drank too much tonic water. Evidently, the quinine in tonic water has a definite effect upon the blood platelets. We were relieved at first, but further research and analysis revealed that I was suffering from a full blown case of myelodysplasia.

All the work-up examinations had been done in one day; we received the results the following morning.

"You have only three months to live," said the doctor.

"You should never tell anybody when they're going to die," I shot right back, "because you don't know that."

I pointed out that for twenty years I'd taught medical ethics at Tulane Medical School. The very first principle we tried to pound into the heads of the new medical students was never to tell anyone when he's going to die. Why? Because they didn't know that.

"I meant to say," said the doctor apologetically, "that there's no known cure."

"I know what you meant to say, but that's not what you said."

The doctor apologized.

Dr. Levy and I began to review the medical options in the light of the Mayo report. The first was to stay at Mayo and undergo one of their protocols. However, we felt Mayo was too far from New Orleans; and I had no support group in Minneapolis.

The second option was M. D. Anderson in Houston; they had many possible protocols, and it would certainly be closer to New Orleans. M. D. Anderson it was. We thanked the doctor for his concern and returned to the hotel. That evening we had dinner and reminisced about our illnesses.

His wife Susan had been our curator during the Vatican Pavilion. There were 3,000 volunteer docents; she trained all them. Through this relationship we became good friends.

Subsequently, Richard retired, and they moved to the Carolinas, but we stayed in touch. Later she was diagnosed with cancer herself; I had the pleasure of taking care of her. Evidently Richard was most grateful and showed it by coming to my rescue. I was most grateful to him. I thanked him profusely for his kindness. Next day he flew home; I called Joe Canizaro to schedule my flight home. and said goodbye.

Many months later when I was in the midst of my treatments at M. D. Anderson, Eric Levy, the blind son of Susan and Richard, called me on the day I was having the most difficulty; my breathing was agonizing, and he attempted to console me. It was a providential moment. This young man who'd had spent all of his life being blind was cheering me up. He urged to be grateful that I was still very much alive and, in spite of my infirmities, able to enjoy my life more or less.

On this occasion and on many similar ones I was struck by how the Lord could and would awaken us to new and deeper awareness of how grateful we should be when the infirm come to our help and assistance.

The irony of Eric's problems was that he was blinded through a mistake made by a nurse who washed his eyes with a double solution when he was first born. Such a tragedy would have been enough to do any good spirit in, but he was able to cope with it. What was a decided defect became an asset in his life.

Years earlier when his mother died, I had the memorial service at the Myra Clare Rogers Memorial Chapel on the Newcomb Campus of Tulane University. During the reception he came up to me.

"You know, when I was a little boy, I was sent by my parents to live with my maternal grandmother in New York to learn braille and to live with my blindness. One morning, I rose very early and turned on the radio, and there I heard the rosary being recited. I'd never heard the rosary before. I was no more than seven or eight years old. When I went downstairs, I asked my grandmother what the rosary was. She replied rather dryly, that was something the Roman Catholics had dreamed up and put together to try to convince people that Jesus was the Messiah."

He thought for a moment and then continued.

"You know, as soon as my grandmother said that, in some mysterious way, I began to believe that Jesus was the Messiah. From that moment on, I've believed in him, and he has literally given me the light to follow him in spite of my affliction."

"What a very touching and profound story," I said to him. "Did you ever tell your mother that story?"

"No, regretfully, but I wish I had."

He told me how this conviction had grown through the years, and how grateful he was for it. I told him my story of how I see such providential moments as being the fulfillment of God's love for individuals of the Jewish faith. They somehow find their way understanding intuitively that Jesus was a Jew, is a Jew, and will be a Jew for all eternity. The amazing thing for me is how he chooses some Jewish people to become fulfilled Jews even while honoring and respecting the others.

"Yes," Eric said, "it's a great paradox."

Back from Mayo I found that entering M. D. Anderson wasn't any easier than Mayo. I went to Houston several times, but before I could qualify for one of their protocols, I had to have blood tests and work-ups over time. I passed them all, but there was a final one that would determine everything. That blood test was taken; the results were reviewed. Alas, my blood level had risen to twenty-six, which made me subject to leukemia and ineligible for the myelodysplasia protocols. Just as Dr. Stephan Faderl was telling me the bad news, the hematologist called; there had been a mistake; the blood level was only sixteen.

"Welcome to M. D. Anderson!" the good doctor said.

The roller coaster emotional drop was really worse than the disease could possibly be, at least at this point. From high to low and high again! But that was my first miracle; it gave me restored confidence and renewed hope.

Before treatment began, I had to sign my life away. It was one consent form after another about the runaway side-effects of the drugs they'd use. They were so depressing that I decided not to read beyond the first paragraph. Instead I put myself in the Lord's hands. "What will be, will be.

If it works, it works. If it doesn't, it doesn't." In the meantime, my friends all prayed for me. At the same time, I was receiving transfusions of blood and blood platelets in order to stabilize my condition.

The treatment itself was a series of intravenous injections of Decidivin. Both my doctor and nurse advised me not to raise my hopes. No noticeable improvement would occur until the eighth or ninth sitting. The roller coaster hit bottom again.

Much to everyone's surprise, after the second treatment, my blood platelets had risen from 5,000 to 286,000. I couldn't wait to see my doctor. It was a little unusual to have such results so quickly, he said. However, the nurse was much more candid.

"That's never happened before."

As the treatment progressed, I no longer needed transfusions of blood platelets every visit and only periodically needed blood transfusions.

Fortunately, the side effects of my treatment were minimal. I had no pain; bowel movements were more frequent; sleep was hard to come by. When I notified the doctor, he was good enough to give me a prescription that enabled me to rest without difficulty.

Evidently the secret of my success was a combination of a good protocol properly administered, many good doctors and nurses, and many good prayers.

The nurses at M. D. Anderson, almost all from the Philippines, were outstanding. Apparently this was by design; they had a very cheery and positive attitude, the sort of attitude M. D. Anderson felt was necessary for successful treatment of difficult diseases. Hence, the management regularly recruited promising young nurses for service in Houston. And I as well as others were the beneficiaries. Every morning outpatients flooded into the waiting rooms; some mornings there would be as many as a hundred waiting. The staff was so well organized that they took care of the people within an hour. In fact, they had signs that said, "If you are waiting more than a half hour, please advise the desk"

One morning in the waiting room an attractive, middle-aged couple from Atlanta sat beside me; she and I fell into conversation. She too had myelodysplasia, and she was afraid she'd die from it. I tried to reassure her; she should place herself in the Lord's hands; he would take care of her and heal her or bring her safely home to paradise. She was a devout Baptist, as it turned out; she and her husband were really deep believers. We became good friends. Periodically she asked that I pray over her either for healing or resignation to the Lord's will. Some months later I discovered the treatment didn't work for her; she was in the Lord's good hands.

Around that time I got a call from a dear friend in Seattle, Charles Thomas Yarington; he was a doctor, head of a well-known clinic, and a retired brigadier general. He too was diagnosed with myelodysplasia and wanted to know how my M. D. Anderson treatments were going. I urged him to come to Houston for a consultation. He assured me that the same treatment could be administered in Seattle hopefully with the same positive results. I pointed out that it wasn't just the treatment of Decidivin but the way in which the mixture was administered that apparently made the difference, at least for me. He still thought Seattle protocol could do as well as Houston. His initial diagnosis was in November; he called me several times during his treatment; by April he was gone.

Once the staff discovered I was a priest, I was immediately on call, blessing people, counseling them, hearing confessions, and attempting to bring hope and some resolution to their pain and illness. Before I knew it, I was carrying on a ministry of my own, paralleling the ministry of the doctors and nurses even though they had chaplains readily available within the complex.

M. D. Anderson pioneered outpatient treatment. It was less expensive and more efficient, but it had its logistical problems.

When I first went to Houston, I planned to stay with my Dominican community at Holy Rosary Priory. Unfortunately, our new house was just being built, and there was no room available. Much to my delight, a young couple I befriended some years before as members of the Patrons of the Vatican Museums were kind enough to invite me to stay at their home for the first five months of my treatment. It worked out well. Mornings Dr. Bob Card had to go to St. Luke's where he was a cardiologist. Afternoons, after my treatments for the day were over, his wife Karol Kreymer would pick me up. During this period, we deepened our friendship. I enjoyed not only their warm hospitality but also their great cuisine; both were both gourmet cooks.

One morning I mentioned to Bob that since he was married to a Roman Catholic gal and had gone to Mass with her for twenty-five years, he should become a Catholic himself. I was willing to give him a crash course while I was living there. He responded positively and indeed enthusiastically. Each evening he arrived home around seven. Instruction came next, followed by Mass and dinner. I received permission from the pastor of Holy Rosary, Father Joe Konkel, to receive Bob into the Church. We did this one evening followed by a lovely dinner party at their home with some of our Dominican friends. It was a fitting and enjoyable conclusion to a wonderful visit that made my sagging spirits soar and kept me involved in pastoral ministry.

By this time Holy Rosary Priory was completed. I moved into the newly built Dominican house, where my brothers welcomed me with open arms. I enjoyed their hospitality very much and remained with them until my treatments were completed.

32

Katrina

In between treatments at Houston I'd return to New Orleans. That's where I was the weekend Hurricane Katrina descended upon the city. I was debating with my community and provincial, Fr. Marty Gleeson, as to whether I should return to Houston before the hurricane struck. Fortunately, they convinced me to leave the day before with some of my brothers, going over the Causeway, which was bumper to bumper; we were able to get as far as our house in Ponchatoula. On Monday, August 29, 2005, the wind and rain came. We were without electricity and in total darkness. Two days later I drove to Baton Rouge. I stayed overnight with my friends at the cathedral and flew out the next day to Houston.

It was a good thing my Dominican brothers and I fled. A break in the levee flooded the city, especially the Ninth Ward and the Lakeview area where I lived in St. Dominic parish and priory.

At that time, nobody knew the full extent of the devastation; it took weeks before we realized that total tragedy had struck the city. Lakeview was under twelve feet of water, and so was the first floor of our priory and church. The statue of St. Dominic in front of the church was covered with water up to his uplifted hand.

The first time I returned to the city after the hurricane, I was devastated to see, in the center of Pontchartrain Boulevard, a mountain, two to three stories high, of debris taken out of houses and buildings. Most of the electricity was still out. It was a very depressing experience, to say the least; not good for my spirits or indeed my body. I was immediately ordered back to Houston lest the contamination and mold endanger my health and my lungs.

My brother Dominicans gradually came back to the city to begin the arduous task of restoring St. Dominic's and St. Anthony's parishes. At last there was something I could do. I could raise funds for the restoration.

RICHARD COLTON'S CONVERSION

Dick Colton and I had been good friends since he first came to New Orleans to work with the Lykes Steamship Company as a vice-president. He was a nephew of Libby and Jack Carrere; after Sunday Mass, I'd meet him at the Carrere's for lunch and a swim.

Katrina, as it had with so many others, sent Dick to Houston. He escaped the storm itself, but he couldn't escape its after-effects. He began to realize that no matter what one may have, it didn't mean much unless one had deep faith to sustain one.

Dick took refuge in the Hilton Hotel nearby. Occasionally we'd meet for lunch or dinner; he'd speak of the emotional and spiritual impact the hurricane had on him; he wanted to deepen his belief. One day he announced it was time for him to become a Roman Catholic. He'd been raised a devout Presbyterian, but he wasn't unfamiliar with Catholicism; his grandmother and many of his relatives were Roman Catholic.

Of course I instructed him in the fundamentals. By the time we finished, the new chapel at the Dominicans' Holy Rosary was completed; he asked to be received there. He invited a few of his friends from New Orleans, fellow refugees from Katrina. He made his profession of faith at Mass and received his first confession, first communion, and confirmation in friendly surroundings.

SANTA FE CONCERT

In his major work on Hurricane Katrina, *The Great Deluge*, historian Douglas Brinkley graphically illustrated the bravery and breath-taking openheartedness of many people in the biggest hurricane of the new century. Untold suffering created new communities of people who'd lost everything, except perhaps family and friends. They found a new sense of togetherness and a deeper sense of love.

Those of us who haven't suffered great loss or affliction can only say, "Thank God I didn't have to go through that!" But we remain the poorer because of the lack of the suffering experience. As Bob Dylan and Sam Shepard say so well in *Brownsville Girl*, "Strange how people who suffer together have stronger connections than people who are most content." That was certainly true of hurricane survivors like me and doubly true so of those who suffered long bouts of illness as I had at M. D. Anderson.

I decided to organize a hurricane benefit concert for the restoration of St. Dominic's Community Center Parish and Priory. I'd call it, "Come and

Listen and Be Still." It would take place in Santa Fe, New Mexico, at St. Francis Cathedral-Basilica. A dear friend on our IDF advisory board, Ivan Konig in London, England, offered to provide the talent. He recommended the group, *Trio Angelico* and a Louisiana poet, a concert portraying in sound, music, and words, recapturing the chaos, confusion, and solace of Katrina. The artists were Sonja Bruzauskas, a soprano from Germany, Jennifer Keeney, a flautist for twenty years, Anita Kruse, an American pianist, and Ava Leavell Haymon, a poet from Baton Rouge.

The archbishop of Santa Fe, Michael J. Sheehan, Monsignor Jerome Martinez, rector of the cathedral-basilica, and his staff were most hospitable in providing the venue for the concert. Fortunately, we were able to raise $100,000 toward restoration of St. Dominic's. None of this would have happened without the friendship and collaboration of Father Bennett J. Voorhies of Albuquerque (formerly of Lafayette and New Orleans) for orchestrating the concert and helping to make it such a success.

OUR LADY OF HOPE CHAPEL

Much of the restoration of St. Dominic's Church has been completed, except for such works of art as the main marble altar, the marble statues, the great bronze cross, and other bronze statues including the Stations of the Cross and the bronze statue of John the Baptist mounted on the baptismal font. Of course, the onyx base of the baptismal font had to be restored as well. All these are taking place gradually with the donations of interested people who want to see the church restored to its original splendor.

Fortunately, through the generosity of the Hilton Foundation (in honor of Mrs. Gerri Frawley) and the Bricker Foundation (Kathleen and John Bricker) as well as our good friend Richard C. Colton, and others, the former baptismal chapel is now being transformed into Our Lady of Hope Chapel. The title was chosen deliberately to renew the hope of the people after the hurricane and in thanksgiving to Our Lady for her care of the city in spite of all the havoc.

The nationally known American water color artist Henry Casselli accepted our commission and has recently completed a beautifully rendered contemporary Mother of Hope holding her son Jesus in her lap as she fingers the rosary. The work of art will be the focus of the small chapel immediately above the free-standing pillared altar surrounded on either side with two large menorah candelabra recalling the Judeo-Christian connections of our common heritage.

We are indeed blessed by having such a sensitive and moving work of art included in the treasures of St. Dominic.

M. D. ANDERSON AGAIN

My treatment at M. D. Anderson continued into 2006 and 2007. Periodically I'd return home to New Orleans; recovery was slow, both for me and the city.

One day near the end of the treatment for blood platelet disorder, while a technician was drawing blood, I asked Dr. Faderl why they'd never done a PSA on me. It was M. D. Anderson policy, he reminded me, not to do such a procedure unless requested by the patient. Naturally, I requested it. The results were disturbing since it was elevated to a 6.5 level, five points above normal.

The doctor advised me to wait three months before having the test again. Three months later it was elevated to 7.2. When it reached 7.8, they decided I should have a biopsy. The test determined that out of the ten biopsies, nine of them were cancerous and that I should immediately go into treatment. After consultation with Andrew K. Lee, M. D., it was determined I'd go on Lupron immediately and stay on it for three years, concluding in January of 2009; then after further consultation I decided I'd take the radiation treatment at M. D. Anderson.

Among the men who arrived at approximately the same time every day at M. D. Anderson was the Club of Eight; we'd gather in the radiation department, get into our radiation garb, and sit and talk until our turn came to be zapped for fifteen minutes. Hanging in the corridor outside the radiation rooms was a ship's bell. When a patient successfully completed the course of treatments, or so custom dictated, he or she rang the bell. And so I did, after the thirty-seventh treatment and with minimal side effects, I rang the bell with great joy and enthusiasm. Alas, I'd have to continue on Lupron for another five months.

Just as I completed the radiation, another symptom appeared. It was fibrillation of my heart. These fibrillations first occurred three years earlier when I was receiving blood and blood platelet transfusions. Once the blood platelets were stabilized, they disappeared. Therefore, just as I was about to go home to New Orleans and restart my ministry of preaching, teaching, and writing, it was disconcerting to have them reappear.

Fortunately, Dr. Robert Card who'd been my Houston host for a time was also my cardiologist; he advised medications that would control the fibrillations until I returned to New Orleans. Back home I sought out a rhythm specialist; he informed me that the problem was not *per se* fibrillations but irregular palpitations of the heart. To control them he prescribed a new medication called Multaq, which I'm currently using and is effective.

My health journey has taken me from Touro to Mayo to M. D. Anderson to Touro to Ochsner. All these institutions have shown remarkable care and indeed I'm grateful to each of them. As I've said on many occasions, I'm still very much alive because of good protocols, many good doctors, and the prayers of many good people.

At one point in my treatment my dear friend and classmate in the Order, Father Neal McDermott, brought Sister Briege McKenna, a Sister of St. Clare, who was well known for her healing ministry, to St. Dominic's. With her he also brought Paul and Jane Nalty. We gathered in the chapel. Sister turned her attention to Paul and me, since we were both bundles of illness. She laid her hands on each of us in turn, holding a small piece of watered silk from the cuff of Pope John Paul II's cassock and prayed over us for some time. In my case the result was positive. In Paul's case it was as well. Alas, he died on July 16, 2009. May he rest in peace.

Before I left for M. D. Anderson the first time, my provincial and community did the same for me when they gave me the sacrament of the sick. That is well-rounded treatment of the spirit and the body.

DEATH DOES NOT HAVE THE FINAL WORD

Growing older for a priest often means burying family and friends. Faith gives us hope at a time of sadness and death, but it is a bittersweet experience. Recently, this has happened to me, burying my father, my sister, Rosemary, and most recently my brothers Angus and Patrick, and including my sister in law, Clare. On the day of my sister's death, my eldest brother, Jack, asked, "Isn't this a sad day? We have lost both our sister and our mother on the same day." I immediately asked him if he'd ever thanked her for being both our mother and our sister; he said no.

This experience taught me how important it is to say things of gratitude and thanksgiving to people while they are still very much alive and can hear us. Oftentimes when I'm caring and saying Masses for people who are dying, I ask family members to mention the things for which they're most grateful.

In the Christian context of things, death does not have the last word. In fact, if we can muster the courage to see through the sadness of death, death becomes the prelude to eternal life and the door to eternity. As many people like to say, "Oh, yes, I want to go to heaven, but I don't want to die." Death does not have to be our final failure. In the deepest human sense, we are giving ourselves back to God in Christ and in some mysterious way, it is our final gift of ourselves when it is given freely and unconditionally.

As a member of the Order of St. Lazarus, I have preached at the burials of many of our members; each time I think of the biblical Lazarus. Mary and Martha were such friends of Christ's that they had no hesitation about asking him to bring Lazarus back to life, giving him new life even here and now. Oral tradition has Lazarus and his sisters going to Rome with Peter, and then to France. With the first bishop, St. Maximinus, they helped establish the Church in Southern France. In the famous Church of St. Maximon today one can see the tomb of Lazarus, Martha, and Mary.

As I like to say and preach, the bond of Christ for Lazarus is epitomized in every Christian relation with Christ. The Lord has died and risen from the dead and gives us the same power to overcome the fear of death and sin; he even plants within us now his risen glory as a foretaste of our eternal life.

In the context of our Judeo-Christian belief, we are called home in death through the Lord's own risen body, giving us hope and light to illumine us on our way.

It is with these thoughts that I nurture my own hope and the hope of all of those I serve with the expectation that Christ is doing for us what he did for Lazarus and his sisters.

33

The St. Thomas Aquinas Environmental Award

In the first decade of the twenty-first century there has been a challenge to the Judeo-Christian tradition as the foundation of western civilization. It came from the European Community's Commission, which was attempting to form a constitution. The chairman of that commission, the former President of France, Giscard d'Estaing, said that he couldn't in conscience place a reference to God either in the constitution or the preamble. What a remark from a so-called practicing Roman Catholic! It showed how secularized or feebly informed this distinguished French statesman had become.

Responding to his statement, Pope John Paul II went to the Italian Parliament to speak. He urged the members of the European community to reflect upon the fact that the Judeo-Christian belief in the One God was the common heritage of all these nations; that the Judeo-Christian heritage was present in our laws and our beliefs, our culture and our arts. If we didn't affirm these principles as the basis of the European Constitution and acknowledge the fundamental role of God and of man made in the image and likeness of God, Europe ran the risk of falling apart. It was only in the light of the individual's relationship to God that rights were based, defined, and took on significance.

Because of the confused reasoning on this and other fundamental issues, the Chair of Judeo-Christian Studies decided to give an annual award entitled *The St. Thomas Aquinas Environmental Award*. It would affirm the Judeo-Christian religious beliefs as the source of inspiration for the responsibility of the world we live in. Questions of individual rights, the environment, climate changes, and other "green" issues were being asked with greater frequency and urgency and had to be answered.

The St. Thomas Aquinas Environmental Award

The first St. Thomas Aquinas Environmental Award was given in 2007 to Sir John Houghton, considered the leading climatologist in the world. He was the Chair of the United Nations Commission as well as the UK Commission on Climate Changes.

For the second award we thought HRH the Prince of Wales would be appropriate. For decades he had addressed such environmental issues as land and water resources, greenhouse gases, and the sacred in nature. By many he was held to be irrelevant, but in the first decade of the second millennium his efforts were being re-evaluated; he had indeed made a substantial contribution to the discussion on climate warming and sustainability of resources. But how to approach him was my immediate question, and therein lies something of a tale.

In 2005 I went to a celebration in honor of the Canadian Consul General, the Honorable Norris Petis, who came over from Dallas to be with us for a day or so in New Orleans. At that party given by Mrs. Pat Denechaud, Canadian Honorary Consul General, I met my old friend Mr. Joseph C. Canizaro. During our conversation I learned that he was preparing to leave for England to attend a board meeting of the Prince of Wales Foundation, of which he was becoming a member. I pointed out to Joe that the prince has been involved in a variety of environmental projects; Joe pointed out to me that the prince would be an ideal honoree for the environment award.

"Give me a letter," he said, "and I'll be glad to present it to His Royal Highness when we have our meeting."

That evening I went home and prepared the letter. The following day I sent it to Joe for perusal and approval; he delivered it to the prince.

For some time we had no response. Then one day Joe called to inform me that the chief executive officer of the prince's foundation, Hank Dittmar, was coming to town; he wanted to work on a variety of projects in the restoration of New Orleans. At the same time he told me the good news; the prince had agreed to accept the award; all we had to do was work out an acceptable date.

Joe asked me to arrange a meeting with the president of Tulane, Scott Cowen, Mr. Dittmar, himself, and me. The president was kind enough to fit in us into his crowded schedule. We explored the different ways Tulane and Delgado might collaborate; educating their talented young people in the arts of restoration would certainly be one. Scholarships in carpentry and architectural design could be arranged for promising American students at the prince's restoration school in England. Cowen suggested that we consult with Kenneth Schwartz, the new dean of architecture. The meeting was cordial, and progress reports were promised.

As for a date in 2008 for the presentation to the prince, I discovered I'd be in England in early September; in Manchester I'd be attending the general elective chapter for the Military and Hospitaller Order of St. Lazarus of Jerusalem. I e-mailed my travel plans to Hank Dittmar.

When I arrived in England, I contacted Hank's office and told him the days I'd be in London. He consulted the prince's schedule; time for a meeting didn't seem promising. While in London I stayed with my Dominican confreres; there followed a flurry of calls from Hank. On the afternoon of September 9, 2008, his secretary called to inform me that a time had been arranged for the following day. The presentation would be made privately in the prince's residence at Clarence House, which had been the residence of the Queen Mother and was given to the Prince of Wales after her death; it wasn't too far from Buckingham Palace. Naturally I was delighted and pulled from my luggage the gold-plated award, suitably inscribed, along with a binder containing my remarks.

The following day I met Hank at a nearby café at four o'clock. After refreshments we made our way down Green Park around to Kensington Palace and into the back entrance of the compound that leads to the prince's home. We presented two pieces of identification before passing through security and proceeding to Clarence House. There we were welcomed by the prince's equerry. He led us to a first-floor drawing room. We were briefed for fifteen minutes and then ushered upstairs.

As we entered the prince's study he greeted us enthusiastically. He invited us to sit down, and immediately we were served tea. I gave him the greetings of Sue Ellen and Joe Canizaro, which he reciprocated. He was pleased to meet with me, he said, even though it would be brief; in a few hours he was speaking to two hundred business leaders at Guild Hall on how their manufacturing facilities affected the environment. Since our presentation was an informal one, I simply shared why we chose him for the award. When I finally presented the gold medallion, he was absolutely delighted.

"Father, you must understand that this award means a great deal to me. I've spent most of my life being concerned about the environment, and here

The St. Thomas Aquinas Environmental Award   147

you present me with one of the few environmental awards I've ever received. I want to thank you for acknowledging that role."

Immediately he dove into the projects he'd been involved in, especially at his estate, Highgrove, and at Poundhaust. After some discussion of land and water resources and sustainability, he invited me to return at a later date and to bring some friends, if I liked, who would be interested to see what he had done not only on his own properties but in some of the nearby towns.

We discussed a collaborative effort among people interested in improving the environment. We spoke about how this could be done by helping to restore New Orleans both environmentally and architecturally. He then deferred to his private secretary about following up on some of these matters and collaborating further with Hank Dittmar.

We then went down to the Morning Room where the photographer had set up his camera and directed us in front of the fireplace. There he took several photographs until the session was completed.

I thanked his highness for his gracious reception and hospitality. I looked forward to seeing him in the near future. He then left to prepare for his evening commitment. Our fifteen-minute courtesy meeting had turned into an hour-and-a-half of interesting conversation.

As Hank and I strolled out of Clarence House, he showed me the beautiful rose garden the prince had established in front of the entrance.

Subsequently, the prince's foundation established relationships in New Orleans with the Preservation Resource Center (PRC), Delgado College, and the Louisiana Carpenters' Regional Council. The foundation also implemented a training program for carpenters' apprenticeships to help restore damaged houses in the Ninth Ward and to receive proper training in the arts of restoration.

34

Surprise Birthday Party

April 21, 2009, would be my eightieth birthday. Perhaps a quiet get-together with my confreres would be nice. But I didn't mention it to anybody for fear they'd think I'd want a party. The Dominican community at St. Dominic's did have a lovely do for me a few days before the actual birthday.

Mark Edney of our community reminded me that we had a date on my actual birthday; he and my good friend, Dick Colton, were going to take me out to dinner; it was set at Le Petite Grocery. I made note in my iPod and looked forward to it.

As time drew close, people began to ask what I was going to do for my birthday, and I'd say, "Nothing much." I was busy finishing up the treatments for my prostate cancer at M. D. Anderson and following up with some post-treatment sessions with Lupron, plus endless blood tests and monitorings.

But I did have one appointment on my birthday docket, Reyna Tabora, the pedicurist. I'd reached the point in life where I could no longer cut my toenails. Off I went to the pedicurist. While I was sitting in the chair, and Reyna was doing the trimming, we usually solved the problems of the world.

"By the way," she said, "Dick Colton was in here yesterday, and he told me you're having a birthday party tonight."

"I hadn't heard that."

She gasped, I gasped, and we promised each other that we hadn't heard a thing, least of all a surprise party.

That night, when Father Mark was bundling me in the car to pick up Dick Colton, I couldn't resist.

"Why don't we tell Dick that we'll meet him at Le Petite Grocery? That'll save us some time."

Surprise Birthday Party 149

"No, no," said Father Mark. "We have to pick up Dick first. He's expecting us to drive him over."

When we arrived at Dick's house, there were droves of cars parked in the neighborhood and a policeman on duty outside.

"Obviously, someone next door is having a party," said Father Mark.

For a moment I fell for it. Dick's verandah wasn't lighted; no light came from the windows. Father Mark didn't bother to ring the bell or knock on the door. He just opened it to a burst of light and a great shout!

"Happy Birthday!"

There in front of me was a host of people, all of whom were dear friends greeting me with great warmth and affection, including my host, Dick Colton. Some had come from as far away as Connecticut, but most were from New Orleans. We spent hours greeting and embracing each another and just chatting each other up. Everyone had to know whether the party was a real surprise or not. It reminded me of Sherlock Holmes and Dr. Watson.

"It's the curious case of the tight-lipped pedicurist."

"What's so curious about that?"

"Pedicurists are never tight-lipped."

Though I knew the party was coming, it was still a grand surprise beyond my imagination. Not only my favorite friends but also my favorite foods. And, of course, freshly-squeezed orange juice, which has become the hallmark of my presence at any party.

After having filled ourselves with the delicious foods and just before cutting the three-tiered cake with the Dominican shield on top and *Best Wishes* for my eightieth birthday, I thought I'd say a few words of thanks.

> When I was a little boy growing up in London, Ontario, I revealed to them, my sister and I took piano and singing lessons. I assured the crowd I could sing and told them they were about to hear the recital of a lifetime.
>
> "My Favorite Things" from *The Sound of Music*.
>
> I'd heard that Julie Andrews, on the occasion of her birthday celebration at Manhattan's Radio City Music Hall, had new lyrics for this old song, lyrics more appropriate to her age and mine.
>
> In my best voice I began to sing!

Maalox and nose drops and needles for knitting
Walkers and handrails and new dental fittings
Bundles of magazines tied up in string
These are a few of my favorite things

Cadillacs, cataracts, hearing aids and glasses
Polident, Fixodent and false teeth in glasses
Pacemakers, golf carts and porches with swings
These are a few of my favorite things

When the pipes leak, when the bones creak, when the knees go bad,
I simply remember my favorite things and then I don't feel so bad

Hot tea and crumpets, and corn pads with bunions
No spicy hot food or food cooked with onions
Bathrobes and heat pads and hot meals they bring
These are a few of my favorite things.

Back pains, confused brains and no fear of sinnin'
Thin bones and fractures and hair that is thinnin'
And we won't mention our short shrunken frames
When we remember our favorite things.

When the joints ache
When the hips break
When the eyes go dim
Then I remember the great life I've had.

    Following the entertainment, we had the cutting of the cake and a few more comments. I thanked the unindicted co-conspirators behind the party: Father Mark, Dick Colton, his secretary, Kim Perrot, and my own assistant, Nancy Tatarski.
    Especially memorable were Paul Nalty's remarks. Like me he'd been through a long illness and was now enjoying good health; it was the last time I saw him alive.

Father Mark was kind enough to bring me a personal note from the Master of our Order, Father Carlos Aspiroz Costa, O.P. Here's what it said.

Rome, March 4, 2009

Dear Val,
Greetings from Rome just to celebrate your birthday! I give thanks to God for your life, for your "call" to be our brother, for your ministry and work for the Order.
Thank you very much for all you have done in many fields for the good of your Province and for the whole Order.
With the blessing of our father Saint Dominic and my prayers,

Your brother,
P. Carlos O.P., Magister Ordinis

The party finally broke up with me leaving a bit early to get home for my own rest, but it was a joy to behold and a night to remember.

A photographer memorialized the wonderfulness of the evening.

35

Avocations

The Sisters of St. Joseph who taught me in grade school discovered my talent for drawing and painting. As a result of their cultivation, they set me on a track to study art at the Banff School of Fine Arts in Alberta, Canada, and Queens University in Kingston, Ontario; later on in my life to study art from historical and philosophical points of view concentrating on the philosophy of aesthetics.

Banff was a summer session in the Canadian Rockies where the scenery was spectacular. There I studied under Mr. W. J. Phillips, the well-known Canadian water colorist, and American painter Henry Taubs.

Years later when I was visiting friends in Palm Beach, I entered the drawing room, and there above the fireplace was a magnificent painting by Henry Taubs. When I identified it, the host was startled and wanted to know how I knew. Not only was he impressed, but he actually gave me two smaller works by Taubs, which now hang in our rec room at St. Dominic's in New Orleans.

In the center of the town of Banff was a mountain called Rundel; it was one of the first paintings I did that summer school. I was under the influence of the Canadian painters called the Group of Seven. A. Y. Jackson and others painted bold landscapes; I did the same. My *Rundel* received first prize as best student painting; it was awarded by the Canadian Pacific Railroad, which reproduced it on the menus in its dining cars. CPR also offered a free weekend at their beautiful Sunrise Lodge, which I enjoyed immensely.

The following year I went to the School of Fine Arts at Queens University where I studied under Andre Bieler, a well–known Canadian painter. He had asthma; in the midst of a lecture he'd bring out the atomizer to ease his breathing. Fortunately, he was a great painter; we benefited much from his tutelage and on-site sketching around the St. Lawrence River.

One day we went to the home of the owners of the Canadian Steamship Company, which was located at the confluence of Lake Ontario and the St. Lawrence River. We spent the afternoon sketching; one of mine caught Bieler's eye; I had promise, he said, and should definitely go to art school.

Later that summer Philip Azziz, a well-known Canadian artist who'd just finished studying at the Harvard School of Fine Arts, came to visit me at my home in London; on seeing some of my paintings he urged me to go to Harvard to study. But by this time I'd already made my decision to become a Dominican.

In giving up my avocation for art, little did I know at the time that I'd be using it in many diverse ways. As I've already described, I did my doctorate in the philosophy of art, analyzing the aesthetic loophole in John Dewey's philosophy of pragmatism.

When I first arrived in New Orleans and became the Chairman of the Fine Arts Committee for the Louisiana Council for Music and the Performing Arts and subsequently the President, I wrote several monographs on the arts, the main one being, "Taste and See: Louisiana Renaissance, Religion, and the Arts." This was an attempt to show how from ancient times both in Jewish and Christian worship the arts were always employed in religious ritual to enhance the glory of God's presence.

As I've mentioned previously, my interest in art and religion led me to call on Archbishop Hannan to bring about the Vatican Pavilion at the 1984 Louisiana World Exposition; my work, *Treasures of the Vatican*, summarizes the contents of that exhibition. At the same time the volume published by the Archdiocese of New Orleans, entitled *Cross, Crozier, and Crucible*, contains the story of the making of the Vatican Pavilion and the key role it played in the Louisiana World's Fair.

The follow-up to the Vatican Pavilion was the establishment of the Patrons of the Vatican Museum first in the South, then throughout the various parts of the country such as New York, Chicago, San Francisco, Los Angeles, and New Orleans, and in Canada itself, as I have already noted.

Fortunately, I have been able to collect some superb works of art; all given to me at one point or another in my career. Most of these hang in the priory of St. Dominic's in New Orleans. Perhaps the most important one is the sculptured gold cross with the inlaid cloisonne enamels of the Crucifixion of one side and the Descent of the Holy Spirit on the other; it was created by the famous German artist, Egineo Weinert; he has a whole room in the Contemporary Museum of the Vatican Collections. I also have two additional inlaid cloisonne enamels entitled "The Tree of Life" and "The Resurrection of Christ." These were all gifts at the time of the Vatican exhibition.

From a local point of view, the beautiful painting by Ellsworth Woodworth, the founder of the School of Fine Art at Newcomb, depicts a Dominican brother meditating; this work was executed when the artist lived in Munich, Germany, in the late 1890s. The collection also includes a seventeenth-century Mexican wooden sculpture of Our Lady of Guadalupe, two watercolors of St. Dominic, one of Dominic himself, the other at the side of his mother, Blessed Jane D'Aza, both by the distinguished Dominican watercolorist, Sr. Mary of the Compassion, a print collection of Pere J-M Coutourier renditions of the "Seven Days of Creation," as well as two Inca-style tapestries of angels depicting the seven sacraments.

In the priory itself we have several of Jack Chambers' seriographs, in particular "Diego at the Dining Room Table" and "The Dormer Tribute." There are two beautiful icons, one from the eighteenth century of St. Michael the Archangel and a nineteenth-century copy of Our Lady of Kazan, the celebrated Russian icon, the patroness of Russia. Pope John Paul II, before his death, returned the original icon to Russia as a gift to celebrate his yearning for reunion with the Russian Orthodox Church. Finally, a beautiful small contemporary Greek icon of Christ entering Jerusalem on Palm Sunday. All these belong to the community of St. Dominic's Priory.

My other avocations of tennis, painting, and traveling have been helpful as well. Tennis has kept me limber until the latter years. of my life. Travel on one business or another has been continuous, but in each and every trip I've found marvelous moments to paint of joy and prayer. There are few places in the world I haven't been. But as every traveler and every pilgrim knows, there's always something new on the horizon.

Epilog

As I look back over the many years of being a Dominican friar/preacher, I find that my inspiration has been St. Dominic's charism of preaching.

You may remember "Memories," that song in Andrew Lloyd Weber's musical, *Cats*. Its haunting melody conjures up all the memories of our past. They're the fabric of our lives; without them we wouldn't have an identity of our own. And so it has been in my life. My memoirs are the memories of my immediate family and my Dominican family both confreres and consoeurs, the Order of St. Lazarus, and Tulane University.

Similarly, in the early Church, Christians delighted in telling their stories and their memories of the main events in the life of Jesus; they preached them for thirty to forty years before Mark, Matthew, Luke, and John began writing them down; they were the community memories of their own respective groups and experiences which have come to be known as the Gospel stories.

The sermons recalled the main events in the life of Christ. His nativity and the wonderful events surrounding it; his public life with the miracles in it, and most of all, his passion, death and resurrection and the commissioning of the apostles to go forth and preach the Word.

Biblical scholars have given us many insights into how the Gospel stories grew from rather primitive accounts to more sophisticated ones, giving more and more detail, stressing various aspects of Christ's journey to Calvary and his triumph over death and sin.

Finally, there is the Gospel of John. It abandons to a certain extent the historical perspective and takes on the perspective of a divine point of view, as it were, looking at things from the perspective of God himself. That's why John is called the Divine Eagle.

John describes the New Creation by paralleling the old creation of Genesis revealing the eternal word becoming flesh in Jesus and dwelling among us. Now the Tree of the Garden of Good and Evil becomes the sign of fall, while the Tree of the Cross becomes the sign of triumph and healing. The fruit of the Tree of the Cross becomes the healing source of the New Creation, washing away the sins of the world and giving meaning and purpose to life.

It has been important for me from time to time to rediscover our sources not only in Sacred Scripture but also in the Order of Preachers. We must claim again, as it were, and rediscover what our relationships with God and Christ are all about. That's why in the early sources of the writings of Dominic, his life is best summed up in the simple sentence,

He was always speaking with God or about God.

Dominic saw the need to channel the great forces at the turn of the thirteenth century, popular energies and aspirations, into a new creative inspiration of preaching the Word of God. He was preaching the Good News, namely, forgiveness of our sins through the passion and death of Christ, and the significance of his life. Christ enjoins on his followers, and St. Paul put it in his own words.

They will not believe in him unless they have heard him; they will not hear of him unless they have a preacher, and they will never have a preacher unless one is sent. (Romans 10:15-16)

Christ was always involved with motivating people with his zeal for his Father's House. From my earliest days in the Order, it has occurred to me that the fruit of a good preacher is manifested in different ways. Conversion of believers and unbelievers. A radical change of heart and attitude in the hearer. People receiving the Holy Spirit in abundance. A profound interior change witnessed by going to confession.

It is not simply responding to the preacher, but to the grace of God operating in the preacher's words. I believe it is in this sense that Christ came to "cast fire upon the earth," as Luke proclaims it (12:49). The preacher, therefore, is sent by Christ in the power of the Holy Spirit with the same mission of Christ Himself. It is not sufficient for the preacher just to give information, but he must set us on fire. That is to say, the fire of charity and of divine love.

St. Bernard says in one place, "unless you are yourself ablaze with love, you cannot kindle the fire in others." The fire blazes up because it is placed among fuel, and the flame rises up from the two of them together. So it is with the preacher who must be among his hearers as fire is among its fuel. For the mendicant preaching friar and for all of his tales, that is the tale alone that counts.

Appendices

APPENDIX A

INTERNATIONAL DOMINICAN FOUNDATION BOARD (IDF)
2003

HONORARY MEMBERS

Most Reverend Father Carlos Azpiroz Costa, O.P.
Master of the Order of Preachers
His Eminence Francis Cardinal George, O.M.I.
Archbishop of Chicago
His Eminence Theodore Cardinal McCarrick
Archbishop of Washington

MEMBERS

Most Rev. Edwin F. O'Brien
Archbishop for the Military Services, U.S.A.
Most Rev. Thomas C. Kelly, O.P.
Archbishop of Louisville
Most Rev. Timothy M. Dolan
Archbishop of Milwaukee, Chair
Most Rev. Donald W. Wuerl
Bishop of Pittsburgh
Most Rev. Robert J. Carlson
Bishop of Sioux Falls
Very Rev. Fr. Edmund C. Nantes, O.P.
Treasurer and International Coordinator, IDF
Very Rev. Fr. D. Dominic Izzo, O.P.
Prior Provincial, Eastern Province of St. Joseph
Very Rev. Fr. Edward M. Ruane, O.P.
Prior Provincial, Central Province of St. Albert the Great
Very Rev. Fr. Martin L. Gleeson, O.P.
Prior Provincial, Southern Province of St. Martin de Porres
Very Rev. Fr. Roberto Corral, O.P.
Prior Provincial Western Province of the Holy Name

Rev. Msgr. James F. Checchio
   Vicar for Administration, Moderator of the Curia
   Diocese of Camden
Very Rev. Fr. Neal W. McDermott, O.P.
   Secretary, Director of Christian Formation
   Archdiocese of New Orleans
Very Rev. Fr. Val A. McInnes, O.P.
   President, National Coordinator, IDF
Mr. William E. Simon, Jr.
   William E. Simon and Sons Investments L.L.C.
   Los Angeles

INTERNATIONAL DOMINICAN FOUNDATION
INTERNATIONAL ADVISORY BOARD (IDF-IAB)
2007
HONORARY MEMBERS
His Eminence Christoph Cardinal Schonborn, O.P.
   Archbishop of Vienna, Austria
Very Rev. Wojciech Giertych, O.P.
   Papal Theologian, Vatican City State

MEMBERS
Most Rev. Carlos Azpiroz Costa, O.P.
   Master of the Order, Chairman
The Right Rev. Malcolm McMahon, O.P.
   Bishop of Nottingham, UK
Very Rev. Edward Ruane, O.P.
   Vicar of the Master, Socius for the USA
Very Rev. Allan White, O.P.
   Socius for Northwest Europe & Canada
Very Rev. Mark Edney, O.P.
Very Rev. Val A. McInnes, O.P.
   President Emeritus and Representative of the Master
M. Michel Bon
   Paris, France

Appendix A

Mr. Joseph and Mrs. Marilyn Calderone
  Toronto, Canada
Mr. Francis Davis
  Chair, International Young Leaders Network
  Oxford, England
Robert J. Card, M.D., and Ms. Karol Kreymer
  Houston, Texas
Ms. Donna Miller Casey, DM, LHS
  San Francisco, California
H. E. Jacqueline de Cossé
  Duchess of Brissac, France
Dr. Jacques Delacave, FKC, FRSA
  London, UK
Senator Mario d'Urso
  Rome, Italy
Mr. Francisco C. Eizmendi, Jr.
  Manilla, Philippines
Dr. Nikolaus Hohmann
  Berkeley, CA
Dr. John Patrick Jordan, O.P., KCHS, and
Mrs. Louise H. Jordan, O.P., LCHS
  New Orleans, Louisiana
The Honorable, Mr. John Kane
  Honorary Consul General, Ireland
  Houston, Texas
Mr. Ivan Konig
  London, UK
Mr. Mitchell L. and Mrs. Lynn D. Lathrop
  San Diego, California
Lady Potter, A.O.
  Melbourne, Australia
Professor David Robertson, MA, PhD
  Oxford, UK
Mrs. Elizabeth Robertson, MA, JD
  London, UK
Mr. Roger Sahni
  Houston, Texas

Dr. Eugene and Mrs. Jean Stark
Coral Gables, Florida
Mr. Eric Waldman
New York, New York

INTERNATIONAL DOMINICAN FOUNDATION BOARD
2009
HONORARY MEMBERS

Most Reverend Carlos Azpiroz Costa, O.P.
Master of the Order
His Eminence Francis Cardinal George, O.M.I.
Archbishop of Chicago
Most Rev. Timothy M. Dolan
Chairman Emeritus, IDF
Archbishop of New York

MEMBERS

Most Rev. Donald W. Wuerl,
Chairman of IDF
Archbishop of Washington DC
Washington DC
Very Rev. Mark Edney, O.P.
President-IDF and Vice-Chairman IDF-IAB
Ms. Donna Miller Casey, DM, LHS
San Francisco, California
Most Rev. Robert J. Carlson
Archbishop of St Louis
St Louis, Missouri
Rev. Msgr. James F. Checchio
Rector
Pontifical North American College
Vatican City State
Most Rev. David R. Choby, DD
Bishop of Nashville
Nashville, Tennessee

Very Rev. Fr. Martin J. Gleeson, O.P.
Prior Provincial
Southern Dominican Province
Metairie, Louisiana
Very Rev. Fr. D. Dominic Izzo, O.P.
Prior Provincial
Eastern Province of St. Joseph
New York, New York
Dr. John Patrick Jordan, O.P., KCHS
New Orleans, Louisiana
Mother Ann Marie Karlovic, O.P.
Prioress General
Nashville, Tennessee
Very Rev. Michael J. Mascari, O.P.
Prior Provincial
Central Province of St. Alfred the Great
Chicago, Illinois
Very Rev. Val A. McInnes, O.P.
Representative of the Master
Metairie, Louisiana
Most Rev. Thomas J. Rodi
Archbishop of Mobile
Mobile, Alabama
Most Rev. Michael J. Sheridan
Bishop of Colorado Springs
Colorado Springs, Colorado
Mr. William E. Simon, Jr.
William E. Simon and Sons Investments L.L.C.
Los Angeles
Dr. Eugene Stark
Coral Gables, Florida
Most Rev. Kevin W. Vann, JCD, DD
Bishop of Fort Worth, Fort Worth, Texas
Very Rev. Emmerich Willian Vogt, OP
Prior General Western Province of the Holy Name
Oakland, California

APPENDIX B

MY MEDJUGORJE EXPERIENCE, 1988
by Cherie Banos Schneider

Medjugorje seems to have been torn from the pages of biblical history, for there is so much in it that is reminiscent of the Holy Land. It is one of several whitewashed villages nestled in a fertile green valley surrounded by rocky mountains. The stark white houses with terra cotta roofs and well-tended grape arbors are modest by western standards but completely in keeping with the simple humble lives of their occupants. They are farmers, and this tiny corner of Yugoslavia, now Bosnia-Hercegovina, is agricultural. Fields of tobacco and grapes spread across the valley like a patchwork quilt of green and gold; along the dusty roads that line the fields one sees an occasional herd of sheep being led home from pasture.

It was in this pastoral setting that the Blessed Mother chose to appear to the young village children Ivanka, Mirjana, Ivan, Yakov, Vicka and Marija on that June evening in 1981. Since that moment the four hundred or more inhabitants of Medjugorje, Bijakovici, Miletina, Surmanci, and Vionica have been singularly blessed, and the "Gospa" (as the Virgin Mary is called) continues to grace them with her presence.

When I meditated on her apparitions and the great gift that has been given to these humble villages, I thought how Mary herself was chosen from the tiny village of Nazareth—and how through the ages she has chosen virtually unknown and remote corners of the world in which to appear: Lourdes, Guadalupe, Fatima, and now, in the waning decades of the twentieth century, Medjugorje, hitherto an insignificant part of communist Yugoslavia. Her very appearance there has been the cause for an unbelievable influx of people as pilgrims come by the thousands from all over the world. There is continuous prayer in the large parish church of St. James from early morning until late evening; the celebration of the Eucharist in various languages alternates with the recitation of the rosary. It was both inspiring and impressive to see so many people packed into this large church and overflowing into the ample courtyard outside.

Certainly it seems as though Medjugorje and its neighboring villages have been overtaken by pilgrims hungry for prayer. Some come, I suspect, as merely curious spectators, unbelievers, skeptics; others, as journalists eager to write the extraordinary happenings as they see them or to capture on film the unique miracle of the sun or the spinning of the giant cross atop Mt. Krizevac. Some come burdened with the pain and discomfort of their physical infirmities hoping and praying for a miraculous cure. Others come for inner peace, spiritual healing. Still others come simply to pray and give thanks at this modern day shrine of Our Lady. Certainly this holy place, devoid of the materialism of our own way of life, gives enough spiritual food to nourish these hordes of pilgrims; no one seems to go away hungry.

In our group of ten pilgrims two were returning to Medjugorje for the second time. The rest of us were told that the usual tourist amenities were almost non-existent; there were no hotels or motels, only a few modest snack bars; we went prepared to be without our creature comforts. We were pleasantly surprised when our guide, Marija Uraic, checked with the Yugoslav Intourist and gave us the good news; we would be staying in one of the larger houses, all ten of us, in the neighboring town of Citluk some minutes away from Medjugorje. Distance was no problem as we had our own bus and would be able to come and go as often as we wished.

"Our house" was a delightful surprise. It was typical of the many we had seen on arriving, but it was quite a bit larger and boasted three stories instead of the usual one. There was a well-tended grape arbor at the front entrance with a garden of lettuce and cabbage below it. Chickens wandered about the small enclosure at random; they became our early morning "wake up call!" Each of us had a bedroom and bath modestly but neatly furnished with two bleached pine beds and a night table; there were no windows, but an ample skylight let me enjoy the blue afternoon sky and the starry nights. The dining room and kitchen combination was on the second floor; it was there that we shared our thoughts, ideas, and prayers with one another.

"Our family" was in a sense matriarchal, presided over by Yaya, the lady of the house. The only time we saw her husband and son was the day we arrived; they were there to greet us and help us with our luggage. (There was so many bags and all of them so heavy, except for Father McInnes's; he had long ago learned the joys of detachment from material things. For me, this was a stark realization of how far I had yet to go to reach that stage of detachment from worldly goods!)

Yaya, her two daughters Daniella and Ivana, and her widowed sister-in-law presided in the kitchen and dining room. We began each meal with grace, which we said in English; Yaya and her helpers followed with their version in Croatian; theirs was much more musical than ours and also much longer! They prayed with their eyes closed and their hands folded in "a prayerful attitude" as the nuns taught us many years ago in grade school.

Breakfast was always a welcome beginning to each new day. The rich smell of Yaya's Turkish coffee was like a magnet that attracted us to the second floor dining room where we feasted on the simple fare they set before us, thick slices of bread with homemade grape jelly and usually some sort of sweet pastry to delight our palates.

There are two hills in Medjugorje where the apparitions took place; as pilgrims we were eager to climb both. We decided to tackle the smaller one called Podbrdo first; it was a wise decision for the mountains are rocky and filled with thorn bushes. We climbed the larger hill, Mt. Krizevac on May 1st, Labor Day in the communist world and a national holiday. The already narrow path became a steady procession of people coming and going, adding to the danger of a missed step.

The fourteen bronze Stations of the Cross are strategically placed to serve as both a pause in the journey to stop and pray and also as a place to stop and rest before continuing on. The path grew narrower and rockier at the twelfth station; the sun was hotter, and the air became noticeably thinner. Though hot and tired, we managed to press on, grateful for the occasional cloud cover that blotted the sun's scorching rays and gave us some moments of relief.

It was inspiring to see people of all nationalities climbing along with us. There were babies carried on their parent's backs, elderly men and women supported by walking staffs determinedly making their way to the top; still others depending on those stronger than they for support. The most impressive sight by far was the crowds of young people, teenaged boys and girls, some climbing barefooted, others carrying guitars, praying and singing the Lord's praises along the way.

After what seemed like an unending last twenty minutes, we finally reached the huge cross at the top where many pilgrims had already gathered. The large stones below the cross were filled with votive candles' plaques that said "thanks"; there were photographs of loved ones and floral offerings. After our own prayers of petition, our meditation, our special prayers for those at home who had asked us to present their needs to the Blessed Mother on this holy mountain, we found a clearing among the rocks, emptied our backpacks and shared our food and drink, our impressions and our prayers high above the valley below. The clusters of tiny whitewashed houses looked as small as the ones we used in the game of Monopoly, we were so high up! We felt refreshed both physically and spiritually and offered a quiet prayer of thanksgiving for having reached the top of the mountain.

When Marija, our guide, first met us at the Mestrovic Museum on our way to Medjugorje, I wondered about her beliefs. Was she a Christian? Could a dedicated communist also be a Christian? I sincerely doubted it, especially when she began to give us the political background of Yugoslavia heavily laced with communist propaganda. It wasn't until a day later that I came to realize that this first impression of mine was completely inaccurate.

That morning we were to have had an interview with Vicka, one of the young visionaries, but it was unfortunately canceled because Vicka had suffered severe burns in a fire the day before in her own kitchen and was not able to see pilgrims. Marija was visibly disappointed, and I sensed that she wanted to do something special for us since we were unable to talk with Vicka. It was then that she offered to try to arrange an interview with Father Jozo Zovko, the former Franciscan pastor of the Church of St. James where the visionaries continue to see the apparitions of Our Lady. He is the same Father Jozo who was imprisoned for eighteen months for hiding the visionaries from the police. He was later ordered away from the parish of St. James by the Bishop of Mostar who even today does not lend his approval to the extraordinary happenings in Medjugorje. He was sent to a small parish church where he lives quietly among his parishioners and rarely sees pilgrims. Marija herself had often wanted to talk with him but dared not even try; it was known that he was not in the habit of granting interviews to tour guides as so many of them are non-Christians.

Somehow she learned that he was coming to Medjugorje that afternoon to perform a wedding ceremony, and announced that she would try to see him. I feel as though the Lord certainly answered her prayer for their meeting was miraculous and a real act of faith on her part.

"I entered the sacristy where he was vesting for the ceremony," she said, "and I approached him saying 'praise the Lord', and in that moment he seemed to know that I was a Christian and that he need not be afraid."

Father Jozo asked her what it was that she wanted from him; she responded by saying that she was guiding a group of pilgrims from North America including a Dominican priest; they would welcome the opportunity to see him. She also said that she herself had hoped to meet him one day but somehow never had the courage to seek him out. When he suggested that she bring us to his church that evening at six o'clock, she was overjoyed. Our excitement and anticipation when we heard the news were equally as great as Marija's; the thought of being in the presence of this holy man inspired us all.

Once inside the church, Marija stood beside Father Jozo to act as his interpreter; we took seats in the front pews of the church. It amazed me that Marija's command of English was as good translating spiritual thoughts as translating political facts about communism. Through her we were not only able to understand but also to appreciate fully the subtle nuances of Father Jozo's thoughts. He himself is a visionary with remarkably expressive eyes that seemed to be looking directly at me as he spoke. While talking with us about his association with the visionaries and about the messages of Our Lady, I kept wondering if the other nine pilgrims had the same experience of feeling that he was talking with each one of us personally.

"You didn't come to Medjugorje on your own," Father Jozo told us. "You have received a special invitation from the Gospa to follow her to Jesus and then to the Father."

These words startled me at the moment they were spoken; they have had such an impact that it has changed my life. I can never be the same person that I was before hearing them, and I shall always be grateful to Father Jozo for this message.

Briefly and simply he gave us the revelations given by Our Lady to the visionaries.

Pray – pray – pray for sinners and for the world. Pray from the heart – pray the rosary, Mary's special prayer.

Learn again the ancient custom of fasting...it's salutary. Not just the physical fast of bread and water but fasting by renunciation. Do penance by surrendering our idols. Give up those things in our lives which keep us from being closely united with Christ and his Blessed Mother.

Live the Mass.... It's the greatest prayer we can pray and in addition to praying the Mass we must also live it. Live the sacrifice just as Christ sacrificed for us. Bring Christ to all those who are a part of your lives.
Read the Bible.... It contains all the messages we need to live a holy life.
Find time each day to meditate.... Your lives will be richer for it.

As he spoke Father Jozo was the image of the true Franciscan in his simple brown habit radiating love with a wonderfully warm smile. After his conversation with us, he graciously permitted us a few moments to photograph him and the statue of Our Lady.

Thank you, Father Jozo, and thank you, Marija, for having had the courage to seek out Father Jozo and to find him for us. You gave us something truly memorable.

And thank you, dear Lady, for having invited us to be with you during the month of April, one of the year's most beautiful months everywhere in the world, one that has inspired poets and songwriters throughout the years. It's a time filled with promise when the Father's creation is bursting with new life, and nowhere was this more evident than in Medjugorje. The daily soft spring rains nourished the fertile fields and the bright new tendrils on the age-old grape vines were just a hint of the bounteous harvest yet to come.

I too felt the promise of spring in that special place and the rich harvest Our Lady has in store for us. She herself has told the visionaries "Peace – Peace – Peace" in your hearts and in your world. It's the peace of reconciliation and conversion given to all who ask for it. It's that "pearl of great price," one of the heavenly blessings that I brought back from Medjugorje; a peace that entered my whole being and that I pray will stay with me always. Thank you, Queen of Peace, for this bounteous gift.

The afternoon before we were to return home from Yugoslavia, we arrived in Dubrovnik with grateful hearts for all that had been given to us in Medjugorje, not the least of which was the bond that had been forged among the ten of us. Suzi and Billy, Colleen and Roy, Susan, Beth, Ruthie, Marilyn, and Val; each one of you has a corner of my heart, and I shall never forget you. But we didn't know that our Blessed Lady had yet another blessing in store for us.

We had arrived at our hotel, Villa Dubrovnik, after a short sight-seeing tour of the medieval city. It was here from our own balconies that we were blessed with seeing the extraordinary miracle of the sun. It was late in the afternoon when suddenly I noticed from my balcony that the usually bright yellow sun had become a symphony of colors. Bright blue, deep pink, and soft violet shafts of light radiated from the outer ring. The center itself was pulsating like a giant heart that was beating with life. I was amazed that I was able to see without any of the usual brightness associated with looking directly into the sun. I cannot explain what was happening scientifically. I only know that for me it was the culmination complete and entire of what the Medjugorje journey had been, the bright beauty of a new beginning, the discovery of a new spiritual journey ahead.

APPENDIX C

TULANE UNIVERSITY
Chair of Judeo-Christian Studies

THE PUBLIC LECTURES
1980-2009

1980

APRIL 14, 1980
    William David Davies, Duke University Divinity School
    "Jewish Territorial Doctrine and A Christian Response"

SEPTEMBER 4, 1980
    John MacQuarrie, Oxford University, England
    "The Idea of a People of God"

SEPTEMBER 25, 1980
    John MacQuarrie, Oxford University, England
    "Heidegger's Philosophy of Religion"

OCTOBER 29, 1980
    Edward P. Sanders, McMaster University, Canada
    "Paul and Judaism"

NOVEMBER 12, 1980
    Edward P. Sanders, McMaster University, Canada
    "Jesus and Judaism"

1981

JANUARY 26, 1981
    Jakob J. Petuchowski, Hebrew Union College, Cincinnati
    "Towards a Jewish Theology of Christianity"

MARCH 5, 1981
    Ernan McMullin, Notre Dame University
    "Interactions of Natural Sciences and Religion Today"

APRIL 1, 1981
Raymond Brown, S.S., Union Theological College, New York City
"The Struggle between Christianity and Judaism"
APRIL 23, 1981
Langdon Gilkey, University of Chicago
"Science, Technology and Religion"
OCTOBER 21, 1981
Roger Le Deaut, C.S.P, Biblical Institute, Rome
"Jewish Tradition and New Testament Interpretation"
NOVEMBER 18, 1981
Roger Le Deaut, C.S.P., Biblical Institute, Rome
"The Greek Bible: Hidden Treasure for Jews and Christians"

1982

MARCH 4, 1982
Harald Riesenfeld, University of Uppsala, Sweden
"Sons of God and Ecclesia: An Intertestamental Analysis"
MARCH 23, 1982
Harald Riesenfeld, University of Uppsala, Sweden
"The Hermeneutic Circle—Uses and Abuses in Translating the Bible"
SEPTEMBER 14, 1982
Geza Vermes, Oxford University, England
"The Gospel of Jesus the Jew: An Historical Approach"
SEPTEMBER 21, 1982
Geza Vermes, Oxford University, England
"Jesus and Christianity"
OCTOBER 18, 1982
Edward Schillebeeckx, O.P., University of Nijmegen, Holland
"The Judeo-Christian Interpretation: An Historical and Critical Approach" (Canceled due to illness)
OCTOBER 19, 1982
Edward Schillebeeckx, O.P., University of Nijmegen, Holland
"The Judeo-Christian Interpretation: An Hermeneutical Approach" (Canceled due to illness)

OCTOBER 26, 1982
   David Daube, University of California School of Law
   "The Old Testament in the New: A Jewish Perspective"

1983

FEBRUARY 22, 1983
   Ernan McMullin, University of Notre Dame
   "The Inter-Relationship between Creationism and Evolution Today"
FEBRUARY 28, 1983
   Robert Soloman, University of Texas
   "The Nietzschean Challenge to the Judeo-Christian Tradition"
MARCH 17, 1983
   Daniel Callahan, Director, The Hastings Center
   "Science and Human Values: The Uneasy Connection"
APRIL 7, 1983
   John T. Noonan, Jr., University of California
   "Religion and Public Policy"

1984

OCTOBER 12, 1984
   Cecilia Weyer-Davis, Newcomb College
   "Roman Churches and Their Saints, Male and Female."
OCTOBER 13, 1984
   Symposium on the Painted Word in conjunction with the Vatican Pavilion and the New Orleans Museum of Art
   Frederick Hartt, University of Virginia
   "Raphael's Religious Experience"
   Alfred Moir, University of California
   "Caravaggio's Religious Paintings: Outrageous but Conforming"
   Jonathan Brown, New York University
   "El Greco: A New Interpretation"
   Robert Rosenblum, New York University
   "From the Sacred to the Secular"
   Val A. McInnes, O.P., Tulane University
   "Towards the Revival of Religious Art"

1985

JANUARY 25, 1985
  Norman St. John–Stevas, MP, London
  "The Law and Religious Conflicts Today"
FEBRUARY 4, 1985
  Bernard McGinn, University of Chicago
  "The Language of Love in Christian and Jewish Mysticism"
MARCH 14, 1985
  Vernon Walters, Ambassador, U.S. Department of State
  "Religion in Politics Today"

1986

JANUARY 22, 1986
  Vernon Walters, U.S. Representative to the United Nations
  "The United States and Central America Today"
MARCH 3, 1986
  Arthur Peacocke, Oxford University, England
  "A Christian Materialism? Some Reflections on the Relation to Cognitive Sciences"
APRIL 16, 1986
  Robert Wilken, University of Virginia
  "The Love of God and the Pursuit of Virtue: Early Christian Ethics"
SEPTEMBER 11, 1986
  Sean Freyne, University of Dublin
  "First Century Christians in a Jewish World"
OCTOBER 16, 1986
  Sean Freyne, University of Dublin
  "The Age of Constantine and Beyond: Jesus in a Christian World"

1987

MARCH 23, 1987
  Henry Chadwick, Oxford University, England
  "The Early Christian Church and Authority"

1988

MARCH 20, 1988
> Rabbi Jakob J. Petuchowski, Hebrew Union College, Cincinnati
> *"A Rabbi Looks at the Lord's Prayer"*

APRIL 13, 1988
> Jurgen Moltmann, University of Tubingen, Germany
> *"Christology in the Christian-Jewish Dialogue"*

APRIL 26, 1988
> David Jenkins, Bishop of Durham, England
> *"The Reality of God and the Future of the Human Project"*

SEPTEMBER 29, 1988
> Robert Russell, Center for Theology & Natural Sciences, Berkeley
> *"Science and Religion"*

OCTOBER 20, 1988
> Emilie Dietrich Griffin, American Author
> *"Propositions Regarding the Necessity of Reinventing God"*

NOVEMBER 14, 1988
> Wolfhart Pannenberg, Munich, Germany
> *"God as Spirit and Natural Science"*

1989

FEBRUARY 16, 1989
> Frank T. Birtel, Tulane University
> *"This I Believe—Choosing God and Choosing Man*

MARCH 2, 1989
> Michael Zimmerman, Tulane University
> *"This I Believe—The Redemption of the Body"*

MARCH 9, 1989
> Phillip Hefner, University of Chicago
> *"This I Believe—Crossing New Terrain"*

OCTOBER 23, 1989
> Chaim Potok, American author
> *"This I Believe: Choices in the Modern World"*

NOVEMBER 7, 1989
> Arthur Peacocke, Oxford University, England
> *"This I Believe: From DNA to DEAN"*

NOVEMBER 27, 1989
Barbara Boggs Sigmund, Mayor, Princeton
Paul E. Sigmund, Princeton
"This I Believe: Politics and Religion, Theory and Practice"

1990

MARCH 5, 1990
Rosemary Haughton, "Wellspring House,"
St. Catherine's, Canada
"This I Believe: In the Catholic Tradition"

MARCH 19, 1990
Thomas F. O'Meara, O.P., Notre Dame University
"This I Believe: Two Different Views of Christianity—Fundamentalism and Catholicism"

MARCH 26, 1990
Harvey Cox, Harvard University
"This I Believe: The Lord and Giver of Life"

OCTOBER 23, 1990
Anne Muggeridge, Canadian Author
"The Apocalyptic Days of the Church"

NOVEMBER 15, 1990
Robert Wilken, University of Virginia
"The Christian Intellectual Tradition"

DECEMBER 6, 1990
Anthony Flew, University of Reading, England
"Forty Years of Falsification"

1991

MARCH 19, 1991
Rev. Dr. Lawrence Frizzell, Seton Hall University
Rabbi Dr. Asher Finkel, Seton Hall University
"Twenty-five Years of Progress—An Evaluation"

MARCH 20, 1991
Rabbi Dr. Asher Finkel, Seton Hall University
Rev. Dr. Lawrence Frizzell, Seton Hall University
"Expectations for the Judeo-Christian Dialogue—The Year 2000"

March 21, 1991
    Francis B. Schulte, Archbishop of New Orleans
    Jewish-Christian Prayer Service
September 11, 1991
    Martin Marty, University of Chicago
    "Power Shift: Changes In and Around American Protestantism"
October 24, 1991
    Rabbi Marc H. Tanenbaum, American Jewish Committee
    "Pope John Paul II and the Jewish People"
November 7, 1991
    Richard P. McBrien, University of Notre Dame
    "The Future of Catholicism in the Unites States"

1992

March 19, 1992
    William F. May, Southern Methodist University
    "The Split between Private and Public Life—Religion as Culprit and Solution"
March 26, 1992
    Claude Geffre, O.P., Institute Catholique, Paris
    "New Trends of French Theology Today"
April 9, 1992
    John J. Carey, Agnes Scott College, Atlanta
    "Sexuality Issues in the American Church"
October 12, 1992
    Richard F. Greenleaf, Tulane University
    "Columbus and the Age of Discovery"
November 9, 1992
    Gustavo Gutierrez, Lima, Peru
    "Bartolomeo de Las Casas—The Theology of Las Casas, Father of Human Rights and International Law"
November 16, 1992
    Helen Rand Parish, University of California, Berkeley
    "Las Casas—The Untold Story"

1993

MARCH 4, 1993
  Avery Dulles, S.J., Fordham University
  "Interrelation of Faith and Culture"
MARCH 18, 1993
  Rabbi David R. Blumenthal, Emory University
  "The Holocaust as Paradigm of the 20th Century"
MARCH 22, 1993
  Brian Davis, O.P., Oxford University, England
  "God and Some American Philosophers"
APRIL 4, 1993
  Charles O'Neill, S.J., Rome
  The Tulane–Archdiocese of New Orleans Bicentennial Lecture
  The Church in the United States—200 Years of Growth—Baltimore and New Orleans"
OCTOBER 14, 1993
  Mary Jo Weaver, Indiana University
  "Feminists and Patriarchs in the Catholic Church: Dysfunctional Discourse or a Common Language?"
OCTOBER 27, 1993
  Jean C. Felts, John J. Kelly, Alden J. Laborde, and Edward A. Lupberger
  "Is Business Ethical? Case Discussions on Ethical Decisions in Business Practice"
NOVEMBER 11, 1993
  Benedict M. Ashley, O.P., St. Louis University
  "A Theology of Intellectual Life"
NOVEMBER 18, 1993
  John S. Spong, Episcopal Bishop, Diocese of Newark, NJ
  "The Gospels as Examples of Jewish Midrash"

1994

FEBRUARY 24, 1994
  Avi Granot, Israeli Embassy, Washington, D.C.
  David-Maria A. Jaeger, O.M.I, Austin, Texas
  "A Major Diplomatic Accomplishment—The Fundamental

Agreement Between the Holy See and the State of Israel: A Catholic Perspective/An Israeli Perspective"

MARCH 8, 1994
Elaine Pagels, Princeton University
"Satan and the New Testament, A Social History of Satan"

MARCH 10, 1994
Jaroslav Pelikan, Yale University
"Russian Roots in the American Spirit"

NOVEMBER 16, 1994
A Dialog.
Fred Kammer, S.J., Catholic Charities, Alexandria, VA
"The Doctrine of Church and State: Should Religion Be Involved in Politics?"
William Barnett, Loyola University
"The Doctrine of Church and State—Should Religion be Involved in Politics?"

NOVEMBER 17, 1994
A Dialog.
David D. Friedman, University of Chicago
Alma H. Young, University of New Orleans
"Government and the Poor—Who Should be Providing Care for the Poor?"

1995

MARCH 9, 1995
Michael Novak, The American Enterprise Institute, Washington, D.C.
Gilbert Meilaender, Oberlin College
"Veritatis Splendor—Roman Catholic and Lutheran Perspectives in Dialogue"

APRIL 6, 1995
George Weigel, Washington, D.C.
Peter Ochs, Drew University
"Religion and Moral Decline in Contemporary American Society—Disintegration or Rejuvenation?"

OCTOBER 12, 1995
   Don Drowning, University of Chicago
   "Religion, Politics and the American Family Debate"
NOVEMBER 16, 1995
   Marcus Borg, Oregon State University
   "The Work of the Jesus Seminar: What Is Its Purpose and Does it Matter?"

1996

MARCH 7, 1996
   David Novak, University of Virginia
   Richard John Neuhaus, New York City
   "Messianic Expectations—A Jewish and Christian Point of View"
MARCH 14, 1996
   J. Wentzel van Huyssteen, Princeton Theological Seminary
   "Truth and Pluralism in Religion and Science Today—The Post-Modern Challenge"
OCTOBER 31, 1996
   Philip Kennedy, O.P., Oxford University, England
   "The God Question in Our Post-Modern Age"
NOVEMBER 25, 1996
   Raymond E. Brown, S.S., Union Theological Seminary
   "New Testament Treatment of the Jews"

1997

Panel Discussion on Three Dates with the Same Participants
Participants:
   Rabbi Edward P. Cohn, Temple Sinai
   Val A. McInnes, O.P., Tulane University
   Jean A. Meade, St. Andrew's Episcopal School
   Steven Meriwether, St. Charles Avenue Baptist Church
Moderator:
   Frank T. Birtel, Tulane University
FEBRUARY 27, 1997
   "Post-Modern Concepts of God—The Problem of Worshiping the One God Today"

MARCH 6, 1997
Transcending the Divisive—Removing Obstacles to Ecumenical Dialog"

MARCH 13, 1997
"Jesus as Messiah: Christian Yes; Jewish No—Messianic Expectations Today"

OCTOBER 16, 1997
Robert J. Collier, M.D., Monsanto Company, St. Louis
"Science and Technology in Cloning, from Sheep to Humans—What are the Real Possibilities of Human Cloning?"

OCTOBER 23, 1997
Dr. Albert Moraczewski, O.P., Pope John XXIII Medical-Moral Research and Education Center, Houston, Texas.
"What are the Ethical and Religious Implications of Human Cloning?—A Judeo-Christian Perspective"

NOVEMBER 13, 1997
Sondra Ely Wheeler, Wesleyan Theological Seminary
"The Impact of Cloning on Family Values—Making Sexual Reproduction Obsolete?"

1998

MARCH 5, 1998
Vernon Gregson, Jr., Loyola University
"Images of God and the Unconscious: Origins andTransformations"

APRIL 16, 1998
Daniel Holcomb, New Orleans Baptist Theological Seminary
"Images of God and Contemporary Literature—Impact and Significance"

OCTOBER 29, 1998
Gordon D. Kaufman, Harvard University
"Re-Imaging God in Light of Today's Evolutionary/Ecological Consciousness"

NOVEMBER 12, 1998
Patrick Henry, Institute for Ecumenical and Cultural Research, Collegeville, MN
"Images of God in Space and Time"

1999

FEBRUARY 25, 1999
Gary Macy, University of San Diego
"The Church in the Middle Ages"

MARCH 25, 1999
Andrew Greeley, Sociologist and Author
"Images of God and Religious Imagination"

APRIL 12, 1999
Francis Cardinal George, O.M.I, Archbishop of Chicago
"Images of God in the Writings of Pope John Paul II: A Spirituality for the New Millennium"

OCTOBER 7, 1999
Benedict M. Ashley, O.P., Aquinas Institute of Theology, St. Louis
"Gender Images and the Mystery of God"

NOVEMBER 3, 1999
Steven T. Katz, Boston University
"Jewish Images of God in the Post-Holocaust Era"

NOVEMBER 11, 1999
Brennan R. Hill, Xavier University, Cincinnati
"Images of God from the Earth and its People: An Environmental Theology"

2000

MARCH 16, 2000
Peter Storey, Duke University
"Resistance and Reconciliation: The Church's Ecumenical Role in Ending Apartheid"

MARCH 27, 2000
Timothy Radcliffe, O.P., Master of the Order of Preachers, Rome
"Where Are We Going? Christian Faith in the Face of an Unknown Future"

APRIL 13, 2000
Anthony M. Matteo, Elizabethtown College, PA
"The Promise and Perils of Evolutionary Ethics"

Appendix C 183

OCTOBER 12, 2000
  John R. Quinn, D.D., Archbishop Emeritus of San Francisco
  "Possibilities of a New Papal Primacy"
OCTOBER 26, 2000
  Rabbi Joseph Ehrenkrantz, Sacred Heart University, Fairfield, CT
  "Strengthening Jewish-Christian Relations—A Jewish Perspective on the Recent Papal Visit to Israel"

2001

MARCH 12, 2001
  Wolfhart Pannenberg, Munich, Germany
  "God the Spirit and Natural Science"
APRIL 5, 2001
  Philip D. Clayton, California State University, Sonoma
  "Reading the Past, Projecting the Future: Science and Theology on the Emergence of Spirit"
MAY 24, 2001
  Christoph Cardinal Schonborn, O.P., Archbishop of Vienna
  "Judaism and Christianity: New Perspectives After the Holy Year"
OCTOBER 4, 2001
  Phyllis Zagano, Co-Chair, Roman Catholic Group of the American Academy of Religion
  "Women Deacons? Past, Present and Future—An Exploration of the Tradition and History of Diaconal Ordination"
OCTOBER 22, 2001
  Mark Guscin, Spanish Center of Sindonology, Madrid
  "Reputed Burial Cloths of Jesus Christ – How to Determine their Authenticity or Fraud?"
NOVEMBER, 8, 2001
  Philip Hefner, Lutheran School of Theology at Chicago
  "Technology, Theology and New Images of Being Human"

2002

FEBRUARY 7, 2002
  Mahmoud M. Ayoub, Temple University
  "Religion and Violence: The Case of Islam"

MARCH 7, 2002
> Dr. Herbert Benson, Harvard Medical School
> "Timeless Healing: The Power and Biology of Belief"

APRIL 11, 2002
> Frank T. Birtel, Tulane University
> "Evolving Thoughts on Taking Science and Religion Seriously"

OCTOBER 10, 2002
> Richard R. Gaillardetz, University of Toledo, OH
> "What We Can Now See: Ecclesial Reflections on the Current Crisis in the American Catholic Church"

OCTOBER 24, 2002
> Kirk O. Hanson, Santa Clara University, CA
> "Corporate Ethics and Responsibility—Enron and Beyond: Ethical Lessons for American Society"

2003

MARCH 13, 2003
> Joseph A. Galante, Coadjutor Roman Catholic Bishop of Dallas
> "Renewing the Hope and the Trust of the Faithful in the Institutional Church"

MARCH 27, 2003
> Rabbi Jack Bemporad, Center for Inter-Religious Understanding, Secaucus, NJ
> "A Jewish Perspective on the Recent Pontifical Biblical Document, 'On the Jewish People and Their Scriptures in the New Testament'"

SEPTEMBER 11, 2003
> William Cardinal Keeler, Archbishop of Baltimore
> "The New Movement in Christian-Jewish Relations"

OCTOBER 23, 2003
> Robert E. Barron, St. Mary of the Lake Seminary, Mundelein, IL
> "Contemporary Moral and Spiritual Formation through the Eucharistic Liturgy"

NOVEMBER 6, 2003
> George Weigel, Ethics and Public Policy Center, Washington, D.C.
> "Moral Leadership and World Politics in the Twenty-first Century"

2004

MARCH 18, 2004
Marcel Sigrist, O.P., Ecole Biblique, Jerusalem
"*In Today's Secularized World, Is It Possible to Believe in God?*"

MARCH 25, 2004
William B. Hurlbut, M.D., Stanford University
"*Patenting Human Life: Clones, Chimeras, and Biological Artifacts*"

OCTOBER 7, 2004
Christoph Cardinal Schonborn, O.P., Archbishop of Vienna
"*Judaism and Christianity: New Perspectives in the New Millennium*"

OCTOBER 28, 2004
Wesley J. Wildman, Boston University
"*A Review and Critique of the 'Divine Action Project'—A Dialogue among Scientists and Theologians, Sponsored by Pope John Paul II*"

2005

MARCH 3, 2005
Antje Jakelen, Lutheran School of Theology, Chicago
"*Challenges of Science and Religion in the New Millennium*"

APRIL 7, 2005
Martin E. Marty, University of Chicago
"*Fundamentalisms and World Religions—What They Have in Common and How They All Demonize 'the Other'*"

(Fall Lectures were canceled due to Hurricane Katrina.)

2006

MARCH 2, 2006
John Dominic Crossan, DePaul University, Chicago
"*What Does St. Paul Have To Say To The Church Today?*"

MARCH 16, 2006
Dennis Doyle, University of Dayton, OH
"*Pope Benedict XVI, What Impact Might His Augustinian Philosophy Have?*"

NOVEMBER 9, 2006
    Richard Ryscavage, S.J., Fairfield University
    "Immigration and Globalization: The New Face of Christianity"
NOVEMBER 16, 2006
    Robert Blair Kaiser, Vatican II Correspondent for Time Magazine, Newsweek Rome Editor
    "A Case for an American Catholic Church"

2007

JANUARY 25, 2007
    John Houghton, Oxford University, England
    First honoree of the St. Thomas Aquinas Environmental Award given by the Chair of Judeo-Christian Studies
    "Climatic Changes: Challenges to Scientists, Politicians, and Religionists Alike"
MARCH 29, 2007
    Donald W. Wuerl, Archbishop of Washington, D.C.
    "The Enduring Challenge of Faith—What the Church Brings to Today's Youth"
OCTOBER 11, 2007
    Marcel Sigrist, O.P., Ecole Biblique, Jerusalem
    "Why a New Translation of the Bible? – 'The Bible in Its Traditions Project'"
NOVEMBER 8, 2007
    Asher Yarden, Consul General of Israel to the Southwest, Houston
    "On the Road to Reconciling the Israeli-Palestinian Conflicts in the Light of Recent Historical Developments"

2008

FEBRUARY 28, 2008
    Julian Wheatley, New Orleans, Consultant for the Government of Singapore
    "The Lady and the General"—Questions of Religious Freedom and Democracy in Myanmar (Burma)

MARCH 13, 2008
  Roger Haight, S.J., Union Theological Seminary, NY
  "Rethinking the Church and the Churches"
SEPTEMBER 10, 2008
  Bestowal of the Second Thomas Aquinas Environmental Award at Clarence House, London
  H.R.H. the Prince of Wales
NOVEMBER 13, 2008
  Lee Martin Martiny, O.P., Kenya
  "The Future of the Church in Africa—Tribalism and Racism—The Challenge to Church Unity"
DECEMBER 4, 2008
  John F. Haught, Georgetown University
  "Evolution and Faith: A Proposal for the Future"
  (Two-hundredth Anniversary of Darwin's Birth)

2009

JANUARY 22, 2009
  Hank Dittmar, Director for the Prince of Wales Foundation
  "Sustainability, Tradition and Harmony: Building Beautifully and for the Long Term"
MARCH 26, 2009
  C. K. Robertson, Canon to the Presiding Bishop of the Episcopal Church in the United States
  "Leadership in a Time of Conflict: What Does the Future Hold for the Episcopal Church in the U.S.?"
OCTOBER 8, 2009
  Robert Schreiter, Catholic Theological Union, Chicago
  "The Philosophical and Theologian Relevance of Professor Edward Schillebeeckx, O.P., for the Twenty-first Century"
NOVEMBER 5, 2009
  Rabbi David Dalin, Ave Maria University, Naples, FL
  "The Myth of Hitler's Pope: A Jewish Response to the Integrity of Pope Pius XII's Dealings with the Nazis"

APPENDIX D

BOOKS PUBLISHED BY THE CHAIR OF JUDEO-CHRISTIAN STUDIES
General Editor, Val A. McInnes, O.P.

VOLUME 1
Renewing the Judeo-Christian Wellsprings
Edited by Val A. McInnes, O.P.
1987

VOLUME 2
Religion, Science, and Public Policy
Edited by Frank T. Birtel
1987

VOLUME 3
New Visions: Historical and Theological Perspective on Jewish-Christian Dialogue
Edited by Val A. McInnes, O.P.
1992

VOLUME 4
Reasoned Faith
Edited by Frank T. Birtel
1993

VOLUME 5
Religion and the American Experience
Edited by Frank T. Birtel
2005

VOLUME 6
Re-Imaging God for Today
Edited by Val A. McInnes, O.P.
2005

VOLUME 7
Renewing Hope in the Judeo-Christian Dialogue
Edited by Val A. McInnes, O.P.
In preparation

APPENDIX E

RECIPIENTS OF THE ST. MARTIN DE PORRES AWARD
SOUTHERN DOMINICAN PROVINCE, USA

NEW ORLEANS

1986	Ms. Loretta Young	2000	Most Rev. Francis B. Schulte, D.D.
1987	Ms. Helen Hayes		Mrs. Edwin Blum
1988	Mr. and Mrs. Ricardo Montalban	2001	Mr. and Mrs. Danny Abramowicz
1990	Mrs. Bob Hope		Mr. and Mrs. Archie Manning
1991	The Honorable Corinne "Lindy" Boggs	2002	Mr. and Mrs. John D'Arcy Becker
			Mr. and Mrs. St. Denis J. Villere, Jr.
1992	Lord and Lady Fitzalan Howard	2003	Dr. and Mrs. George Cary
1993	Most Reverend Philip M. Hannan and Marguerite Piazza		Mrs. Marilyn Rusovich
			Mr. Basil J. Rusovich, Jr.
1994	Ambassador and Mrs. Raymond Flynn and family		(posthumously)
		2004	Mr. and Mrs. Nat Garofalo
	Mr. and Mrs. David F. Dixon and family		Mr. and Mrs. Ray Naquin
			Mrs. Mary Ann Valentino
1995	Mr. and Mrs. Joseph C. Canizaro	2005	*[Cancelled due to Hurricane Katrina]*
	Sister Lillian McCormack, S.S.N.D.	2006	Drs. Haydee and Nicolas Bazan
1996	Cokie and Steve Roberts		Drs. Marguerite McDonald and Stephen Klyce
1997	The Dominican Sisters of St. Mary's		
	Mr. and Mrs. Alden J. Laborde	2007	Leah Chase
1998	Dr. and Mrs. Norman C. Francis		Richard C. Colton
	Dr. and Mrs. Eamon M. Kelly	2008	Harry Connick, Sr.
1999	Mr. and Mrs. Paul A. Nalty		Harry Connick, Jr.
	Dr. and Mrs. John J. Walsh, Sr.	2009	Mr. and Mrs. John Laborde

HOUSTON

1990	Dr. Paul Chu	2000	Harry H. and Rose Cullen
1991	Ambassador Vernon A. Walters		Very Rev. Val A. McInnes, O.P.
1992	Archbishop Thomas E. Kelly	2001	Katie and Luke McConn
1993	Most Rev. Timothy Radcliffe, O.P.	2002	Mr. and Mrs. Robert R. Fretz, Sr.
	Dr. Robert J. Campbell	2003	Dr. and Mrs. Malcolm Granberry
1994	Fr. Henri J. M. Nouwen	2004	The Serra Club of Houston
	Mrs. Leo Edward Linbeck	2005	Mr. and Mrs. Marion Spiers
1995	Mr. and Mrs. Ernest Cronin	2006	Msgr. Albert Beck
1996	Most Rev. Joseph A. Fiorenza, O.P.	2007	Mr. Arthur F. Holland
	Mrs. David L. Garrison, Jr.	2008	The Catholic Chaplain Corps Archdiocese Galveston–Houston
1997	Sr. Edna Ann Herbert, O.P.		
	Mr. Cornelius O. Ryan	2009	The Correctional Ministries Archdiocese Galveston–Houston
1998	Most Rev. John McCarthy, D.D.		
1999	Mrs. Mary Elizabeth Broussard Donovan		

APPENDIX F

RECIPIENTS OF THE ST. THOMAS AQUINAS
ENVIRONMENTAL AWARD
SOUTHERN DOMINICAN PROVINCE, USA

JANUARY 25, 2007
John Houghton, Oxford University, England

SEPTEMBER 10, 2008
H.R.H. the Prince of Wales

2009
Not Awarded.

APPENDIX G

"PASSION FOR THE ARTS PLAYS BIG ROLE IN POPE'S TEACHINGS"
INTERVIEW WITH FR. VAL A. MCINNES, O.P.,

by James Hodge, staff writer, *The New Orleans Times-Picayune*
Monday, August 24, 1987; page A-1.

As a youth, Karol Joseph Wojtyla played soccer as a goalie, took daredevil swims across flooded rivers, did expert impersonations of his teachers, and above all had a love for the theater.

His overriding ambition was to study literature and become a professional actor, and he didn't give up that goal without a fight.

His dream was first stymied by the Nazis, who outlawed the study of Polish drama in the 1940s. But the young Wojtyla and his college friends kept alive an underground drama group called *The Rhapsodic Theater* at the same time he was helping Jews find refuge from the Nazis.

To support himself, the young man who would become Pope John Paul II worked as a stonecutter and unloaded lime from railroad hoppers.

Wojtyla never considered a religious vocation until he was hospitalized after a streetcar accident. However, he resisted the call, and as soon as he recovered, he persisted in believing his talents lay in the theater. But soon after his release, he was hit by a German army truck, his brother died, then his father died, and he reconsidered the priesthood.

While Wojtyla did leave the world of the theater for the service of God, he never abandoned the arts and has used them "in a way that no other modern pope has ever dared to do," the Rev. Val McInnes said Sunday at Tulane University in a papal lecture sponsored by Xavier University.

His involvement in the theater has had "a deep-rooted and lasting influence on his personality," McInnes said. "He became a drama person as opposed to a picture person, who sees light as something unfolding, not fixed in place with no action."

During his pastoral visits, John Paul tries whenever he can to awaken his audience with a sort of dramatization of the church's teachings, McInnes said.

John Paul sees the arts as "the indispensable complement to the role of evangelizing," he said. They are the vehicles of "inculcating the drama of salvation, clothed in the various styles of the ages through which man travels on his pilgrimage home to the Lord."

The pope sees the role of the artist as one of helping man find "the ultimate beauty, who is God," McInnes said.

"Art is important for human development, because in creating beauty, it transmits the enchantment of pure spirituality—a glimpse into God himself," McInnes said, quoting John Paul.

The pope believes that the source of the inspiration for every great work of art is essentially religious, he said.

The universal appeal of an artwork depends upon the intensity of the inspiration and "how it speaks to the complex dimensions of the human personality," he said.

John Paul recently created the Pontifical Council for Culture, McInnes said, which underscores his notion that "the cultural arena is crucial for the survival of human values and for the church's evangelizing mission."

The pope feels the cultural diversity in the world provides the "matrix not only for the artist, but for the faith as well."

John Paul himself has penned six plays and translated Sophocles' "Oedipus" into Polish.

One of his plays, "Job," deals with the Old Testament figure, while a three-act work, "The Jeweler's Shop," relates the travails of three couples and will be produced on Broadway this fall.

John Paul also wrote several key Vatican II documents and as pope has published several encyclicals.

Today, the pope "channels most of his creative energies into his homilies which he writes himself," McInnes said.

The lion's share of the pope's speeches, which he edits and rewrites, are put together largely by his private secretaries, various bishops' conferences, and Vatican officials, McInnes said.

APPENDIX H
CURRICULUM VITAE OF VERY REV.
FATHER VAL AMBROSE MCINNES, O.P., PH.D.

Founding Pastor of the Tulane University Community of St. Thomas More. Member of the Dominican Order of the Province of St. Martin de Porres. Founder of the Chair of Judeo-Christian Studies, Tulane University, Director and Executive Secretary. Former Promoter of Development for the Southern Dominican Province of St. Martin de Porres and President of the International Dominican Foundation for the Order of Preachers (2001-2007), now President Emeritus.

Born. April 21, 1929, London, Ontario, Canada. Son of Angus J. McInnes, Sr., and Genevieve Rodgers McInnes.

UNIVERSITIES ATTENDED & DEGREES
Banff School of Fine Arts, University of Alberta;
  Painting (1949).
University of Fribourg, Switzerland;
  Philosophy (1950).
McGill University;
  French and French-Canadian Political Life (1951).
Assumption College of the University of Western Ontario;
  Honors B.A. in Philosophy and History (1952).
Leyden University, Holland; International Law (1953),
  Diploma, International Court in The Hague.
Assumption University of Windsor;
  M.A. in Philosophy (1954).
Aquinas Institute;
Philosophy, Ph.B. (1957), Ph.L. (1958), Ph.D. (1966).

ACADEMIC POSITIONS & ADMINISTRATION
Lecturer in Theology, College of St. Thomas,
  St. Paul, MN (1962-65).
Chairman of the Philosophy and Theology Departments,
  King's College, University of Western Ontario, and
  Associate Director of the Newman Apostolate on the same
  campus, London, Ontario (1965-66).

Seminar in Tulane Medical School on Psychology,
    Psychiatry and Medical Ethics (1968-82); Human Values and
    Decision-Making in Medicine (1973-82).
Consultant in the Tulane School of Architecture on Contemporary
    Ecclesiastical French Art and Architecture, and Sometime
    Examiner for the Master of Fine Arts, School of Art,
    Newcomb College, New Orleans (1967-75).
Professor, University College,
    Tulane University (1970-78).
Homiletics Professor, Notre Dame Seminary,
    New Orleans (1975-79).
Founder, Director, and Executive Secretary,
    Chair of Judeo-Christian Studies Tulane University (1979-).
Director, New Orleans Vatican Pavilion at the
    Louisiana World Exposition (1981-84).
Board Member, Aquinas Center of Theology,
    Emory University (1992-99) and Vice Chair (1996-99).
Advisory Board, Vatican Museums (1985-).
Founder and First President of the Patrons of the
    Vatican Museums in the South (1986-96).
President of the International Dominican Foundation and
    National Coordinator for the International Campaign
    for Global Priorities for the Order of Preachers (2001-2007),
    President Emeritus (2007-).

PASTORAL POSITIONS

Solemn Profession, Order of Preachers (Dominican),
    Province of St. Albert the Great (1958).
    Ordained to the priesthood,
    St. Rose of Lima Priory, Dubuque, Iowa (1961).
Associate Chaplain, University of Western Ontario (1965-66).
Director, Tulane Catholic Center (1966-70).
Founding Pastor of the Tulane University Community of
    St. Thomas More (1970-79).
Member of the St. Albert the Great Provincial Liturgical
    Commission (1973-77).

Member of the Admissions Board to the Dominican Order (1973-79.)
Member of the St. Albert the Great Provincial Liturgical Art Commission (1977-79).
Chaplain, the Southern Commandery of the Military and Hospitaller Order of St. Lazarus of Jerusalem (1977-).
Senior Chaplain, Grand Priory of America, Military and Hospitaller Order of St. Lazarus of Jerusalem, U.S.A. (1979-).
Elected Prior of the Dominican Community of St. Anthony of Padua Priory, New Orleans (1976-79). Re-elected (1979-82).
Elected Prior of the Dominican Community of St. Dominic Priory, New Orleans (1999-2002). Re-elected (2002-06).
Promoter of Development, Southern Dominicans (1985-2000).
Chaplain Knight Commander of the Equestrian Order of the Holy Sepulchre of Jerusalem, Southern Lieutenancy, U.S.A. (1991-).
Member of the Provincial Council (1997-2006).
Member of the Economic Council (1997-2006).

AWARDS & HONORS, 1997-2006

UNESCO Scholarship to study International Law at Leyden and at the International Court in The Hague (1953).
Canada Council grant to study the life and influence of Pere J.-M. Couturier, O.P. on Contemporary French Ecclesiastical Art and Architecture (1966).
Omicron Delta Kappa Society, member, Tulane University (1973).
National Endowment for the Arts grant for the Development of Louisiana Renaissance, Religion and the Arts, (1977-80).
Louisiana Council for Music and the Performing Arts medal (1978).
Louisiana Council for Music and the Performing Arts: state and federal grants to inaugurate the program "Louisiana Outreach, Arts for the Handicapped" (1978-82).
Vatican Museums, the Canova Medal, in recognition for the organization of the Vatican Pavilion, 1984 Louisiana World Exposition (1980-85).
Institute of Human Understanding Award (1987).
The Outstanding Volunteers New Orleans Award (1988).

St. Martin de Porres Award, Houston, Texas (2001).
Elected member of the General Chapter for the Order of Preachers, Providence College, Providence, Rhode Island (June-July 2001).
Fra Angelico Award, New Orleans Museum of Art (2002).
Krakow International Dominican Chapter (2004). Cited for the outstanding contributions to the establishment and the success of the International Dominican Foundation.
Bogota International Dominican Chapter (2007). Cited again for continuing contributions to IDF with much gratitude.

COMMITTEES & CONSULTATIONS

Vice Chairman and Member of Executive Committee, Henry Edward Dormer Centennial Celebrations (1966).
Chairman, Fine Arts Committee of the Louisiana Council for Music and the Performing Arts and Board Member of theame (1967-78).
Consultant, Government of Ecuador on Church-State Problems (1969).
Chairman, Religious Staff Association of Tulane University (1969-73).
United States Roman Catholic Delegate, First World Conference On Religion and Peace, Kyoto, Japan (1970).
Member, Committee on the Use of Human Subjects in Research, Tulane University Medical School (1971-78).
Catholic Consultant, World Conference on Religion for Peace; Consultations over Bangladesh, United Nations (October 1971).
Catholic Delegate, North American Consultation on Religion for Peace, Wingspread, Racine, WI (October 1972).
Delegate, St. Dominic's Priory to the Dominican Chapter, River Forest, IL (1973).
Member, Board of Admissions to the Province of St. Albert the Great (1973-78).
Catholic Representative, Second World Conference on Religion and Peace, Louvain, Belgium (1974).
Panel Chairman, "Future of the Arts in the U.S.," Direction '74, Tulane University (1974).

Participant, Justice Conference on the "Violations of Human Rights," Lima, Peru (1975).
Member, Arts Commission for the Dominicans of St. Albert the Great Province (1977-79).
Vice-President, Louisiana Renaissance, Religion, and the Arts (1977-78); President (1978-80).
President, Louisiana Council for Music and the Performing Arts, Inc. (1978-88).
Chairman, President's Committee to Establish the Chair of Judeo-Christian Studies, Tulane University (1977-79).
Executive Secretary, Chair of Judeo-Christian Studies, Tulane University (1979-); later, Director (1989-), and Chair (1998-2011).
Chairman, Minority Religion Committee for the World Conference on Religion and Peace Meetings, Princeton University (1979).
Chairman, Committee on establishing the National Shrine of St. Lazarus, Old Ursuline Convent, French Quarter, New Orleans (1979-80). Member of Chapel committee (1980-).
Member, Council of the New Dominican Province of St. Martin de Porres (1980-83).
Consultant, Dominican Studies Center of the South, Emory University (1983-84).
Consultant, Australian Ambassador to the Holy See, re Vatican Pavilion, World's Fair 1988, Brisbane, Australia (1985).
Member, Committee for the Fourth World Foundation.
Member, Committee on the International Traveling Exhibition of The Shroud of Turin, entitled "Science, Mystery, and Art" (1985-90).
Member, Southern Dominican Foundation Board (1985-).
Consultant, Vatican Pavilion, Brisbane, Australia (1985-86).
Member, Advisory Board, Vatican Museums, Vatican City, Europe (1986-).
Member, Committee to celebrate the twin centenary of Christ Church Cathedral and Sacred Heart Academy, New Orleans (1987).
Consultant to Robert Evans, Paramount Studios, on the production of the life of Pope John Paul II, "The Power of Faith" (1987).

Consultant, Vatican Pavilion, Barcelona, Spain (1988-89).
Member, Regional Ecumenical Access Channel—REACH Television Board (1988-98).
Participant, "Faith to Faith," television series; with Rabbi Edward Paul Cohn as Chair, [DATE???].
Coordinator, International Exhibition of Belgian Dominican artist, Pere Albert Carpentier, O.P., Historic New Orleans Collection, New Orleans (1990).
Member, Board of Trustees, Aquinas Center for Theology, Emory University, Atlanta, Georgia (1991-96); Vice-Chair (1996-99).
Member, Fra Angelico Foundation Board, Chicago (1990-94).
Consultant for the Establishment of the Center of Jewish-Christian Studies, Sacred Heart University, Fairfield, CT (1990-96).
Consultant, Columbia University, The American Assembly Consultation on the Government and the Arts, Arden House (Fall 1990).
Chairman, seminar at Tulane University celebrating the Twenty-fifth Anniversary of the Vatican II document *Nostra Aetate* (1991).
Roman Catholic Participant, U.S. Delegation of Religious Leaders to The Republic of China (Taiwan) (1991).
Member, Papal Delegation to the United Nations (Vatican Museums Advisory Board) on the occasion of Pope John Paul II's visit (1995).
Vice Chair of Board of Trustees, Aquinas Center of Theology, Emory University (1995-99).
Member, Executive Committee Aquinas Board of Theology developing "A New Vision for a New Millennium: A Proposal" (1999).
Board member, Fourth World Foundation, Fairfield, CT (1996-). Consultant, Designing the Building of a Grand Statue of St. Martin de Porres on St. Maartin Island (1999-2000).
Coordinator and Director, National Millennium Sacred Art Project (1998-).

PUBLICATIONS
Books

The Philosophical Basis of Aesthetic Criticism. Unpublished, 1954.
A Return to a Living Christian Art. Unpublished, 1966.
The Aesthetics of John Dewey. Aquinas Institute, 1966.
A Thousand Arrows. University of Windsor Press, 1970.
Humanizing Through the Arts; Creation and Recreation. Louisiana Department of Education, Art and Environment, 1973.
Taste and See: Louisiana Renaissance Religion and the Arts. Harvey Press, New Orleans, 1977.
Releasing the Artistic Talents of Our Handicapped: A Report on the Project, Louisiana Outreach—Arts for the Handicapped. Harvey Press, 1982.
Treasures of the Vatican, Editor and Contributor. The New Orleans Vatican Pavilion Publishers, 1987.
Renewing the Judeo-Christian Wellsprings, Editor. Crossroad Publishing Company, 1987.
Religion, Science and Public Policy, General Editor. Crossroad Publishing Company, 1987.
To Rise with the Light: The Spiritual Odyssey of Jack Chambers. University of Toronto Press and Ontario College of Art, 1989.
New Vision, Historical Perspectives in the Jewish-Christian Dialogue, Editor and Introduction, Crossroad Publishing Company, 1992.
Reasoned Faith, General Editor. Crossroad Publishing Company, 1993.
Re-Imaging God for Today, Editor with Introduction, New City Press, 2005.
Religion and the American Experience, General Editor, New City Press, 2005.
Resurrection Fern: Tales of a Dominican Friar. Southern Dominican Books, 2010.

Articles

"Henry Edward Dormer." *The Torch,* 1954.
"The Doctrine of the Image of God in Man." Aquinas Institute, 1960.
"A New Saint for Our Day: St. Martin de Porres." *America,* 1961.
"Reality," *Dedication,* 1962.
"Liturgy of the Word and the Rosary." *Ecclesiastical Review,* 1962.
"Ivan Mestrovic on Christian Art." *Liturgical Arts,* 1963.
"Ivan Mestrovic on Christian Art." *Country Beautiful,* 1963.
"An Experience in Biblical Theology." *America* Magazine, 1964.

"The Liturgy of the Word and the Rosary." *The Immaculate,* 1965.
"The Faith-Learning Dilemma." New Orleans Baptist Workshop Conference, 1969.
"Moral Aspects of Sex Counseling." *Journal on Human Sexuality,* 1967.
"Henry Dormer, A Saint for Our Times." *Dominican Life,* 1968.
Order of St. Lazarus, Quarterly Newsletter, 1978-1990.
"The Making of the Vatican Pavilion, 1984." Archdiocese of New Orleans, *Cross, Crozier, and Crucible,* Editor, Glenn R. Conrad, 1993.
"Frontiers of Contemporary Religious Experience and Secular Ideologies." INFO, Dominican Publication, 1998.
"The Great Jubilee Prayer, The Dominican Rosary." Southern Dominicans, 2000.

PAPERS, ADDRESSES AND SERMONS

"Problems of Unrest in the University." University of Arizona, 1969.
"Consultations Concerning the World Conference on Religion and Peace." Stockholm, London, Paris, Tokyo, Kyoto, 1970- 80."
"The Significance of the World Conference on Religion and Peace." University of Houston, 1971.
"Ecumenism and the World Conference on Religion and Peace." Aquinas Institute, 1971.
"A New Vision for Ecumenism." Grenada and Barbados, Caribbean, Ecumenical Consultation for Development, January 1972.
"Impact of the Second World Conference on Religion and Peace." Tulane University, 1974.
"The Power to Heal." *The Christian Revolution,* 1974.
Northeastern Louisiana University, Conference of Baptist Ministers, "How Baptists Should Better Utilize the Liturgy of the Word and the Liturgy of the Word Made Flesh," 1974.
Tulane University Medical School, "Medical Care and Immortality"; talks to medical students 1974.
International Law and Second World Conference for Religion and Peace," Wingspread, Wind Point/Racine, WI, 1975.
"Malta, Jerusalem, Rome: Talks on the Spirituality of the Order of St. Lazarus of Jerusalem." *The Order Quarterly* 1977-90.
"Is Islam at Loggerheads with Christianity?" New Orleans, 1980.
"Allowing Your Children to Grow and Go" 1980.
"The Myths of Communism," 1980.

Preaching, Ecumenical Week. New Orleans Christ Church Cathedral, 1986; Presbyterian Church, 1987.

"Reactions and Evaluation of the Papal Visit." The New Orleans Presbyterian Ministry, 1987.

"Fr. Angelo Zarlenga, O.P., Promoter of the Arts." Chapter for commemorative volume, 1987.

"The Artistic Legacy of Pope John Paul II." Paper in the series Pope John Paul II, The Man and the Pope, 1987.

"Miracle of the Sun Experience." Sermon, Medjugorje, Yugoslavia (Bosnia and Hercegovina), 1988.

Sermon in conjunction with the opening of the Vatican Exhibition at the Museum of Western Art. St. Mary's Cathedral, Tokyo, 1989.

"A Christian Perspective of the Holy Land: Why the Holy See Has Not Recognized Israel." Talk, Kenner Presbyterian Church, 1991.

Preaching, Order of St. Lazarus International Meetings. Angers, France, 1990; Toronto, 1992; Vienna, 1994; New Orleans, 1996; Atlanta, 1998; Los Angeles, 2000; Chicago, 2002; New Orleans, 2004; Houston, 2006; Vienna, 2007; Chicago, 2008.

"Homilies from the Holy Land," Order of St. Lazarus. DVD, 2008.

TELEVISION

Interview with Pere de Vaux on the Dead Sea Scrolls. St. Thomas College, St. Paul, Minnesota, 1964.

"Faith to Faith" Series with Rabbi Edward P. Cohn and others (1990–1994).

DVD

"Homilies from the Holy Land." The Military and Hospitaller Order of St. Lazarus of Jerusalem, 900th Anniversary of the Founding of the Order of St. Lazarus, 2008.

MEMBERSHIPS

Catholic Philosophical Society (1966-79).
Catholic Theological Society (1968-74).
World Conference on Religion and Peace (1967, 1971, 1975, 1977).
Louisiana Council for Music and the Performing Arts, Inc. (1967-).
Catholic Campus Ministry Association (1966-79).
Ecumenical Campus Ministry (1966-79).

New Orleans Museum of Art (1966-).
Society for Human Values in Medicine (1966-82).
Louisiana Renaissance, Religion and the Arts (1977-80).
Military and Hospitaller Order of St. Lazarus of Jerusalem (1976-).
Friends of the Kennedy Center (1972-80).
Patrons of the Vatican Museums in the South, Inc., (1985-).
Patrons of the Vatican Museums on the West Coast (1986-).
Vatican Museums (1985-).
Equestrian Order of the Holy Sepulchre of Jerusalem, Southern Lieutenancy, U.S.A. (1991-).
Catholic Commission on Intellectual and Cultural Affairs.

AWARD ORIGINATOR

Founder, St. Martin de Porres Social Justice Award for the Southern Dominican Province. Designed by Fr. Thomas McGlynn, O.P., and Fr. Ambrose McAlister, O.P. (1986-).

Founder, St. Thomas Aquinas Award for Dominican Benefactors of the International Dominican Foundation. Designed by Fr. Thomas McGlynn, O.P., and Fr. Ambrose McAlister, O.P. (2001-).

Founder, St. Thomas Aquinas Environmental Award given by the Chair of Judeo-Christian Studies, Tulane University. Designed by Fr. Thomas McGlynn, O.P. (2007-).

First Honoree: Sir John Houghton (2007).
Second Honoree: H.R.H., the Prince of Wales (2008).

TRAVELS

North and South America: United States, Canada, Alaska, Mexico, Honduras, Panama, Peru, Columbia, Venezuela, Brazil, Argentina, Paraguay.

Europe: British Isles, France, Spain, Switzerland, Italy, Germany, Malta, Soviet Union, Scandinavia, Ukraine.

North Africa: Egypt.

Middle East: Israel, Jordan, Turkey.

Asia: Hong Kong, Japan, Thailand, Australia, New Zealand.

Pacific: Fiji, Hawaii.

HOBBIES

Painting, tennis, walking, reading.

APPENDIX I

PATRONS OF THE VATICAN MUSEUMS IN THE SOUTH AND THE SOUTHERN DOMINICANS PRESENT CANADIAN SERIGRAPHS TO THE VATICAN MUSEUMS

On the twelfth of November, 1997, at the conclusion of the annual Vatican Museums Advsory Board meetings, in the Hall of the Holy Spirit of the Vatican Galleries, Fr. Val Ambrose McInnes, O.P., and Mr. Carlo Capomazza presented to Dr. Carlo Pietrangeli, Director General of the Vatican Museums, and to Dr. Walter Persegati, the International Coordinator for the Patrons of the Vatican Museums, two valuable serigraphs entitled "The Dormer Tribute" by Canadian artist Jack Chambers. A serigraph is a sophisticated form of silk screen.

The Chambers serigraphs, depicting young people laying roses on a grave, memorialize a young English army officer named Henry Edward Dormer; he died in London, Ontario, Canada, in 1866 as a result of a cholera epidemic. On leaving the army he planned to enter the Dominican Order.

The two Dormer serigraphs, silver-framed and matted, are twin works, one unfinished, the other showing a transparent overlay of the last of twenty-five colors that would have completed the work. Unfortunately, the artist died of leukemia before this could be accomplished.

"Isn't it remarkable," wrote Chambers before his death, "that young people a hundred years after the death of another young person would be moved to come and lay roses at his grave in the middle of winter? This gives me the inspiration to do my long-desired religious work, not a crucifixion or a resurrection, but a work that captures the experience of young people's faith."

"The Tribute" is celebrated for its dreamlike, visionary images and the realistic presentation of the London cemetery. The unfinished work leaves the figures outlined but undefined, thus giving the whole work an ethereal impression.

Chambers died in 1978 at the height of his career; his paintings were selling for forty-, fifty-, sixty-thousand dollars apiece.

The seriographs were presented as a gift on behalf of the Southern

Dominicans and the Patrons of the Vatican Museums in the South.

Fr. McInnes also presented a copy of his recent work entitled *To Rise Wtth the Light: The Spiritual Odyssey of Jack Chambers* to each member of the Vatican Museums Board.

In 2007 his niece Mrs. Marilyn Coles Calderone presented a similar framed "Dormer Tribute" to the Bishop of London, Ontario, the Most Rev. Ronald P. Fabrro, C.S.B.

INDEX

Abramowicz, Claudia & Danny, 189.
Adams, Franklin, 95.
Ambrose, O.P., Brother, 36.
Anderson, Matt, iv.
Anderson, M. D., 133 & fllg., 133, 141& fllg.
Andrews, Julie, 149.
Ann, Princess of Bourbon-Parma, 117.
Annenberg, Leonore & Walter, 117.
Anterior and Posterior Analytics, 42.
Anthony, C. N., 32.
Arbour, Verna, 95.
Aristotle, xxi.
Arnold, Claude, 15, 46.
Art as Experience, 49.
Ashley, OP, Benedict M., 42-43, 49, 182.
Assumption College, Windsor, Ont., 10, 15, 26, 28, 48, 55.
Augustine, 29 & fllg.
Ayoub, Mahmoud, 184.
Azziz, Philip, 153.

Ballestrero, Anastasio, 86.
Banff School of Fine Arts, 152.
Barnett, William, 180.
Barron, Robert E., 185.
Basilian Fathers, 10, 16, 41.
Bazan, Haydee & Nicolas, 190.
Beck, Albert, 191.
Becker, Mary Jane & John D'Arcy, 190.
Bemporad, Jack, 185.
Benson Herbert, 185.
Bernadin, Joseph, 104.
Bible in Its Traditions, 100.
Biblical Studies, xix.
Bieler, Andre, 152.
Birtel, Frank, 61-62, 175, 180, 184, 188.
Biskup, George J., 45.
Bittista, Ned, 93.
Blenheim Palace, 53.
Blitch, Ron, 81, 95.
Blum, Lucile, 75, 189.

Blumenthal, David R., 178
Bochenski, O.P., I. M., 18.
Boggs, Barbara, 176.
Boggs, Corinne "Lindy," 75, 81, 189.
Bon, M. Michel, 161.
Bonee, O.P. John Thomas, 42.
Bonniwell, William R., O.P., 40.
Bontempo, O.P., Richard, vi.
Borg, Marcus, 180.
Bowles, George "Corky", 121 & fllg.
Branfield, Michael J., 119.
Brescia College, 13.
Brenner Pass, 54.
Breuer, Marcel, 33.
Bricker, Kathleen & John, 61, 140.
Brinkley, Douglas, 139.
Brown, Jonathan, 173.
Brown, Raymond E., 171, 180.
Brown, O.P., Victor, 91.
Brownsville Girl, 139.
Bruckberger, O.P., Raymond L., 37.
Bruzauskas, Sonja, 140.
Buckingham Palace, 146.
Bullard, John, 81, 84.
Buonarotti, Michelangelo, 76, 86, 88.
Burgess, Clare & Bill, 119.
Burka, Julia Woodward, vi.
Butler, O.P., Richard, 49.

Caesar, Julius, 18.
Calderone, Marilyn & Joseph, 161, 206.
Callahan, Daniel, 173.
Camara, Helder, xviii, 129.
Campbell, Robert J., 190.
Canizaro, Sue Ellen & Joseph C., 99, 132, 145 & fllg., 189.
Canova Medal, 104.
Canterbury Tales, 25.
Capomazza, Rosemonde & Carlo, 205.
Caputto, Salvador, 131.
Caravaggio, Michelangelo, 76.

206 Resurrection Fern

Card, Karol (Kreymer) & Robert J., 136, 142, 161.
Carey, John J., 177.
Carlson, Robert J., 159.
Carmelite Order, 27.
Carrere, Ernest, 127-128.
Carrere, Libby & Jack, 139.
Carter, G. Emmett, 48, 49, 65.
Carty, Arthur, 49, 66.
Carty, Olive, 49.
Cary, Beth & George, 106, 112, 168 & fllg., 189.
Caseroli, Agostino, 81
Casselli, Henry, iv, 95, 140.
Casey, Donna Miller, 161.
Catholic Center, Tulane, 50, 56 & fllg.
Catholic Chaplain Corps, Archdiocese Galveston-Houston, 190.
Catholic Doctors Guild, 58.
Cats, 155.
Celio, O.P., Victor, vi.
Center for World Religions, 62.
Chadwick, Henry, 174.
Chagall, Marc, 51, 103.
Chambers, Jack, 48, 49, 66, 92, 154, 205.
Chase, Leah, 189.
Checchio, James. F., 160.
Christian Brothers of St. Jean Baptiste de la Salle, 8.
Christ the King College (King's College), 47, 50, 51, 64.
Churchill, Winston, 53 & fllg.; 86.
Chu, Paul, 199.
Clarence House, 146.
Clayton, Philip D., 183.
Clark, Eugene, 79-80, 104.
Club of Eight, 141.
Cohn, Edward P., 180.
Cody, John, 56.
Coles, William, 10.
College of St. Thomas, 47, 64.
Collier, Robert J., 181.
Colton, Jr., Richard C., 87, 89, 139 & fllg.; 148 & fllg., 189.
Colton (Howell), Mrs. Richard C., 88.
Comeau-Hart, Judy, 99.

Condon, O.P., Thomas M., 71.
Congar, O.P., Yves, 64.
Congregation of St. Basil, 10.
Connick, Jr., Harry, 189.
Connick, Sr., Harry, 189.
Constitution on the Sacred Liturgy, xviii.
"Consummatory Experience" in John Dewey's Philosophy, 49.
Contemporary Museum of the Vatican Collections, 154.
Cooke, Terence, 79.
Corral, O.P., Roberto, 160.
Correctional Ministries, Archdiocese Galveston-Houston, 190.
Costa, O.P., Carlos Aspiroz, 151, 159, 160.
Coutourier, O.P., Joseph-Marie, 49, 51, 95, 97, 154.
Cowen, Scott, 145.
Cox, Harvey, 176.
Creative Intuition in Art and Poetry, 16.
Cronin, Mr. & Mrs. Ernest, 190.
Crossan, John Dominic, 185.
Cross, Crozier, and Crucible, 81, 153.
Cullen, Rose & Harry H., 91, 190.
Cunningham, O.P., Louis Bertrand, 45.
Curse You, Jack Dalton!, 8.
Curtis, Nathaniel "Buster", 81, 95.

Dalin, David, 187.
Daube, David, 172.
Davies, W. D., 62, 171.
Davis, O.P., Brian, 178.
Davis, Francis, 161.
Davis, Hampton, 73.
Day, Dorothy, xix.
D'Aza, Jane, 154.
De Barrio-Ochoa, Valentine, 35.
De Borbon, Don Carlos, 128.
De Borbon, Francesco, 128.
De Cosse, Jacqueline, 161.
Decree on Ecumenism, xviii.
De Gaulle, Charles, 37.
Delacave, Jacques, 161.
Delgado, College, 147.
DeMille, Cecil B., 114.
Denechaud, Pat, 145.

Descartes, Rene., 29.
Desmond, John, 62.
D'Estaing, Giscard, 144.
DeToqueville—A Hundred Years Later, 37.
De Vittorio, O.P., Francesco, 27.
Dewey, John, 49, 153.
Dextra, Beau, 75.
Dialogues of the Carmelites, 37.
"Diego at the Dining Room Table," 154.
Discalced Carmelites, 121.
Dittmar, Hank, 145 & fllg, 187.
Dixon, David F. & family, 189.
Dolan, Timothy M., 159.
Domingo, Placido, 83.
Dominican Center, Brussels, 98.
Dominican Rosary College (Dominican University), 18.
Dominican shield, iv, 149.
Dominican Sisters of St. Mary's, 189.
Donnelly, James, 70.
Donnelly, Maria-Helena Sampar, 70-71.
Donovan, Brian, O.P., 68, 71.
Donovan, Mary Elizabeth Broussard, 190.
Dormer, Henry Edward, 65 & fllg.
"Dormer Tribute, The," 154, 205.
Doyle, Dennis, 185.
Dozier, Carroll T., xviii, 129.
Drowning, Don, 180.
Dubrovnik, 107 & fllg.
Duke of Windsor, 27.
Dulles, Avery, 178.
D'Urso, Mario, 161.
Dwyer, Wilfred, 15.
Dylan, Bob, 139.
Dziwisz, Stanislaw, 77.

Ecole Biblique, xix.
Ecumenical Movement, xviii.
Edmonds, Karen, 95.
Edney, O.P., Mark, vi, 102, 148 & fllg., 160.
Ehrenkrantz, Joseph, 183.
Eizmendi, Jr., Francisco C., 161.
El Greco, 96, 123.
Emery, Lynn, 95.
Equestrian Order of the Holy Sepulchre, 196, 206.

Fabro, Ronald P., 206.
Faderl, Stephan, 134.
Fanjeaux, 102.
Farrell, John Kevin, 10, 31, 40, 65.
Felts, Jean C., 178.
Feibleman, Julian B., 93.
Filmore, Lorin, 19, 33.
Finkel, Asher, 176.
Finn, O.P., Chrys, vi, 99.
Fiori, O.P., Cajetan, 34.
Firebird, 24.
Fiorenza, O.P., Joseph A., 190.
Fitzalan-Howard, Lord & Lady, 189.
Flannery, Msgr., 10, 46.
Flew, Anthony, 176.
Flood, Patrick, 15, 29.
Flynn, Mr. & Mrs. Raymond, 189.
Fountain, Pete, 116.
Fox, O.P., Joseph, 99.
Fra Angelico, 96.
Francis, Blanche & Norman, 189.
Frawley, Gerri, 140.
French, Ron, 131.
Fr. Jozo, 106 & fllg.
Fr. Philip, 106 & fllg.
Fretz, Sr., Mr. & Mrs. Robert R., 190.
Freyne, Sean, 174.
Friedman, David D., 179.
Frizell, Lawrence, 95, 176.

Gaillardetz, Richard R., 184.
Gaisman, Catherine & Henry J., 61.
Galante, Joseph A., 184.
Garavani, Valentino, 123.
Garofalo, Jennifer & Nat, 189.
Garrison, Jr., Robin & David, 190.
Garvey, Edwin, 15.
Geffre, O.P., Claude, 176.
George, Francis, 72, 159, 182.
Giertych, O.P., Wojciech, 160.
Gilkey, Langdon, 172.
Gilson, Etienne, 16, 41.
Gleeson, O.P., Martin, vi, 138, 159.
Glennon, Susan (Suzi) & Billy, 106, 111, 168 & fllg.
God and the Unconscious, 43.

Goetz, Stephen, 73.
Gospa, 163
Grable, Betty, 81.
Graham, O.P., Gilbert, 32.
Granberry, Margaret & Malcolm, 190.
Grand Priory of America, 128.
Grand Priory of Canada, 128.
Grand Priory of France, 128.
Grand Theatre, 8.
Granot, Avi, 178.
Great Deluge, 139.
Greeley, Andrew, 182.
Green Book, 128.
Greenleaf, Richard F., 177.
Green Park, 146.
Gregorios III, 128.
Gregory, Angela, xix, 95.
Gregson, Jr., Vernon, 181.
Griffin, Emilie Dietrich, 175.
Griffin, Emilie & William, vi.
Groeschel, Benedict, 119.
Group of Seven, 152.
Guscin, Mark, 183.
Gutierrez, O.P., Gustavo, 177.

Hackney, Sheldon, 61.
Haight, Roger, 187.
Hamer and Brothers, 46.
Hamilton, Douglas, 55.
Hannan, Philip H., 56, 76, 81, 86, 104, 189.
Hanson, Kirk O., 184.
Harris, William "Billy", 58.
Hartt, Frederick, 173.
Harvard School of Fine Arts, 153.
"Harvesting Excellence: The Spirituality of the Aging," 14.
Haught, John F, 187.
Haughton, Rosemary, 176.
Haymon, Ava Leavell, 140.
Hayes, Helen, 189.
Hebert, Sister Edna Ann, 91.
Hefner, Philip, 183.
Helen (Aunt Helen) [Rodgers] Sister St. Sebastian, Sisters of St. Joseph, 1 & fllg.
Henry Moore Foundation, iv, 89.
Henry, Patrick, 181.

Herbert, O.P., Sister Edna Ann, 190.
Highgrove, 147.
Hill, Brennan R., 182.
Hill, Carol & Paul, 104.
Hirt, Al, 116.
History of the Dominicans in the United States, 40.
Hodge, James,192.
Hohmann, Nikolaus, 161.
Holcomb, Daniel, 181.
Holland, Arthur F., 190.
Holmes, Sherlock, 149.
Holy Name of Jesus parish, 57.
Hope, Dolores & Bob, 105 & fllg, 117 & fllg., 189.
Hope, Linda, 119.
Hope, Kelly, 119.
Hope, Mildred, 119.
Hotel Busby, Nice, 22.
Houghton, John, 145, 186, 191.
Hurlbut, William B., 185.
Hurricane Katrina, 71, 138 & fllg.

Ingraffia, Colleen & Roy, 106, 169 & fllg.
Institute for Higher Studies, 101
Interfaith Inter-Race Society, 11.
International Dominican Foundation, 98 & fllg.
International Dominican Foundation, Advisory Board, 140.
International Dominican Foundation, International Advisory Board, 160.
International University Services, 26.
Introduction to Philosophy, 16.
Ivan, visionary, 107 & fllg, 163 & fllg.
Ivy family, 49.
Izzo, O.P., D. Dominic, 159.

Jackson, A. Y., 152.
Jackson Square, 115.
Jaeger, David-Maria, 178.
Jakelen, Antje, 185.
Japanese, Buddhistic, Shintoist Studies, 62.
Jeffreys, Gordon, 65.
Jenkins, David, 175.
Jerusalem Bible, xix, 100.
John XXIII, xix, xx, xxii.

Johnson, Myrtle, 57.
Jordan, Louise H. & John Patrick, 161.
Joyal, Serge, 77.
Judeo-Christian Studies, xviii, 61 & fllg, 93, 144.
Jung, Carl, 43.

Kaiser, Robert Blair, 186.
Kammer, Fred, 179.
Kane, John, 161.
Kant, Immanuel, 29.
Karsh, Yousuf, 77 & fllg.; 85.
Katz, Steven T., 182.
Kaufman, Gordon D., 180.
Kearney, Hal, 95.
Keeler, William, 182.
Keeney, Jennifer, 140.
Kelly, Margaret & Eamon, 61, 116, 189.
Kelly, Grace, 123.
Kelly, John J., 176.
Kelly, Thomas C., 159, 190.
Kennedy Galleries, 103.
Kennedy, O.P., Philip, 180.
Khan, Aly, 123.
Kiev Institute for Higher Education in Christian Theology, 98.
Kilroy, O.P., Antoninus (Tony), 34, 36.
King (King's) College, 47.
King, McKenzie, 78.
Klyce, Stephen, 189.
Knight, James, 58.
Kohlmeyer, Ida, 95.
Konig, Ivan, 140, 161.
Konkel, O.P., Joseph, 91, 137.
Kreymer, Karol, 136, 142, 161.
Krizevac, 164.
Kruse, Anita, 140.

Labatt, Bessie (Mrs. John S.), 65.
Laborde, Margaret & Alden J., 61, 89, 178, 189.
Laborde, Karen, 95, 189.
LaGrange, O.P., Joseph-Marie, xix, 100.
Laghi, Pio, 81.
Laragh, Brian, 9, 15, 28.
Lathrop, Lynn D. & Mitchell L., 161.
Lavelli, Mimi & Giovanni, 51 & fllg.

Lawrence, John, 95.
LeBel, Eugene, 15.
Le Corbusier, 51.
Le Deaut, Roger, 171.
"Legacy of the Vatican Museums," 104.
Leger, Fernand, 51, 103.
Lemann, Bernie, 95.
Leo XIII, xix.
Le Petit Grocery, 148.
Leuer, O.P., Mark, 34.
Levy, Eric, 133 & fllg., 133.
Levy, Susan & Richard, 131.
Lewis, C. S., 97.
Leyden, 26 & fllg.
Linbeck, Pattie Ruth (Mrs. Leo Edward), 189.
Liturgical Reform Movement, xvii.
Liturgy of the Eucharist, xvii.
Liturgy of the Word, xvii.
Loiten, F., 19.
London Little Theatre, 65.
London, Ontario, 2 & throughout.
London Symphony Orchestra, 66.
Long, Russell B., 75.
Louisiana Carpenter's Regional Council, 147.
Louisiana Council for Music and the Performing Arts, 75, 95.
Louisiana Renaissance: Religion and the Arts, 95.
Louisiana State Arts Council and Endowment for the Arts, 75.
Lourdes, 24 & fllg.
Luce, Clare Booth, 81.
Lupberger, Edward, 178.
Lydon, O.P., John, 71.
Lykes, Margaret K. (Mrs. Joseph T.), 87.
Lykes Steamship Company, 139.

MacNeill, Edith & Robert, 75.
MacNeill, Marjorie, 75.
MacQuarrie, John, 171.
Macy, Gary, 182.
Mahoney, A. P., 5, 10, 48, 49.
Mahoney, Roger, 119.
Manfrini, Enrico, 92.
Manning, Olivia & Archie, 189.
Marcinkus, Paul, 86, 103.

Mardi Gras, 155 & fllg.
Maritain, Jacques, 15, 41.
Maritain, Raissa, 15, 41.
Markey, O.P., John, 71.
Martin, Paul, 75.
Martiny, O.P., Lee Martin, 187.
Martinez, Jerome, 140.
Marty, Martin, 185.
Mary (Aunt Mary) [Rodgers], Sister St. Mary, Sisters of Charity, 1 & fllg.
Masson, Andre, 51, 103.
Masterson, O.P., Reginald, 45.
Matilda Chapel, 111.
Matisse, Henri, 97, 103.
Matteo, Anthony M., 182.
Maximinus, 143.
Maximom, 143.
May, William F., 177.
Mayo Clinic, 131 & fllg., 131.
McBrien, Richard P., 177.
McCabe, Babe, 49.
McCallum, Jackie, 29.
McCallum, Jason, 28.
McCance, Murray, 46.
McCarrick, Theodore, 119, 159.
McCarthy, John, 190.
McConn, Katie & Luke, 190.
McCormack, Sister Lillian, S.S.N.D., 189.
McDermott, O.P., Neal W., 92, 142, 159.
McDonald, Marguerite & Stephen Klyce, 189.
McDonnell, Henry J. F. "Chum," O.P., 44.
McDonnell, O.P., John J. "Benie," 45 & fllg.
McGinn, Bernard, 174.
McInnes, Sr., Angus J. (Father), 1 & throughout.
McInnes, Jr., Angus J., v, 8, 91, 142.
McInnes, Ann, 91.
McInnes, Carol Ann, 91.
McInnes, Clare, 142.
McInnes, Genevieve Rodgers, v.
McInnes, James A., 000.
McInnes, John C. ("Jack"), 46.
McInnes, Maureen, 91.
McInnes, Patrick R., 4, 8, 40, 46, 142.
McInnes Coles, Rosemary, 4.
McInnes, O.P., Valentine Ambrose.

BOOKS *Continuing Dialog between Christians and Jews*, 000. *Environmental Awareness through the Arts*, 000. *New Visions: Historical and Theological Perspectives on the Jewish-Christian Dialog*, 000. *Homilies of the Holy Land*, 129. *Releasing the Artistic Talents of Our Handicapped*, 000. *Re-Imaging God for Today*, 000. *Renewing the Judeo-Christian Well Springs*, 000. *Taste and See: Louisiana Renaissance, Religion and the Arts*, 153. *To Rise with the Light: The Spirituality of Jack Chambers*, 48, 66. *Treasures of the Vatican: The New Orleans Vatican Pavilion*, 81.
McInnes Scholarship Fund, 94.
McKenna, Sister Briege, 142.
McMahon, O.P., Malcolm, 160.
McMullin, Ernan, 171, 173.
Meade, Jean A., 180.
Medeiros, Humberto Sousa, 79.
Medjugorje, 106 & fllg., 163 & follg.
Medjugorje children. Ivan, 163. Ivanka, 163. Marija, 163. Mirjana, 163. Vicka, 107, 163. Yakov, 163.
Meilaender, Gilbert, 179.
Melkite, 128.
Merchant of Venice, 9.
Meriwether, Steven, 179.
Mestrovic, Ivan, 82, 84, 167.
Michael, King-Prince of Romania, and Ann, Princess of Bourbon-Parma, 117.
Miller, Ann (Mrs. Richard K.), 80, 104, 117 & fllg., 121 & fllg.
Miller, Dick, 117.
Milner, Ginny, 80, 104, 124.
Miracle of the Sun, 107 & fllg.
Moir, Alfred, 173.
Moltmann, Jurgen, 175.
Monastery of Carmel, Des Plaines, 126.
Montalban, Georgiana & Ricardo, 189.
Moore, Henry, 87.
Moraczewski, O.P., Albert, 181.
Morial, Dutch, 87.
Morin, Roger, 73.
Mother St. Michael, O.S.U., 13.

Much Hadham, 88-89.
Muggeridge, Anne, 176.
Musee de Quebec, 77.
Museum for Modern Religious Art, 103.
Murphy, O.P., Richard T. A., 44, 47.
Muslim Studies, 62.
Mussolini, Benito, 51 & fllg.
Myra Clare Rogers Memorial Chapel, 62, 133.

Nalty, Jane & Paul, 132, 142, 150, 189.
Nantes, O.P., Edmund C., 159.
Napoli, Jana, 95.
Naquin, Ruth & Ray, 189.
National Catholic Conference of Bishops, 100.
National Catholic Education Association, 116.
N'Awlins, 114.
Nelligan, Charles Leo, 66.
Neuhaus, Richard John, 180.
Newberger, Grace & Ken, 131.
Newcomb College, 133.
Newcomb School of Art, 95.
New Deal, xix.
New Orleans Museum of Art, 81.
New Orleans Times-Picayune, 114.
Nice, French Riviera, O.P., 22 & fllg.
Nogar, O.P., Jude, xxi.
Noonan, Jr., John T., 173.
Northup, Ruth, 169.
Nostra Aetate, xviii.
Nouwen, Henri J. M., 190.
Novak, David, 180.
Novak, Michael, 179.

O'Brien, Edwin F., 159
O'Brien, O.P., Scott, 71.
Ochs, Peter, 179.
Old Tea House, 56.
O'Meara, Martin, 9, 66.
O'Meara, Thomas F., 176.
O'Neill, Charles, 79, 178.
One Sky to Share, 37.
Order of St. Lazarus of Jerusalem, 118 127 & fllg., 143, 146, 155.
O'Reiley, Philip, 19.
O'Rourke, O.P., Michael, vi.

Oriental Institute for Moslem and Christian Dialogue, 98.
Our Lady of Hope Chapel, 140 & fllg.

Pagels, Elaine, 179.
Pannenberg, Wolfhart, 175.
Parish, Helen Rand, 177.
Patrons of the Arts in the Vatican Museums, 104, 136, 153.
Peacocke, Arthur, 174, 175.
Pelikan, Jaroslav, 179.
Penza, Claude, 9.
Percy, Walker, 113.
Perennial Philosophy, 16.
Perrot, Kim, 150.
Persegati, Walter, 79, 86, 104, 204.
Petacci, Clara, 54.
Petis, Norris, 145.
Petuchowski, Jakob J., 171, 175.
Peterson, Karl, 74.
Phelan, W. J., 31.
Philip II, King of Spain, 27.
Phillips, W. J., 152.
Piazza, Marguerite, 189.
Picasso, Pablo, 48, 51, 103.
Pietrangeli, Carlo, 104, 205.
Pizzello, Chris, iv.
Plotinus, 29 & fllg.
Pond, Jo & Bob, 119.
Pontifical Institute of MediÆval Studies, St. Michael's College, 16.
Pope John XXIII, xix & fllg., 48.
Pope John Paul II, 85, 114 & fllg., 142, 154, 192 & fllg.
Pope Paul VI, 103.
Pope Pius, XII, 20.
Potok, Chaim, 175.
Potter, Lady, 161.
Pound, Hazel, 5, 7.
Pound, Stella, 5, 7.
Poundhaust, 147.
Powell, O.P., Ralph, 42.
Precious Blood Sisters, 11.
Preservation Resource Center, 147.
Prince and Princess of Wales, 78 & fllg., 145 & fllg., 145, 187, 191.

Priory of Holy Rosary, Houston, 136.
Priory of St. Albert the Great, Minneapolis, 47, 64.
Priory of St. Dominic, Dubrovnik, 107.
Priory of St. Dominic, New Orleans, 56, 139, 153, 154.
Priory of St. Peter Martyr, Winona, 35.
Priory of St. Rose, Dubuque, 46.
Prouilhe, France, 102.
Province, St. Albert the Great, xxii, 94.
Province, St. Martin de Porres, xxii.
Province, St. Joseph, 94, 99.

Queen Juliana, Holland, 27.
Queens University, Kingston, Ontario, 152.
Queens University School of Fine Arts, 152.
Quinn, John R, 81, 125, 183.

Radcliffe, O.P., Timothy, 91, 98, 182, 189.
Radio City Music Hall, 147.
Rahal, Bendigal, 27.
Raphael (Raffaello Sanzio da Urbino), 19, 82.
Raymond, Christian brother, 8.
Religious Staff Association, Tulane, 59.
Rerum Novarum, xix.
Resurrection fern, xv.
Riesenfeld, Harald, 172.
Roberts, Corinne (Cokie) & Steven, 189.
Robertson, C. K., 187.
Robertson, Elizabeth & David, 162.
Rodi, Thomas J., 72.
Rogers, Myra Clare & James Mitchell, 62.
Romeo and Juliet, 9.
Rosenblum, Robert, 173.
Rost van Tonnigen, Admiral, 25.
Rost van Tonnigen, Nicholas, 25.
Rottier, Kitty, 19.
Rouault, Georges, 51, 109.
Roxborough, O.P., Gilbert, 56.
Royce, Josiah.
Ruane, O.P., Edward M., 159, 160.
Rusovich, Jr., Marilyn & Basil J., 106, 169, 189.
Russell, Robert, 175.
Ryan, Cornelius O., 190.
Ryscavage, Richard, 186.

Sabat, Michel, 101.
Sahni, Roger, 161.
Sanders, Edward P., 171.
San Francisco Chronicle, 121.
San Francisco Symphony, 125.
Santa Fe Concert, 139 & fllg.
Santa Maria Supra Minerva, 76, 86 & fllg.
Santa Sabina, 51.
Sargawic, Paul, 5.
Schillebeeckx, O.P., Edward, 172.
Schlesinger, Henry, 68.
Schmeck, Ted, 65.
Schmidt, George, 95.
Schneider, Cherie Banos, 106, 163 & fllg.
Schonborn, O.P., Christoph, 160, 183, 185.
"*School of Christ,*" 46.
Schreiter, Robert, 187.
Schulte, Francis B., 177, 189.
"Science of the Saints," 11.
Scott, Flo, 9.
Scullion, O.P., Raymond, 40.
Second Vatican Council, xvii-xviii, 59, 128.
Seidenberg, Jean, 95.
Sense et Nonsense, 16.
Serra Club of Houston, 190.
Serrano, O.P., Sergio, vi.
Sertillanges, O.P., Antonin-Gilbert, 41-42.
"Seven Days of Creation," 154.
Shakespeare, William, 11, 12.
Shanahan, O.P., Daniel, vi.
Sheed, Frank, 19.
Sheehan, Michael J., 140.
Sheen, Fulton J., 79.
Shepherd, Sam, 139.
Shondel, O.P., Roger, vi.
Show Boat, 9.
Shroud of Turin, 86.
Sigmund, Paul E., 176, 186.
Sigrist, O.P., Marcel, 185, 186.
Silver, Stuart, 84-85.
Silverman, Arthur, 95.
Simon, Jr., William E., 160.
Sister Mary of the Compassion, 154.
Sister Mary Theophane Wallace, Precious Blood Sisters, 11.

Sister St. Mary, Sisters of Charity (Aunt Mary), 1.
Sister St. Sebastian, Sisters of St. Joseph, (Aunt Helen), 1.
Sisters of St. Joseph, 1 and throughout.
Sistine Chapel, 103.
Sinatra, Frank, 105.
Social Justice, xviii.
Solomon, Robert, 173.
Song of Bernadette, 24.
Sound of Music, 149.
Southern Dominican Galas, 112.
Southern Dominican Province, 73, 91 & fllg.
Sovereign Order of St. John of Malta, 127.
Spiers, Maria & Marion, 190.
Split, 106.
Spong, John S., 178.
Springbank Park Amusement Centre, 11.
St. Angelus High School, 9.
St. Albert the Great, 45.
Stark, Jean & Eugene, 162.
St. Basil the Great, 127.
St. Bernadette Soubirous, 24.
St. Bernard of Clairvaux, 156.
St. Catherine of Siena, 45.
St. Charles Borromeo, 19, 52.
St. Clare Retreat Center, 117.
St. Dominic, 45, 102, 112, 154, 155.
St. Ignatius Loyola, 92.
St. John the Baptist, 140.
St. John-Stevas, Norman, 174.
St. Margaret Mary Alacoque, 17.
St. Martin de Porres, xix, 94.
St. Martin De Porres Award, 91.
St. Martin of Tours Parish, 5.
St. Mary Magdalene, 37.
St. Mary's Dominican High School, 56.
St. Mary's School, 5.
St. Michael's College, Toronto, 10.
St. Peter's Seminary, 31.
St. Thomas Aquinas, 45.
St. Thomas Aquinas Environmental Award, 144.
St. Thomas More, university parish, 62, 71 & fllg.
Stall, Susan, 106, 169.
Steers family, 49.
Stern, Edith, 75.
Stewart, Frank, 85.

Storey, Peter, 182.
Stream, Matilda & Harold, 81, 127-128.
Stritch, Samuel, 41.
Stuart, Mary, queen, 53.
Stuart, Mary, novelist, 53.
Sullivan, Jackie, 81, 84.
Stravinsky, Igor, 24.
Swan, Peter, 15.
Sweeney, Mary Helen, 9.
Swiss Guard, Vatican, 18.

Tabora, Reyna, 148.
Tanenbaum, Marc H., 176.
Tatarski, Nancy, vi, 150.
Taubs, Henry, 152.
Teilhard de Chardin, Pierre, 58.
Thames River, Ontario, 4.
Thatcher, Margaret, 118-119.
Thousand Arrows, A, 66.
Toronto Fall Exposition Oratorical Competition, 8.
Trapolin, Tim, 95.
Trio Angelico, 140.
Tulane Catholic Center, 50, 55 & fllg.
Tulane University, 48 155.
Twentieth Century Art Museum, 103.

University of Fribourg, 17 & fllg.
University of Leyden, 26 & fllg.
University of St. Thomas (Angelicum), Rome, 98, 99.
University of Western Ontario, 10, 48.
Uraic, Marija, 164 & fllg.
Ursulines, Canada, 13.

Valentino, Mary Ann, 189.
Van Huyssteen, J. Wentzel, 180.
Vanier, Governor General & Mrs., 65.
Van Rijn, Rembrandt, 97.
Vatican Curia, 48.
Vatican Museums, 104 & fllg., 205.
Vatican Palace, 104.
Vatican Pavilion, 76 & fllg; 83 & fllg.
Vatican Museums, 103 and fllg.
Vermes, Geza, 171.
Vicka, visionary, 107.

Villere, Jr., Margie & St. Denis J., 189.
Voorhies, Bennett J., 140.

Walden, Henry, 123.
Waldman, Eric, 162.
Wales, Preston, 68.
Walker, O.P., Bernard, 40.
Walsh, Sr., Gloria/Dorothy and John J., 189.
Walsh, O.P, Nicholas, 35.
Walters, Vernon A. "Dick," 81, 174, 190.
Ward, Maisie, 19.
Wayne, John, 105.
Weaver, Mary Jo, 178.
Weber, Andrew Lloyd, 155.
Weigel, George, 179, 184.
Weil, Simone, 97.
Weinert, Egineo, 154.
Weisheipl, O.P., Athanasius, 42.
Westmoreland, William, 117.
Weyer-Davis, Cecilia, 172.
Wheatley, Julian, 186.
Wheeler, Sondra Ely, 181.
White, O.P. Allan, 160.
White, O.P., Victor, 43.
Wildman, Wesley J., 185.
Wilken, Robert, 174, 176.
Williams, O.P., R. B., 71.

Wilson, Ambassador and Mrs. William, 77.
Wolfe, O.P., Sister Mary Ellen, 71.
World Conference of Churches on Ecumenism, xviii.
World Conference of Religion and Peace, xviii, 129.
Wright, John J., xviii, 129.
Wuerl, Donald W., 159, 186.

Xavier University, 116.

Yarden, Asher, 186.
Yarington, Charles Thomas, 136.
Yakov, visionary, 164.
Yaya, 110, 164.
Yaya's children
    Daniella, 167.
    Ivana, 167.
Young House, 71.
Young, Alma H., 179.
Young, Loretta, 105, 189.

Zagano, Phyllis, 183.
Zarlingo, O.P., Angelo, iv.
Zimmerman, Michael, 175.
Zovko, Fr. Jozo, 167 & fllg.